GHOST SIGNS

GHOST SIGNS: POVERTY AND THE PANDEMIC

Stu Hennigan

Bluemoose

First published in 2022 by
Bluemoose Books Ltd
25 Sackville Street
Hebden Bridge
West Yorkshire
HX7 7DJ

www.bluemoosebooks.com

British Library Cataloguing-in-Publication data
A catalogue record for this book is available from the British Library

Paperback 978-1-910422-96-0

Printed and bound in the UK by Short Run Press

Author's note

There are several different strains of human Coronavirus, some of which produce more severe symptoms than others. The specific virus featured in this book is the one named by the World Health Organisation as COVID-19, which was responsible for the pandemic that swept the globe in 2020 and beyond. In the UK, both in common parlance and in the media, it was known variously as Coronavirus, Corona, COVID-19 and Covid. For the sake of consistency, except when used in direct quotation, it is referred to in the text as Covid or Covid-19.

All names given in the text for service users and Leeds City Council workers (including details of their usual roles) – aside from my own – have been changed. Similarly, any street names and house numbers, where given, are used for illustrative purposes only and do not refer to addresses actually visited.

Any views expressed are entirely my own and are not those of Leeds City Council or its representatives.

S.H.

Introduction

"It is still true that many lives sadly will be lost. And yet it is also true that there is a clear way through." – Prime Minister Boris Johnson's televised address to the nation, Monday 23rd March 2020

In some ways, this is a book that needs no introduction. The Covid-19 pandemic that infected upwards of 439 million people and killed over 5.96 million people worldwide, as of 02.03.22, was a once-in-a-century global catastrophe, the likes of which no one alive today had ever experienced before. It caused a shutdown of the global economy and forced governments the world over to impose strict lockdown measures[1] to try to stem its spread; the social, political and economic upheaval it caused are unparalleled in peacetime, and the ramifications are likely to be felt for decades. It could well mark a turning point in human history, with life being described in terms of the pre- and post-virus worlds.

In the UK, the Government was slow to respond. Lockdown wasn't implemented until towards the end of March 2020, by which point the virus was spreading at an exponential rate. The Government announced early on that if the country came out of the pandemic with less than twenty thousand deaths it would be "a good result"; the official death toll at the time of writing is now more than eight times that figure, with BAME[2] communities, those on low incomes and the elderly being the most affected.

In Leeds, the response from the council was immediate. They set up a Covid information helpline for residents who were worried; they also set up a Food Distribution Centre in a warehouse in the east of the city from which food parcels could be sent out to anyone who was

1   Collins Dictionary declared "lockdown" to be their Word of the Year in 2020, defining it as "the imposition of stringent restrictions on travel, social interaction, and access to public spaces".
2   BAME: Black, Asian and Minority Ethnic.

1

self-isolating.[3] These parcels were delivered directly to people's homes by a team of volunteer drivers recruited from across the wider council.

For over a decade I've worked in an outreach and development role for the library service in the city. When a call went out for volunteers to deliver food parcels, I jumped at the chance. All the city's libraries were closed, and I wanted to do something to help the people of Leeds when they needed it most. I decided right at the beginning to write something about the delivery role; I've always been a diarist and thought it would be good to be able to look back in years to come and read about what I did and how I felt during the crisis.

However, it became apparent immediately that the virus wasn't the whole story. Once the helpline had been up and running for a few weeks, word got out that the council were giving away food and people struggling on low incomes from all over the city were quick to accept the offer of help. By the middle of May, the FDC had distributed almost twenty thousand food parcels to households and third sector partners at an average of nearly four thousand a week. Over the course of five months working Friday to Monday, I drove approximately three and a half thousand miles around the city, with the work taking me into the heart of some of the most disadvantaged estates and onto the doorsteps of some of the city's most vulnerable people. Many of the scenes I saw were horrifying, and in some parts of the city I was confronted by levels of deprivation that are unbelievable in the twenty-first century.

I witnessed how years of Tory government has widened the gap between the haves and the have-nots to levels that are shocking to behold at a time when there's more wealth in the country than ever before; the stark contrast between immense privilege and dire poverty that splits the city – and by extension the country – almost in half. I saw first-hand the effects of austerity, and how the savage cuts that started during the Cameron years have left local authorities floundering, financially unable to cope and lacking vital services when a disaster of this scale hit their communities. I visited people living in slum houses that should have been demolished decades ago, denied decent housing by the eternal diktat of private profit that allows landlords to become rich while people on low incomes live below the poverty line. I saw communities torn apart by drugs and crime, generations

3   This neologism which came to be inextricably linked with the pandemic is defined by the Oxford Learner's Dictionary Online as "the act of avoiding contact with other people in order to prevent the spread of infection."

of families living on benefits because they were born in places where aspiration is low and social mobility is practically non-existent. I met adults who were literally starving; I saw parents struggling to provide basic necessities for young families; I encountered children who looked at everyday food items like they were extravagant birthday gifts; I saw people with severe mental health problems abandoned by the state to fend for themselves. It struck me that something needed to be done to document all this.

According to the key findings of the Institute for Fiscal Studies report *Living standards, poverty and inequality in the UK: 2020*, "The Covid-19 crisis hit at a time when income growth had already been extremely disappointing for some years."[4] It then goes on to describe "a decade of unprecedented poor improvements in living standards, with average income before housing costs having grown less than over any other 10-year period since records began in 1961."[5] A rise in inflation since 2016 is named as a contributory factor to this stagnation of real income growth, which the report states "was partly due to the depreciation of sterling following the Brexit referendum."[6] Furthermore, poverty levels in the UK have been slow to improve through the years of austerity, which is also addressed by the IFS: "The recent lack of progress in reducing absolute poverty[7] is disappointing: it only fell by 1.4 percentage points between 2010–11 and 2018–19 whereas reductions over an equivalent period in previous decades were around 5–6 percentage points on average."[8]

In Leeds the statistics are striking. 114 neighbourhoods (Lower Super Output Areas, or LSOAs) in Leeds are listed as being in the top 10% of the most deprived areas nationally, which equates to 24% of all the neighbourhoods in the city.[9] The Department of Work and Pensions estimates that 157,839 people in the city live in absolute poverty; it also states that 13.7% of households in which one adult is in work are living in poverty. This is borne out by the Office for

---

4   Bourquin, P., Joyce, R., Keiller, A N., (2020) *Living standards, poverty and inequality in the UK: 2020*, Institute for Fiscal Studies: London, p.6.

5   Ibid

6   Ibid

7   Absolute poverty is defined by the United Nations as "a condition characterized by severe deprivation of basic human needs, including food, safe drinking water, sanitation facilities, health, shelter, education and information."

8   Ibid

9   All statistics on poverty in this paragraph are taken from https://observatory. leeds.gov.uk/leeds-poverty-fact-book/

National Statistics, which says 9.9% of the working population of the city earn below the National Living Wage of £8.72/hour. The figures concerning child poverty are also alarming; the Centre for Research in Social Policy estimates that 29% of children under 16 in the city live in absolute poverty which equates to 51,604 children. These statistics paint a bleak picture of the living conditions of huge numbers of people in the city.

Like all cities, Leeds is constantly evolving. Old buildings are torn down, new ones spring up and the city limits creep steadily outwards, eating away at the rolling countryside in the name of progress and the hollow capitalist fantasy of eternal economic growth. The more time I spent driving around, the more I was able to see past the surface of the modern city, and I became fascinated by how much of old Leeds is still visible – the repurposed Victorian buildings; the sprawling mazes of back-to-back housing that have been standing for over a century; pubs, mills, libraries, the ghost signs haunting the gable ends of so many red-brick buildings – Bile Beans on Belle Isle Road, Combe's Ale in Hyde Park, Puck Match on Conway Road and countless others – fading memories of a bygone age. I started to see the city as a palimpsest, juxtaposing the layers in my mind in a kind of psycho-archaeology: on the one hand, throwbacks to the Hovis-advert nostalgia of the industrial North, the Yorkshire of coal pits, cobbled streets, flat caps and brass bands, and on the other, the modern scourges of unemployment, benefit dependency, drug addiction, and teenage pregnancy.

Nothing could have prepared me for what I experienced during those months. I took on the driving role thinking it would simply be a useful way to spend the lockdown – delivering parcels and having a chat with whoever I met along the way. Nothing could have been further from the truth. It was an emotionally draining experience, stressful and bruising at times, unutterably sad at others, always tiring, and with an intermittent threat of violence that took me completely by surprise. I saw some things that will stay with me forever, plenty of which I hope to never see again.

Week 1:
Feelings of failure

Number of recorded deaths: 10,612[10]

"I am sorry if people feel there have been failings. I will be very, very clear about that." – Home Secretary Priti Patel's Downing Street briefing, Saturday 11th April 2020

The week begins with a grim milestone as deaths from Covid-19 pass 5000. On Monday 6th April, the number of reported cases stands at 52,000. Government Chief Scientific Adviser Sir Patrick Vallance says that cases are not accelerating at the predicted rate, but it's too early at this stage to say if the outbreak has reached its peak in this country. The Resolution Foundation – an independent thinktank that focuses on improving living standards for those on low to middle incomes – says that nine million workers are expected to be furloughed under the Government's Coronavirus Job Retention Scheme at an estimated cost of thirty to forty billion pounds. Foreign Secretary Dominic Raab – deputising for Prime Minister Boris Johnson, who has been hospitalised after contracting the virus – says that the impact of lockdown is emerging, but it's too early to talk about lifting restrictions. At the same time, people are encouraged to stay at home over the upcoming bank holiday weekend, despite the glorious weather that has been forecast. On Saturday 11th April, occupancy of critical care beds across the NHS peaks at 58% of capacity, at the same time as NHS staff report a lack of adequate Personal Protective Equipment (PPE). The week ends as it began with another milestone passed – on Sunday, the death toll

10 The statistics for the number of recorded deaths throughout this book are taken from the Department of Health and Social Care's official figures and indicate the total number of deaths recorded up to and including the final day of the given week, in this case Sunday 12th April 2020. These figures include only people who died within 28 days of a positive Covid-19 test.

exceeds 10,000. Health Secretary Matt Hancock calls it "a sombre day".
Boris Johnson is released from hospital on the same day.

Friday 10th April

Good Friday is the first day of deliveries and I'm really not sure what to expect.

The official lockdown was announced on 23rd March so I've been at home for nearly two weeks, and already the days have become the same. The weather's been beautiful and I've enjoyed having some time to spend with my wife and kids – painting fences, *finally* sorting the garden, walking in the park, long afternoons where they've spent the whole time playing nothing but that wonderful game called Let's Lob Waterbombs at Daddy – but I'm excited by the prospect of taking on the new role and looking forward to getting started.

From the outset, it's an unsettling and unnerving experience. The drive to the Food Distribution Centre takes me from home up Meanwood Road and through the bottom of town with not another vehicle in sight. There are loads of roadside signs about the virus even on this short journey, foreboding and faintly totalitarian

Stay Home. Protect the NHS. Save Lives.

Thank you Key Workers

SHN – Stay Home Now

Leeds is like a scene from a sci-fi movie. Across the Eastgate Roundabout I can see the bus station, empty and silent as the tomb of Christ on this Easter weekend. In the middle distance there's the brand new John Lewis and Victoria Gate shopping centre with its multi-story car park, built on the site of the old Millgarth nick, which was bulldozed to make way for it a few years ago as part of the plan to modernise the city centre. To the left, the dazzling new Leeds City College buildings rise up in all their splendour, and on my immediate right there's Eastgate Job Centre, which raises a shudder every time I go near it. Before I started my work for the city's libraries I used to have to queue up there once a fortnight to sign on, and the place holds nothing but bad memories for me. There are a couple of small grotesques stuck to the dirty white stone above the door, leftovers from one of the building's previous incarnations, but instead of the JobCentrePlus logo between them I think there should be a sign saying *Abandon All Hope, Ye Who Enter Here.* On weekdays there are always queues outside, people smoking, swapping gossip and killing time till they get let in, while over the road the masses should be pouring into Victoria Gate ready to make the cash registers sing.

It's like aliens have come down in a spaceship and removed all the people; I've lived in this city for thirteen years and been a visitor here for most of my life, but I've never seen it like this before; it's freaking me out already. The stillness, the silence, the complete lack of sound or motion from anything but my own car, the feeling that we're in the midst of something completely unique and epochal, wondering where the fuck all this is going to end up – it's a real head trip and I haven't even started the job yet.

I carry on, past the College of Music and Leeds Playhouse on the left, past the BBC building, under the sooty arches of the railway bridge and on towards to the bottom of Richmond Hill where the road turns into Pontefract Lane, and from there it's a straight line right into the industrial estate. The first thing I see is Leeds Recycling and Energy Recovery Facility – known to locals as 'the incinerator' – a huge structure of wood and glass that stands at forty-five metres high, rising to seventy-five metres with the thin metal chimney poking out of the top. It opened in 2016 with the aim of reusing black bin waste to generate eco-friendly power. The structure itself is striking enough, but when you drive past you see that most of the road-facing side is covered with a living wall of plants, the yellow, green and purple shrubbery an effort to promote biodiversity and reflect the environmentally friendly aims of the site. I've always found it eerie, like someone's plucked a building from *Metropolis* and dropped it at the edge of the city, but it's even stranger today in the aching quiet.

Cross Green is deserted too. Usually it's a throbbing, clattering hum of HGVs, tankers, flatbeds, artics and fleets of white vans, plus a steady flow of traffic driving to and from the M1, but not today. I cruise past the incinerator, past the William Cook Rail plant with its rusty corrugated roof, flaking blue frontage and yard full of heavy metal, past the vast wasteland where a new development of industrial units is being built. The next major landmark I see is another new development, the Amazon complex at the top end of the estate, which is so big it can be seen from about half a mile away and is situated more or less opposite the FDC. I drive past it, double-taking at the sheer fucking *size* of the thing; with its three warehouses surrounded by wooden stakes, crash barriers and a high-security fence, it looks more like a small airport than a retail facility. There's a car park big enough for hundreds of vehicles, but it's empty. It looks like even Jeff Bezos has given his staff some time off today.

It's half past eight by the time I arrive and slide into one of the few free spaces in the tiny car park at the FDC. I'm feeling weirdly nervous. Other than going out to the park with my wife and the kids, I've not had any human contact for about a fortnight. I'm always shy in unfamiliar surroundings and around people I don't know, so I sit in the car while I try to stop my nerves from jangling. After five minutes or so, I pull myself together and decide to crack on. No point sitting out here when there's work to be done, and I *did* volunteer to be here after all.

The first thing I see are handwritten signs scrawled on A4 paper in black marker, stuck to the glass doors with blu-tac.

WASH YOUR HANDS. SCRUB. RINSE.

It's a reminder, as if I needed one, that the circumstances are far from normal, no matter how hard I'm trying to convince myself that they are. The room itself is pretty spacious – white walls and a hard-wearing blue carpet, a water-cooler in the far corner – and I'm struck straight away by how many people there are. I was told to get here at nine; it's barely twenty to and already there are six or seven other people here – drivers, presumably. I don't recognise any of them, and I don't think many of them know each other either. A few are wearing face masks and everyone's trying to position themselves so they're not standing too close to anybody else. The concept of social distancing[11] is still a new one, and even later when we're weeks into the pandemic I'll never get used to it. There's an awkward atmosphere, everyone staring at their shoes and no one really saying much as a

---

11 Another neologism synonymous with the pandemic. According to Wikipedia, "social distancing, also called physical distancing, is a set of non-pharmaceutical interventions or measures intended to prevent the spread of contagious disease by maintaining a physical distance between people and reducing the number of times people come into close contact with each other. It usually avoids keeping a certain distance from others [...] and avoiding gathering in large groups."

security guard with a bald head and hi-vis vest who I'll later come to know as Johnny comes round with his signing-in sheet.

I've been told to report to Sharon, who I assume is the woman sitting at a desk next to the window, staring at a computer and speaking to someone on the phone while simultaneously having another conversation via Skype messenger. Eventually she stops both and turns round.

Morning everyone, she says, smiling. Sorry about that. We've got a lot to get out today and I've got some job sheets ready so we can get cracked straight on. Walk this way...

Shuffling feet, the slow forming of an orderly queue, no one really wanting to be first and everyone still trying to avoid everyone else, like a posse of drunks at a silent disco. While I'm waiting a door opens at the back of the room and I spy Dale, a lad I used to manage once upon a time. I'm pleased to see a familiar face and it breaks a bit of the tension I've been feeling. We have a quick chat about work and how things are going. We work at opposite ends of the city now so we don't see each other much, but he's a good guy and it's nice to catch up. We're talking quietly, almost in a whisper so as not to break the silence in the room. He keeps moving slightly away from me, and I keep moving towards him because I can't properly hear what he's saying. By the time we finish speaking, we've moved about five feet away from where we started; I've lost my place and have to go to the back of the queue.

When it's my turn, Sharon is all smiles.

What's your name? Stu? Jane said you were coming. It's your first day, innit?

I nod.

You'll be right, there's nothing to it. Drive round to the warehouse, give this list to the people there, and they'll sort you out. When you've delivered all the parcels, come back here, see me and I'll give you another list, alright?

Sure.

I walk outside, looking at the paper in my hand. It's a list of names, addresses and phone numbers, with a single digit number – 1 or 2 – next to each one. All the addresses on this sheet have an LS14 postcode – Seacroft – which is handy, because I've worked around the estate for years and know it well.

On the other side of the chickenwire fence that borders the car park I can see the rest of the unit – a huge metal structure with two gaping doorways, goods in and goods out. There are a couple of drivers in their own cars loading stuff into their boots, but most of the people I can see are in Leeds City Council vans. I was offered one when I said I'd take on the role but politely declined, preferring to use my own vehicle. I hang around for a few minutes, wait for most of the drivers to pull out, then drive into the warehouse yard and back the car up to the goods out door. The guy at the warehouse is chatty and friendly, asks if it's my first day. I tell him it is, embarrassed and feeling like I don't really know what I'm doing.

Give us your list here, he says. Right, let's have a look. This number here – that's how many dry bags you get for each house, so that's one for this one and this one, two for here...

He goes down the list, confirming the numbers.

Right, so as well as that, everyone gets a bag of fruit and veg, and a bag of fresh stuff out the fridge. Dry bags are over there – grab yourself some of them and I'll go get the rest. We've got some bread today an' all, so you need one of them for each address.

He turns and wanders off, leaves me gaping in astonishment at the size of the place. It's massive, pallets of food everywhere, tins of soup, bags of rice, cases of Pot Noodles, boxes of chocolate bars and breakfast cereal, packets of tea piled in stacks four and five feet high. I'd like to have a proper look round, but the warehouse man comes back with my stuff.

Here y'are. Stick these in the boot. Did you get your dry bags and your bread?

I shake my head.

Over there. He points to some more wooden pallets with what I'd estimate to be at least a couple of hundred Morrisons carrier bags on them. Next to them are some plastic trays packed with wholemeal Hovis loaves.

Grab what you need, bud, I'll see you in a bit.

I take the parcels he's brought me – a mixture of lumpy fruit and veg bags and some cold food that's just come out of the fridge – and put them in the back of the car, then go back for some of the carrier bags. They're packed to the top with pasta, rice, tins, teabags, biscuits – including an Easter egg in each one – and pretty heavy, but I used to work on a building site moving plasterboards for a living in one of my former lives so I grab as many as I can manage without breaking the handles and throw them in the boot on top of the other stuff before going back and collecting some bread. I'm keen to crack on.

Seacroft is one of the biggest housing estates in the country, and the second biggest in Yorkshire (behind Bransholme in Kingston upon Hull). It was built in the 1950s as an extension of the existing Seacroft Village, starting with traditional red-brick houses and then adding some prefabs and high-rise tower blocks in the 1960s as the city expanded in the wake of World War 2. These days it's a densely packed urban jungle that's often taken to include the Whinmoor and Swarcliffe estates, all emanating out from the Seacroft Green shopping centre with its busy bus station and gigantic Tesco. Some parts of it are extremely deprived, with drugs and crime rife.

I first started working in the area after a library restructure and small promotion in 2015. Back then the only time I'd visited the area was to have my first ever interview for a library job in the office of the old Seacroft library, hidden away next to the working man's club behind Tesco; both buildings have long-since been closed and bulldozed.

As far as first mornings on the job go, it's not too bad. I've had a skeg through the list and I know where all the addresses are so I won't have to rely too much on my satnav. The first name on the list is a house on a street off South Parkway, one of the main thoroughfares that bisects the estate. It was home to a community of Irish travellers until about eighteen months ago when the council cleared them off the waste ground they'd been living on and fenced it all in, ready to build more new houses to go with two other new developments in a part of the estate that was already packed.

There's a note on the job sheet saying the gentleman is disabled and may take a while to come to the door. When I get there, the door's already open so I give him a shout and he wheels himself over from where he's sitting in front of the telly watching one of those shows where people hunt for antiques at car boot sales. He's an oldish man, in his 60s probably, red faced, balding and with a tractor tyre of flab bulging out around his waist. I'm not sure if I'm supposed to go into people's houses but I offer to carry the bags in for him anyway. He's not bothered.

Just chuck it down there, kid. He points to a spot inside the front door, roll-up on the go and fag ash dropping all down the front of his string vest. I'll shift it when you've gone.

No worries, chief.

The time passes quickly. I cross the estate a couple of times, dropping parcels off at different addresses, including one for an old woman whose house has five or six jumbo bags of cat litter piled up at the bottom of the staircase and who said she wasn't worried about feeding herself but wondered how her cats were going to cope.

I wasn't sure how many people there'd be about, but it's hard to tell yet if the lockdown has made any difference as a lot of people on the estate are usually still in bed at this time, and it's not uncommon to see people walking the streets in their dressing gowns even in the middle of the afternoon. It's a pleasant morning, hot already, and there's a smattering of people around, mostly young men in the estate uniform of dirty grey tracky bottoms and matching top, always worn with the hood up whatever the weather, usually with a baseball cap as well. There are a few mums too, toddlers with clutching hands and cuddly toys, but it doesn't really look or feel all that different to any other day.

One of the drops takes me into a narrow crescent of semis in the Boggart Hill area, one of the most deprived parts of the estate. I remember being at a multi-agency meeting in the area once, where a policeman told me that over the weekend he'd had someone from near here in his custody. They'd told him, I'll bite your fucking nose off and spit it back in your face, you cunt. The person in question was a ten-year-old boy.

It looks like a war zone. In common with much of the rest of the estate there are shopping trolleys crashed all over the place and rubbish everywhere, strewn all over the grass verges in front of people's houses. All of the small front gardens – and I mean *all* of them – are absolutely trashed, overgrown, choked with weeds. Every other garden has a smashed TV set being devoured by the undergrowth, and the ones that don't are scattered with old mattresses, their springs rusting and their foamy viscera spewing out. The road is so narrow that it's hard to park the car, and in the end I ditch it in the middle of the road and run to the drop. My knock is answered by a woman in a dressing gown, probably about my age – late thirties -, sucking on a fag and smelling like she's had a vodka and tonic for breakfast. The house stinks of smoke and there's dogshit all over the yard, mouldering in the morning sun. I say hi, try to hold my breath and give her the food as quickly as I can. She's swaying a little on her feet as she gives me some effusive thanks, then shuts the door in my face.

It's nearly dinnertime already, but there don't seem to be many more people about as I drive through the estate and back to the FDC. There are a couple of the other drivers sitting drinking brews and waiting for Sharon to give them another job sheet. It's a similar atmosphere to this morning, muted and awkward.

After about an hour, Sharon gives me another sheet. It's a long one, drops in Tinshill, West Park, Moortown, Alwoodley, Wetherby, Garforth, Kippax, Rothwell and Swillington. The areas are spread out all over the city and it's clear that this will probably take all afternoon.

Tinshill is an area I'm not hugely familiar with. I know where it is and how to get there, but I've no real sense of what the community is like. When I get there, it's a mixed bag; Tinshill Lane has some gigantic houses on it, big semis that look like they have four or five bedrooms, one with a full-sized wooden playhouse being erected in a huge tree that overlooks the main road. But once you get away from there, there are lots of winding little Crescents, Closes, Mews, Views and Garths lined with parked vehicles on both sides of the street and practically impassable, even in a smallish car like mine. I manage to find the address I'm looking for and park a good couple of hundred yards away – no problem usually, but not quite as convenient when you're carrying three bags of heavy shopping.

Like so many streets in Leeds, this one consists of a row of red-brick semis, with many of them having been turned into flats, so the occupier of the downstairs uses the front door, and the upstairs uses the one at the back. The address I have must be for the upstairs flat as I can't see the number from the street.

I head down the side of the house, past the overflowing bins and overgrown patch of moss and weeds that passes for a lawn. Whatever paint or varnish has been used on the back door is long gone, leaving bare timber tinged with green fungus that's dried out in the sun. I knock, having no idea what to expect. The door opens the tiniest crack, a couple of pink fingertips the only sign that there is anybody inside. A cloud of verdant, fragrant weed smoke billows out, then a disembodied male voice croaks, Who are you and what do you want?

I introduce myself and the door swings open, revealing an emaciated man of about fifty, with shortish grey hair and patches of stubble stuck all over his face. His eyes are red from the weed he's been smoking, but they're wide and staring too, like a cornered animal. As soon as he's opened the door he backs away and points to the mat. Just leave it there, he says.

I do as he says and ask how he's doing.

I'm glad you've brought all this, he tells me, this stuff will last for *weeks*. I never was much of one for eating. I fuckin' hate going out an' all. Here, let me tell yer what happened to me when I tried to go shopping on Monday...

So saying, he launches into a tale about how he'd gone to Asda up at Holt Park and been kicked out by security because he kept calling the other customers fucking crazy bastards when he didn't think they were socially distanced enough.

I mean, like, this fella was standing about as far away from me as you are now, right, but then he came to walk right past me and I was like whoa! he says, jumping backwards onto the staircase, *Mission Impossible* style, to demonstrate how he got out of the way. It's comical really, but you can already see the effect that the pandemic is having on some people. I'm assuming that this man is slightly paranoid at the best of times, possibly somewhere near agoraphobic judging by his story, but it's clear that this has been exacerbated by the new social distancing rules.

The following three drops are all sheltered housing complexes for older people, a couple in Alwoodley and one all the way out in Wetherby, which is a ten-mile drive away. The ride to Wetherby is as picturesque as usual, and I've got the road to myself here too. There isn't the same end-of-the-world feel here as there is in the city centre though – if I really try, I can convince myself it's a normal, peaceful drive in the countryside and that there's no cataclysmic threat to the health of the nation, the lush fields rolling by in the roiling heat of the early afternoon as prettily as they would on any other day.

The woman I'm delivering to is ancient and looks like she's being eaten by her armchair, huddled beneath a blanket despite the blazing heat. I'm greeted by a bewhiskered, white-haired Scottish man in his 70s who smiles and manages, Just pop it down there, lad, but that's all I get out of him by way of conversation.

The next couple are in Garforth, which is an area generally considered to be one of the more affluent in the city. The house is a big semi with a tidy front garden, a beautifully manicured lawn surrounded by colourful flowers and two cars with 2019 number plates parked on a spacious drive.

No one answers the door so I ring up and speak to a man who sounds like he could be in his late 50s or early 60s, but it's difficult to tell over the phone. He's well-spoken and polite, hugely grateful for the help, and asks how much it costs. I tell him it's a free service and he's gobsmacked. He asks if I can leave the parcels on the step for him so I oblige, and half an hour later I get a text from him and his wife thanking me for my help.

For the next drop, I go to the wrong house. I knock on the front door of a run-down semi, white paint flaking off and much of it covered in grey-green patches of damp. There's no answer so I knock again and wait. Still no answer, so I call the number on the sheet.

Yeah? A low voice on the end of the phone, suspicious and wary.

I tell him who I am and why I'm there.

Ah sound, cheers mate. The voice brightens instantly. Door's open. D'yer mind just sticking it inside? I'm disabled and I can't lift a lot.

No worries, I reply, but when I try to open the door, it's locked. I tell him this, but he says it definitely isn't.

Have you got a Mondeo on the drive? I ask, looking at the rusty green hulk next to me.

Fuck no, mate, I can't drive. I can barely walk half the time.

Ah bollocks. Hang on. Can you confirm the address for me again?

Turns out I've come down the wrong street, although thankfully it's only a thirty-second drive for me to get to the right house. I pull up outside, push the door open and call inside. The house is wrecked, judging by what I can see from here. There's no carpet on the floor, and no gripper rods to indicate that there has ever been one, just a load of splintered floorboards caked in a thick layer of dirt; there's nothing on the walls either, bare plaster showing through thin layers of paint, chunks gouged out of the walls where they've been bumped by some sharp implement or other, a few wires poking out like veins from a severed limb. On the floor next to the door, piled the best part of a foot high, flops months of unopened mail and circulars. Everything I can see is covered in a layer of gritty grey dust, like someone's opened a bag of cement and hit it with a cricket bat.

The man who comes out is a little younger than me, mid-30s probably, wrapped in a black towelling dressing gown. He's leaning on a thin cane, gaunt-faced and eyes half-vacant, not quite the thousand-yard stare but definitely well on its way. There's a powerful reek of fag smoke and body odour, and not for the first time today I find myself holding my breath.

Thank you so much, our kid, he's smiling. I'm absolutely fuckin' starvin'. I can't remember when I last ate.

This last bit chills me; it's the first indication that the food parcel service isn't going to be solely for those who are isolating because of the virus. There are a lot of people out there struggling to feed themselves and they're in desperate need of help.

I wish him all the best and head back to the car. I'm a bit shaken, wondering how on earth he's ended up living like that. Before we bought the house we live in now, my wife and I went to look at one that was advertised as being "in need of complete renovation." When we went in, it looked like a lunatic had been at it with a chainsaw. The entire place was levelled – all the furniture was broken, the spindles from the staircase had been ripped out, the plasterboards on the walls were caved in, there were bare wires everywhere and there wasn't a single intact pane of glass in the whole building. One of the rooms had a rock-hard pile of stalagmitic cement in the middle of it; another had a heap of something that looked and smelled like human shit, and we were horrified to find out afterwards that the house was actually inhabited. Prices being what they are in Meanwood, it still sold for over a hundred grand, and that was nearly ten years ago now.

We came out of it wondering what could be going on in someone's life for them to be reduced to that. My wife worked for Shelter at the time and had been inside some horrific properties with her clients, but even she was surprised by the level of devastation in that one. This lad in Garforth clearly isn't that far gone yet, but I get the sense that he could be one day if he hasn't got adequate support, and mental health services are hard to access these days.

The next drop is at another sheltered housing complex in Kippax, a couple of miles from Garforth, heading out towards mining territory on the eastern edge of the city. I struggle to park, and struggle again to get in as I don't have the access code for the door, but two older ladies who are sitting on a bench outside having a socially distanced brew are kind enough to let me in. The person in the flat is an old man, eighty if he's a day, propped up on a three-wheeled walking frame with a basket on the front. He's sallow and bald with a few liver spots on his head and looks like he's about ready to drop dead, but he greets me with a big smile.

Shall I carry them in for you, chief?

Nay bother, kid, just pop 'em down there and I'll take 'em one at a time.

I put the lightest one into his basket and leave the other two by the door.

Have a good day, kid. Will you bring us some more another time?

I tell him to give the helpline a call when he starts running out so we can get him back on the list. It's a sad thing to think of an old man living on his own like that with no one to help with his shopping, and there must be tens of thousands more like him all over the country. So much work has been done by local authorities and third sector organisations over the years to reduce social isolation in the elderly, but all that is being undone now as they're being told to stay home alone for the foreseeable future.

There are still three drops to go this afternoon. I ask the ladies outside if they can point me in the direction of the next one and they do their best, but I get lost in the middle of a tiny estate with streets so tight I can barely get the car down them. The only people around who may be able to help are four lads in sports casuals who are sitting on the bonnet of a Ford Fiesta, banging on cans of Carling and smoking some potent-smelling weed, but the evil eyes they're giving me tell me it's probably best not to ask.

I eventually end up in a similarly cramped street not too far away, houses on both sides creeping up a steep hill into a cul-de-sac so enclosed it's impossible to turn around. I'm not convinced I'm in the right place, so I give the woman a call.

I'm not being rude, love, but I won't come out, she tells me, after confirming I'm at the correct address. Leave it on the back step and I'll get it after.

Sure thing, I tell her.

Can I just ask you something? She sounds apprehensive.

Of course, go ahead.

These parcels – I mean, are they safe?

I hope so. I've been driving round with them in the boot of my car since half nine this morning.

Is it okay that other people have touched them, I mean?

I do my best to reassure her. Truth be told, I've no idea if it's safe or not. I don't know how many pairs of hands these have passed through while being picked and packed in the warehouse; I'm assuming that everything has been rigorously risk-assessed and the people working in there are wearing gloves, but I don't know that for sure. She's happy enough by the time she gets off the phone though, and I've just got time to do the last two drops before home time. I've covered a hundred and sixteen miles in the car today and I'm feeling pretty tired from the heat, but I've enjoyed it for the most part. It'll be interesting to see what tomorrow brings.

Saturday 11th April

After an enjoyable first day yesterday, I wake up in a good mood and I'm keen to get back on the road. Easter Saturday starts off in a similar vein to Good Friday – a lonely drive through the bottom end of the empty city. The first job of the day is a meds run down to Morley. It's the first time I've done one but it's simple; I need to pick up some medication from a pharmacy and deliver it to the person whose name is on it. This should be simple enough, but it transpires that the meds drops never are.

The trip takes me a couple of miles down the M1 and then onto the M62, always busy even at the quietest times and usually a guaranteed nightmare to drive on. Today, I drive the entire twenty-odd-mile round trip without seeing another vehicle. Driving on the deserted motorway and taking it all in, the enormity of the situation really starts to hit me and I realise what a privileged position I'm in. The empty city is one thing, but the empty motorway is quite another. I bet no one has seen this, ever – even when it was being built, there would have always been construction vehicles and transport for the people that were working on laying the thing, but for twenty minutes both ways I've got the entire road to myself. It's unreal. It starts to dawn on me that I've got front row seats to the end of the world, an Access All Areas pass to the entire city, big enough to hold 800,000 inhabitants, at a time when everyone else is being instructed to stay at home and only go out when absolutely necessary. This is akin to how Michael Collins must have felt on Apollo 11 flying solo round the dark side of the moon when Neil and Buzz were taking their one small step. It's mind-blowing.

The drive is punctuated with a fruitless trip to a pharmacy which turns out to be closed, locked up and bolted behind a security fence, but it doesn't feel like a wasted journey. The solitude of the motorways with the countryside flying by and the absolute emptiness of the world around is something to really savour. If I live to be a hundred, I bet it's something I'll never get to see again.

When I get back to the FDC I'm spaced out, lost in a reverie about what I've witnessed, the enormity of the events I *haven't* seen, but I come crashing back to Earth when I turn off the roundabout and slow to a halt behind the enormous queue of vans waiting to get into the Amazon complex. There is a line waiting to get into a car park on the right-hand side of the estate; I find out later that they have to go in there to register before they're allowed near the warehouse on the opposite side of the road, which means that there are now something like 50 vans queuing in either direction, every single one of them making it impossible for me to get back to the FDC any time soon. It seems Jeff's Eastertime generosity to his staff doesn't stretch to a whole weekend.

Eventually I get back and pick up another job sheet. All these drops are in the Richmond Hill/East End Park area, which is only a few minutes' drive away. Richmond Hill is one of the areas of the city that used to house industrial workers, and it remains full of ancient dwellings that have long-since seen better days. Its dubious claim to fame is that in 2012 it was named as one of the worst hit areas for teenage pregnancy in the whole country, with one in ten girls from the estate becoming pregnant before the age of eighteen.

It's a difficult area to drive around. I'm not unfamiliar with it because I used to work around here, but the endless maze can be tricky when half the streets have bollards blocking the ends. The houses are characteristic of so many in the city: tiny, weather-beaten, redbrick back-to-backs stretching out in all directions. These days most of them have additional metal gates across the front doors, a sign of the crime and insecurity that plagues the estate.

There are a few jobs in this area; one of the quirks of the lists is that the addresses aren't given in any kind of logical sequence, they're just grouped together by postcode. I do three drops over the course of this run that are within a couple of hundred yards of each other but are at opposite ends of the list, a bit like trying to do a jigsaw puzzle without a picture to work from and slotting the final pieces in at the end.

East End Park stands in stark contrast to the rest of the estate. Driving round the wide streets, tall trees laden with the most beautiful pink blossom appear out of nowhere, pushing up through huge cracks in the pavement. In the park there's a children's playground;

government legislation has ordered all playgrounds to be closed and many have been taped off or padlocked, but this one is standing alone and unsecured. Anyone who wants to access it can step over the perimeter fence, which is only about three feet high. There's not much there – a broken slide, a knackered climbing frame; it's empty, but for a couple with three kids tossing a basketball into a rusty, netless hoop.

In the middle of this run, there's a drop on York Road. York Road is one of the main thoroughfares that starts down by the Playhouse and goes out to the east of the city, and it's possible to follow it right out of Leeds and all the way to Scarborough. Trying to find the drop is virtually impossible; most of the buildings by the side of York Road are warehouses and shops, plus the beautiful building which used to house York Road Swimming Baths and public library and has been Grade II listed since 1987.

It's a dual carriageway so there's no room for error. I'm looking for an even number in the mid-300s. I drive up and down twice, which takes about half an hour; I can see 324 and 424 but nothing in between. I turn off, park outside a paper shop on a side street and explore a little on foot, but no dice. For some reason, the satnav thinks the place I'm delivering to is somewhere on the central reservation so in the end I have to give up; hopefully another driver will be able to find it later.

From there I have a drop in Gipton, which borders the Seacroft area. It's near the Church of the Epiphany where I've been visiting the food bank once every six weeks for the last four or five years, providing library books to the congregation of older people who meet weekly in the church hall café next door and trying to engage with the food bank users to signpost them to council services that might help them. Anecdotally, there's been a huge increase in traffic through the food bank since I started visiting, and this is clearly backed up by the statistics. According to Leeds Food Aid Network, 20,514 people benefitted from food banks in Leeds in 2014; by 2019, this had rocketed to 33,645.[12]

Food banks like the one I visit were set up to meet an identifiable community need as government benefit changes – including the introduction of ill-fated and widely condemned Universal Credit scheme – started to seriously impact those on low incomes. The place

12 Leeds Observatory (2020), Leeds Poverty Fact Book: Food Poverty [online]. Available from: https://observatory.leeds.gov.uk/leeds-poverty-fact-book/section-6-food-poverty/

is packed every week now, and it's heartbreaking to see young families with newborns pushing their prams up the road to try to get some help. It's impossible to under-estimate the damage done to low-income families by successive Conservative governments, and the rise of the food banks is just one bitter proof of this.

At the drop there's a sign saying to knock at the side door but the path is barred by a gate, maybe five and a half feet high, made of rotten wood and falling off the hinges, with a sign on it saying BEWARE OF THE DOG. I decide to chance it, give the gate a prod with my boot and it swings open with a creak. There's not much of a garden, just three feet of spidery grass growing underneath a hedge that looks like it hasn't been cut in years; the side door has a plastic handle screwed into the wall, the kind that are put in for people with mobility issues to grip when they climb up a step. There are dog turds festering everywhere and more fag ends than I can count.

I knock and wait. Eventually the door opens. I'm greeted by a woman, in her early 70s by the looks of her, roll-up glued to her lip, holding a Schnauzer in a harness – though goodness knows why it needs it. It looks like a lazy, decrepit thing – it's not even pulling and the lead is slack. So much for beware of the dog. The smell from the house is one of fag smoke, damp and dog shit. I ask how she's doing and try to have a chat but she's too busy talking to the dog, waves a hand in the general direction of the grass – leave it there, will yer, love? she says.

The last drop on this run is back in Richmond Hill. It's a narrow street, cutting through the back-to-backs, wide enough to get the car down but not much more than that. It's a gnarly scene. The people here have reacted to the lockdown instructions by having a party; sofas have been dragged outside and grime music slams from a living room window. There are nine or ten people hanging around guzzling bottles of Kopparberg and passing round a spliff the size of a carrot. They clock me a mile off, staring daggers as soon as the car turns the corner, never mind when I park up at the top of the street.

I say hello and ask them if they know where number 48 is, despite the fact that one of the sofas is clearly right outside the front door. They're immediately evasive.

Maybe it's that one over there? one of the girls says. She wears massive hoop earrings and has hair scraped back, pulled so tight you can practically see her skull through her skin. She's pointing at number 57.

I'm trying to be nonchalant but the atmosphere is heavy – the sense of otherness is palpable. I've worked on estates like this across the city for at least ten years, but this feels edgy. Usually when I'm doing outreach work it's in neutral spaces like schools or community centres so I can meet people on an equal footing, but today I'm on their patch and they don't look happy. No one's smiling. They're waiting for me to make a move and I'm not sure how this is going to pan out. It all feels quite intimidating.

Nah, I say. I don't think it's that one.

Who are you looking for? asks a lad with a diamond stud in his ear and biceps the size of my thighs bulging out of his Chicago Bulls vest.

I give them the name on the sheet and they all squint again. Drinks are swigged meaningfully, the joint is passed; one of the men glares at me and spits on the floor like he's Clint Eastwood staring down Lee Van Cleef.

Never mind then, I say, turning to leave. I had some food parcels, so if you see them can you tell them they need to ring the number again and we'll put them back on the list?

The penny drops.

Ah, mate. Did you say number forty-*eight*? That's *us*.

Yeah man, number forty-eight. Stay there and I'll go get it.

They're happier now, a couple of them coming over to help me unload the car.

Safe, brother, thank you so much for bringing this stuff, yer know, yer a proper legend. Someone pats me on the back, another hand ruffles my shoulder; the idea of social distancing obviously isn't one they're on board with.

I'm nodding along. No worries guys, give us a shout when you need some more. In truth, I'm happy to get out of there in one piece.

My next job sheet is Kirkstall and Burley, familiar territory in parts. When I first became a librarian back in 2010, Burley library was one of my branches and I did a lot of work in the community during the time I was there. It was one of the city's Carnegie Libraries, opened in 1926. It would have been a beautiful building once upon a time, with its glass ceilings, wooden shelves and gigantic reading room but, by the time I took it on, years of under-investment had left it a shadow of its former self: a damp, decaying, cobweb-filled place with peeling plaster, crumbling walls and rats in the cellar, the library equivalent of Satis House. I always had a soft spot for the place, but it closed down in 2016 as it was no longer safe to enter. Like the one on York Road, it attained Grade II listed status in 2017, but at present it looks derelict and sad, as if the whole structure is riddled with cancer and can't wait to die.

It's still desolate out and about. There are occasional cars and the odd jogger, but that's about it. I spy a lad sitting on a garden wall, bony shoulders scarlet from the sun; a couple of young women sashay down the road, one in short shorts and the other in a swishy skirt, laughing at something they're looking at on a phone.

The first drop here is for an older woman on crutches wearing a hair net and pink rollers. She's propped up on her doorstep, taking in the sun.

Eeeee I say, is all this for me? she asks when I carry the bags up the steps for her.

It certainly is, I tell her.

There aren't any fags in there, are there?

I crack out laughing and apologise for the lack of cigarettes, tell her that while we're trying to look after people's needs, we don't quite stretch to feeding their nicotine habits.

Don't suppose you've any Rizlas on you, have you, love? she wants to know. I think there's some baccy in t'living room. God, I could *murder* a tab.

I wish I did, because then I could give her a packet and it would make her day, but she's out of luck. She says she used to go to the shops but her arthritis is bad at the moment and she's not so good on her feet.

And anyway, she says, my neighbours will go mad if they catch me out and about with all this lot going on.

Could they not go to the shop for you? I ask.

I'm sure they will, love, but there was no one in when I phoned them up, and I want a fag *now*.

I'm tempted to go to the shop and buy her some Rizlas myself but I've got too much to do, so I say, Well, hopefully they'll be back before too long.

I bloody hope so, love, I'm gasping. By the way, how much do I owe you? You'll have to wait while I get my purse, it's on t'kitchen table.

When I tell her it's free, she's amazed.

This tendency of the older service users to expect to have to pay for the food parcels is something that will crop up regularly as the weeks go by. The older generations are completely unable to grasp the fact that the service is free; conversely, no one of working age ever enquires about the price. To people of this woman's generation, born around the end of World War Two, the idea of any kind of welfare state is anathema – *you never get summat for nowt*. This all changed in the 70s and 80s, when mass unemployment led to huge dole queues; benefits as a precarious means of support has been embedded in certain parts of society ever since. To people who are used to accessing services for free, the idea of asking how much something like this costs doesn't seem to occur.

The next couple are in Kirkstall – famous for its brewery and the spectacular ruins of its Cistercian Abbey – so I drive back past the bottom of the park and head right onto Cardigan Road. Cardigan Road was always beautiful at this time of year when I worked at the library. There are two towering blossom trees at the end of it – an incongruous sight in the middle of such a densely populated inner-city area – and when the wind blew the blossom would flow up the gutters and the middle of the road in a vast pink river. The trees are in full bloom today, but the air is breathless and still so the blossom stays where it is, soft and plump in the sun.

On the way I have to brake suddenly for a lad accompanied by two kids of pre-school age. He's riding on a Segway, one child holding each hand, and they step out into the road without looking. I grit my teeth and wave him on, then follow him down into the complex of flats where the drop is. I get out of the van and tell him which house I'm looking for. It turns out that it's his. He's only young, early 20s I think, in a vest and shorts with stubby, spiky dreads, all smiles, shoving the joint he's smoking behind his back and thinking I haven't seen it. It's a funny scene, him trying to hide the spliff from me while I carry the parcels up the steps to the flats as he follows behind babbling thanks and his kids try to swipe the Easter eggs from the bags. He's extremely polite and grateful for the food, but I can tell that he's freaking out because he's stoned and wasn't expecting the visit.

To get back to the FDC I have to drive past Hyde Park. On a day like this you'd expect it to be rammed with students, plus all the local pot- and pill-heads getting stoned in the sunshine and soaking up some cold ones to the thump of dub music from numerous miniature sound systems and boom boxes. Today it's deserted – there's not a single person anywhere that I can see – and the fact of its emptiness makes it seem even bigger than usual. There's a skate park at one end and even this is closed.

Right on cue, a single skateboarder comes flying up the road in the opposite direction to the one I'm driving, cruising in the bus lane with not a care in the world. The only other person I can see is a kid in the basketball court who must have scaled the chickenwire fence and is shooting hoops on his own. Further on I pass the Parkinson Building, the most visible part of Leeds University with its white clock tower and big steps up the front of it; even on Saturdays the steps are always full of students smoking, drinking brews and eating cheap food from the cafés and fast food places over the road, but there isn't a single soul in sight here either.

There's one last job to do in Woodhouse before home time. The person at the drop is an old man, well into his eighties. He's a bit hesitant to open the door until I tell him who I am, but he soon warms up. As with so many others of his generation he gets his wallet out to try to pay me, but I wave him away.

It's been a long day and I'm glad to get home at the end of it.

Sunday 12th April

Easter Sunday turns out to be a slow day. The council put out a call saying they needed volunteers for emergency deliveries over this weekend, and they've had such a positive response that there are more drivers than work. I arrive at half eight and there are already loads of people waiting.

It's a different atmosphere today. Standing in one corner of the room are four men – joiners by trade, I gather from their conversation – who obviously know each other well, proper Loiners[13] with accents that speak of B&H, rugby league, meat pies, fifteen pints on a Friday night and fifteen more on a Saturday. They're ripping the piss out of everything and everybody, especially themselves.

How're yer gerrin' on wi' t'pubs being shut, like?

What, yer mean yer didn't trip over his tongue on t'way in?

'Ere, how long were that stretch yer did, three years, were it? What d'ya tell us, yer were in t'army? Fuck off. Think yer missing an L, mate. Arm*l*ey more like.

---

13 Loiner is a term used to describe the citizens of Leeds.

The job sheets are dished out on a first come, first served basis. There were already plenty of drivers here before I arrived, so it takes a long time for Sharon to get to me. By half ten, there's only me and one other woman left waiting for something to do.

Who wants to go to Harehills? Sharon asks.

I shrug. I don't mind going, but I don't mind not going either so I ask the other driver what she wants to do.

I'll go, she says. Then, oh, hang on, you'll have to do this one, actually. She hands me the sheet.

Fine with me, I say, standing up. Any particular reason?

She laughs. I work for the anti-social behaviour team and I've had dealings with this lot. Let's just say they won't be pleased to see me, even if I *do* rock up at their house with a load of free food on a Sunday morning...

It'll be interesting to see what Harehills looks like today. It's a densely populated, inner-city area, home to a hugely diverse community which statistically figures in the top 5% of the most deprived electoral wards in the country. The main road that runs through it looks more like a Bedouin market most days, lined as it is with Indian supermarkets, Polish and Romanian shops, stalls on the pavement, people of all different creeds and colours bustling around in tight crowds, everyone talking in a polyglottic babble, smoking, shaking hands, hugging, eating and drinking things from the shops and takeaways. It's been the scene of some violence in recent years, with multiple stabbings in the area in 2017.

Harehills is buzzing. There aren't anywhere near as many people about as there would normally be, but even so there are more people here than I've seen in the rest of the city combined. There isn't much social distancing on display, and there have been rumours going round that the police have had to increase their presence to disperse the groups of people that keep congregating on the streets.

The drop is on a street off the main drag in a warren of redbrick terraces, back-to-back slum housing that looks like it should have been demolished years ago. The last back-to-backs were built in Leeds in 1937[14], so these houses could easily be a hundred years old. There's trash everywhere, the gutters lined with fag ends, broken glass, sweet wrappers, spent lighters, and whippits – small cartridges of nitrous

---

14 Harrison, J., (2017). The Origin, Development and Decline of Back-to-Back Houses in Leeds, 1787–1937. *Industrial Archaeology Review*. 39:2.

oxide that are supposed to be used to charge up whipped cream dispensers but that some people inhale to get high – sparkling in the sun. When I get out of the car there's an arid stench of decomposing rubbish, the sick tang of rotting fruit and bins that are long past overflowing. A couple of houses on the street have broken windows; a few more have doors that have been boarded up; one place over the road is in such a bad state that even the temporary door is hanging off its hinges. At the house next to it, a bearded man in a thobe eyes me casually while smoking a fag out of the side of his mouth.

The house I'm delivering to is one of the few on the street that is completely intact. I bang on the door a few times, step back and wait. No answer. I bang again, but no one comes. I try phoning, but there's no answer there either. This is frustrating for a number of reasons, but the main one is that we're supposed to be delivering to people who aren't capable of leaving the house, so where have they gone?! The other thing is the referral has only just come through – it's probably been less than an hour from the parcel being requested to me delivering it.

On the way back to the FDC, I ponder the fact that Boris Johnson is to be released from hospital today, having been treated in intensive care for Covid-19. There's much talk of "NHS heroes" and the Government have said that money is no object for the health service, although this position doesn't appear to be consistent with the huge cuts that have been made to NHS funding over the past decade. One great unknown about the pandemic is what will happen in the aftermath, especially from an economic point of view. The Government have promised untold billions to help the nation through the crisis, but it's unclear at this stage how they will recoup the money.

The next job is in Burley. It's a long parade of single-floor flats, not much more than expanded bedsits, which look like they could be some kind of sheltered accommodation. The house next door to the one I'm visiting is clearly unoccupied; it has steel shutters on all the windows and doors to deter the local drug users from shooting up in there. Round the front there's an old computer keyboard snapped nearly in half against the side of the overflowing wheelie bin, plus an assortment of rancid old trainers. Weirdly, none of them match.

It's a sleepy atmosphere in Burley. I notice that a few of the eateries seem to be open – the chippy next to the library, a jerk chicken joint, a Caribbean street food place – but none of them have any customers.

The door is opened by a lad in his early twenties, wearing nothing but boxer shorts, looking like he's just got up. He doesn't seem to have much English, but he smiles his thanks before I get back in the car and head off.

Today marks a grim milestone in the history of the pandemic, the day that the official figure for hospital deaths in this country passed the 10,000 mark. When the crisis started it seemed inconceivable that so many people could die, but this is merely the tip of the iceberg. The Government say that their strategy is contingent on a vaccine and treatment, but a vaccine could take a couple of years to develop, and economically speaking there's no way this can carry on for too long, no matter how much money the Government promises to help. Even at this early stage it's apparent that the exit strategy will be dictated by economic rather than public health considerations, but at this point no one really knows how long this could go on for or where it might end.

Week 2:
A National Scandal

Number of recorded deaths: 16,060

*"We're increasing again PPE supplies for social care.
We're creating a supply logistics and distribution
network of unprecedented scale." – Health Secretary Matt
Hancock's press briefing, Wednesday 15th April 2020*

*According to the Office for National Statistics, Covid-19 was linked to
20% of all deaths in the UK for the week leading up to 3rd April. Early
in the week, charities including Age UK and the Alzheimer's Society
raise concerns for the first time that official statistics are only published
for deaths in hospitals and don't include deaths in either care homes
or people's own homes. Official figures estimate that 1,400 care home
residents may have died from the virus, but Care England calculates
the true figure may be closer to 7,500. Health Secretary Matt Hancock
announces a plan for a network to provide PPE for care home staff.
Later in the week, he also announces that testing will be rolled out to
include more key workers, including those employed by the police, fire
service and prison officers.*

*On 16th April, Foreign Secretary Dominic Raab announces that
lockdown restrictions are to be extended by three weeks; on the same
day, confirmed cases pass the 100,000 mark. Doctors' and nurses' unions
raise major concerns about the shortage of PPE and reveal that staff are
being asked to reuse equipment in cases where there isn't enough to go
around. Shadow Health Minister Justin Madders says, "It is a scandal
that so many key workers and public servants still don't have enough
protective equipment." According to Acting Liberal Democrat Leader
Sir Ed Davey, "It has become clear that the Government is failing to
deliver on key promises to NHS staff and key care workers, especially*

over supplies of protective equipment. Ministers look in danger of losing control." Later, he states, "The lack of protective equipment is a national scandal."

In a letter to Chancellor of the Duchy of Lancaster Michael Gove, Shadow Minister for the Cabinet Office Rachel Reeves writes, "The Health Secretary has in recent weeks suggested that PPE was being used inappropriately by health and care workers and that this was the cause for shortages. Many workers within these sectors have been dismayed at what they feel is an attempt to apportion blame for lack of PPE to frontline workers [...] I would strongly urge the Government not to repeat this suggestion [...] when there is no evidence this is a notable factor." Communities Secretary Robert Jenrick announces that 400,000 gowns have been sourced from Turkey and states that they will arrive by the end of the week. They are two days late.

The furlough scheme is extended by a month until the end of June; the Government also promises another 1.6 billion pounds in aid to local authorities, to go with the 1.6 billion they pledged in March. Shadow Communities Secretary Steve Reed responds to the news of extra funding, saying, "The additional money [...] is nowhere near enough. Councils are facing a financial black hole because of the costs of getting emergency help to vulnerable people and years of underfunding of local government. If the Government breaks their promise to fund whatever is necessary then cuts will follow and some of the frontline workers we're cheering will lose their jobs."

At the end of the week on 19th April, the official death toll stands at 16,060. Liberal Democrat Health Spokesperson Munira Wilsons questions the accuracy of government figures, saying, "The frequency of inaccurate information being given out from the Government is becoming increasingly alarming. [...] The fact that repeated concerns have been raised regarding government figures, whether it is the number of tests, deaths or ventilators, reveals that there is either incompetence, or worse, at the heart of the Government's current approach."

Monday 13th April

My first drop of the day is in Kirkstall.

The city is quiet in the cool of the morning. One thing I've noticed about cruising the empty streets is how much harder it is to drive. I'd thought that with no other traffic it would be easy, but the opposite is actually the case. I'm so used to having the road to myself that I get lost in my head, seeing the desolate city through eyes I'll never get to see it through again, trying to take it all in, to process what's going on, to remember every single minute detail, so when I hit a red light I have to jam on the brakes because I'm so caught up in my thoughts I've almost driven through it before I've even realised it's there. Conversely, what few pedestrians there are seem to have lost all road sense; they've grown so used to there being no traffic on the roads that they often step out to cross without looking, so I need to be alert for them too.

The town end of Kirkstall Road looks run-down at the best of times; empty units, old warehouses, construction sites that never seem to get past the stage of being nothing but rubble and bulldozers, but today it's even worse than usual. Everything is closed. There's some fantastic spray-painted street art on many of the metal shutters, but it's hard to get past the fact that a lot of the places look derelict and I find myself wondering how many of them will ever open their doors to the public again.

On and on the road goes, past the remains of Kirkstall Abbey, stentorian and grand against the grey of the sky. It must have seen an awful lot in the nearly nine hundred years it's been standing, but I wonder if it's ever known a period as bizarre as the one we're living through now.

The drop is in a lovely part of the area. It's a crescent full of big semis with beautiful front gardens, blossom trees, drives full of luxury cars. There are lots of Mercs, BMWs and SUVs, often more than one at the same address. I've got three food parcels for a man who looks ashen when he opens the door, and his voice is so hoarse he can barely speak to say thank you. For the first time, I wonder if I'm staring the virus in the face. This man is certainly ill, and whatever he has is nasty judging by the state of him; he looks like he's so weak it's an effort for him to stand up, and he's supporting himself by leaning slightly on the door frame. I leave the bags on his doorstep and wave goodbye, tell him to take care of himself as he croaks a farewell before closing the door.

The next job I get is in Halton Moor, an estate that's only a five-minute drive from the FDC, on a street typical of this kind of area – red-brick semis, cars parked both sides of the road, the outside spaces running wild with bits of broken garden furniture here and there. I knock on the door at the drop and the living room window opens. It's a woman in her 40s who tells me how frightened she is to go out and how she's been worried she wasn't going to be able to feed herself.

I pass her the bags through the window.

Oh, love, I can't believe you're giving me all this. Are you sure it's alright?

Of course. We're here to help.

I know, love, but there's an awful lot here. I promise I'll make it last. It's just I don't know when I'll be able to get out again with all this going on. I'm bad with my nerves, you see. Her lip starts wobbling, her voice cracks. I just can't cope with all this at all. Thank you so, so much, this is brilliant.

I'm sure she's crying when she closes the window. It's humbling how grateful she is, and I've got a lump in my throat as I walk back to the car. I wasn't prepared for the emotional impact that this kind of work would have on me; I was a little shaken by the lad in the wrecked house in Garforth on Friday but somehow I was able to detach myself from it, maybe because he was so remote himself. With this woman it's not so easy to do that as she's visibly on the point of tears, and this is the first time I feel myself getting upset in the course of carrying out the job.

The next one is a long ride away in Rodley. The drive takes me right through the heart of the town for the first time, past the rainbow bridge which marks the end of the annual Pride march – another event that's unlikely to take place this year – and signifies the start of the gay district. It's Bank Holiday Monday and this part of the city should be packed with shoppers and people hitting up the pubs, bars and food joints, but today there's no one around. Onward, past the train station, which is so quiet it looks like it's been cleared by the bomb squad. From there it's back onto Kirkstall Road, across the river and up the hill to Bramley.

Bramley isn't the prettiest area of the city but Fall Park looks beautiful now as the sun comes out and lights up the blossom on the trees that are planted all the way up the side of it, a fat cotton wool pillow of pink and white. Further on I pass Bramley Baths, another wonderful relic of old Leeds. Built in 1904 on the site of an old foundry, it's now the only remaining Edwardian bath house in the city and another Grade II listed building; the old foundry chimney, made from eight thousand Kirkstall bricks, is a prominent feature of the local skyline. It was slated for closure by the council to save money about a decade ago, but since 2013 it's passed into the hands of a not-for-profit community group, and has been thriving ever since.

When I turn into Rodley I find myself looking for the drop somewhere in a narrow cul-de-sac lined with cars. There isn't much room for manoeuvre here. Two neighbours, a man and a woman at the top end of middle age, are chatting over a front garden wall near where I park, so I give them the house number and ask if they know where it is.

Look over there, smirks the man, all tattoos and Leeds Rhinos shirt, pointing to the corner of the cul-de-sac. Yer can't miss it. There's Christmas decorations all over it. And with that, he gets back to his conversation, asking the woman what kind of flowers she's planning on planting this summer.

I start walking over to where he indicated, and he's right – it sticks out like a sore thumb. It's a small semi, painted white but covered in the accumulated slime of the years, looking like it could do with a good power washing and a repaint. Stuck to the house right above the front door are a couple of shiny reindeer, and above those a fat jolly Santa made out of green and red neon tubing, a tangle of wires tumbling knottily out of the bottom. In broad daylight and bright spring sunshine, they look ridiculous.

I knock on the door to be greeted by a skinny woman with grey dreadlocks right down her back and a couple of little yappy dogs of indeterminate breed capering round her feet, their barking just about drowning out the sound of the telly inside. She's accompanied by a billowing cloud of weed smoke so strong I feel like I could get high if I stuck my head through the door.

Bloody hell love, that was a loud knock, she says in a broad Leeds accent. You frightened the piss out of me. And with that, she shuts the door.

The next job is in Kippax. No one else wants to do it because they don't know the area, but I helped refurbish the library up there about five years back so I know my way around a little bit. The house I'm delivering to is at the end of a tight cul-de-sac. Taking up half the driveway is a dilapidated people carrier that has scores of Jesus Saves stickers plastered all over it. Next to it is a caravan, brown with rust and age and completely unroadworthy, with broken windows and great rents torn into the metal sides.

I squeeze my way past it to the front door. The house looks a mess, dirt and damp all over the walls, rotten, blackened wooden window frames with the glass almost falling out. It looks like if you wanted to break in you could put a pair of gauntlets on and lift them out with your bare hands. The door used to be painted green, but a lot of that has flaked off and the timber beneath has started to go black with mould. A tarnished brass plaque on the wall reads *The Lord's my shepherd, I shall not want.* Another one on a gate next to the side of the house says *Beware of the dog.*

When I knock on the door there's a cacophony of growls and high-pitched yelps, then muffled shouting as someone inside admonishes whatever gang of pooches is trying to get out, followed by the dull thud of a door slamming. The man who comes out is about sixty, wearing baggy, grubby tracky bottoms and a stained string vest that barely covers his gut, which is dangling pendulously somewhere around his knees. A blast of fetid air comes out with him, ripe with a smell of dog shit so powerful it's hard not to retch. He tries to shake my hand before I leave, but I politely decline.

So ends the first stint. I've covered something like three hundred miles in four days, but this is only the beginning. It's been a hugely interesting experience so far, and one I'm glad I volunteered to do. I've covered a wide variety of areas and met people from a whole raft of backgrounds, seeing in the process the first signs of the stark inequalities of wealth and social class that divide the city – for example, the contrast between the relative affluence of a place like Garforth with the poverty of Harehills.

At this stage, at least, it seems that helping victims of the virus is still paramount to the council in terms of the aims and objectives of the Food Distribution Centre, but this will quickly begin to change.

Wednesday 15th and Thursday 16th April

After my first weekend on the job I have a few days at home. It's felt strange to have been out working for nearly a week after being stuck at home for so long, and I appreciate my family time all the more for it. My wife is glad to have me back too. Having two children at home all the time was hard enough when we were both there, but with me out delivering most of the time my wife has had to do everything herself and she's feeling pretty tired as a result; it's good for her to have some respite while I'm off. The weather has been beautiful again so we've spent most of the time pottering around the garden while the kids attack me with their water pistols. I've been pretty tired from the driving too, so a couple of quiet days off together does us all good.

Friday 17th April

Today is an interesting day in that it marks a real change in the communities I'm asked to deliver to. Up until now there's been a reasonably wide variety of demographics across the city, but this is when I really start to get into the more deprived areas. Word has got out on the grapevine that the council are delivering food parcels, so a lot of low-income families are requesting help irrespective of the virus. The day starts with three drops at some tower blocks in the Burmantofts area of the city, near St. James's Hospital – known to locals as Jimmy's.

On the way to the first one I get a bit boggled by the road system where it splits into five and nearly get shunted by a taxi. A loud screech of tyres, a prolonged beep of horn; it's my fault entirely because I cut across the lanes without looking and the poor driver nearly goes right up my back end. I wave a sheepish apology and drive on. At the next set of lights we're parked right next to each other and the window of the taxi comes down. Oh shit, I think, I'm going to cop it now.

The driver sticks his head out of the window and calls to me with a smile, Are you lost, my friend? Next to him, I can see the man in the passenger seat pissing himself laughing.

Really sorry, chief. Just lost sight of where I was. I know where I'm going now.

He laughs and we have a quick chat about the weather while we're waiting for the lights to change. The exchange gives me a warm glow inside; there's so much negativity and anger around, and he'd have been well within his rights to call me a right stupid prick, but the fact that it ended amicably has made my morning. Especially with the blocks I'm about to visit, this could end up being the only high point of my day.

The first is called, somewhat disarmingly, Gargrave Court. I know Gargrave – the real Gargrave – well. It's an idyllic village a couple of miles away from where I was born, and home to one of my favourite pubs, the Masons Arms. My grandma on my mum's side was born in a tiny cottage a couple of doors up from there in the 1920s and got married in the stone church over the road.

This Gargrave is of a totally different stripe, being as it is some fourteen stories of flats with a carpet of broken glass, whippits and spliff ends littering the ground outside. I give the woman a call on the intercom and ask if she can come down for the parcel, but she can't. She says has a bad back and has been displaying symptoms of the virus for two days. She sounds ill, her voice dry and scratchy.

The first thing that hits me upon entering is the eerie atmosphere. There are hundreds of people living here, but it's totally silent. There's a smell in the air of something like hospital disinfectant, overlaid with the lingering perfume of eau de fag smoke and the heady tang of weed. There are holes in the ceiling with bare wires poking down from them and I duck, mindful of catching my head.

I don't really want to get in the lift in case it breaks, but she's on an upper floor and there's no way I can tackle the stairs with three bags of food. The lift is a cramped, dark, smelly thing with a couple of spliff ends crumpled up on the floor and a faint whiff of piss, but it moves smoothly enough. When the door opens, the woman is waiting for me. She's about thirty but looks much older. She has a ravaged face, huge black circles under her eyes and a pasty, spotty complexion, greasy and grey. She's wearing a red dressing gown that's open at the top to reveal a tattoo on her chest, but her skin is wrinkled and saggy so I can't tell what it depicts.

How are you feeling? It's only polite of me to ask, but it's obvious that she's unwell.

Fuckin' rough, mate. She coughs into her sleeve. I did my back in a couple of weeks ago and then two nights ago I started with this. *Cough cough cough.* Had a three-hour nosebleed last night an' all. I need to get back to bed.

I ask if she's okay to carry the bags; if she tells me she can't manage them, I'll take it back to her flat for her. She says she's alright but I wait until I've seen her pick it up to make sure she can carry it before I get back into the lift.

Torre Green is a tower block that's virtually identical to Gargrave Court. I park by the garages at the bottom, hoping that none of the broken glass pops my tyres. I call on the intercom again, and this time the man comes down to meet me. He's not so old, maybe in his 50s, but he only has a couple of teeth in his head and an untidy beard, brown and matted with nicotine which gives him a truly grizzled look. He's as skinny as a rake with bad skin and sunken eyes, his expression a curious mixture of vacant and wild. He's trying to ask me something about who phoned up for the parcel but I struggle to make out the words. It sounds like he's asking if it was his niece, but the lack of teeth makes it hard to understand him and I've no idea who called anyway.

The last of the high rises is Naseby Grange. When I buzz up and speak to the woman she sounds fucked, her rasping drawl scarcely louder than a whisper. So it proves. She buzzes the door open to let me in and I stand downstairs and wait for her, noticing as soon as I go in that this place has an identical feel to Gargrave Court. Save for the faint hum of the lift, there's not much sound in here either; the bare wires hanging from the roof and the smell of disinfectant, weed and smoke are an exact replica too.

When the lift arrives she's so wasted I'm amazed she can stand up. She's in her early 20s, black eyes, head little more than a skull topped with knotted dark hair. She has pin-prick pupils locked into a cold, fixed stare, limbs dragging in a jerky shuffle as if she's trying to move her whole body through a sea of treacle. She sees me straightaway but it takes her some time to properly register my presence.

Got your food parcels. I point at the bags on the floor.

Right, she whispers, barely opening her mouth.

How she manages to pick the bags up will forever remain a mystery but somehow she does and drags her carcass, wraithlike, back into the lift. I bet later on she'll find the food in her flat and have no idea at all how it got there.

The tower blocks done, I have a look to see what's next on the sheet. The next drop is right in the middle of Harehills, not far from The Compton Centre and Library – another place I was based at a few years back. It's swamped with litter, bins overflowing, graffiti everywhere, many of the houses in terrible states of repair. The place I'm delivering to is one of the worst.

I pull up outside a dilapidated terrace with a six-foot wooden gate that falls off its hinges, collapses into the yard and breaks in half when I open it with my foot. It's probably the sturdiest thing about the place. When I see the house my jaw hits the floor. Every single window – including all the upstairs ones – has been smashed and boarded up; the main door has been kicked in repeatedly; this has probably been replaced with a temporary one at some point, but this is missing too and the only thing covering the hole is a piece of splintered MDF held on by some ragged pieces of string. There's the obligatory smashed TV next to the bins, as well as cigarette butts and fag packets spread all over, and the whole yard reeks of stale baccy, piss, puke and mouldy rubbish.

The two young women who come to the door are in as sorry a state as the house. The smaller of the pair hangs back while her friend comes to greet me. She's excruciatingly thin, all bone, arms a mess of bruises, scars and track marks. She's nearly as tall as me – I'm six foot two – and she looks like you could knock her down with a feather. Burned-out eyes bulge from sunken sockets. It looks like she's cut her hair herself, right back to the wood; it's started growing back in erratic patches, blonde clumps emerging from the fuzz like tufts of grass on an uneven lawn.

The inside of the house looks as bad as the outside – no carpets, no wallpaper, nothing but dust, detritus and damage. From where I'm standing on the third step I can see into the kitchen and it looks like the ruined house my wife and I went to look at all those years ago. Cupboards hanging off walls, the floor a mess of fag ends, pot noodle cartons, bits of foil and blackened spoons, empty bottles and cans.

When I introduce myself and tell her why I'm there, there's such a look of relief on her face she looks like she's going to throw her arms around me and give me a hug. I don't know the exact circumstances these women are living under, but it's obvious even from this fleeting encounter that trying to help them with a couple of bags of food is like trying to staunch a bullet wound with a sticking plaster.

She's gushing in her thanks, clearly wrecked but utterly sincere with it and I'm lost for words. I mumble something about phoning up when they need some more and head back to the car, choked with a mixture of unbelievable sadness and inarticulate rage that anyone should have to live in conditions like these. It's unbearable to imagine what kind of life these women must be living, this twilight world of addiction, sickness and starvation. There are thousands more like them all over the city, replicated in towns and cities nationwide. The numbers must be staggering, an unimaginable human tragedy in one of the wealthiest countries on earth.

I have to hang around a bit waiting for a job when I get back. There are a lot more people at the FDC today; the warehouse was operating on a skeleton staff last weekend because of the bank holidays, but today there are about fifteen people inside, doing all the picking and packing to get the parcels ready, plus the people sorting out the food to load onto the vans. It's clear from the size of the place and the number of people what a big operation this is, and it's worth bearing in mind that all of them have volunteered to be here. Every single one of them could be working from home if they chose to. Everyone's working hard to make sure the people that need the most help get it, but when the Government look to make cuts, this could well be where they'll start; when the gaping holes in Council finances become really apparent, tough decisions about public services will have to be made by authorities across the country and jobs will have to go.

The first drop is across the city in Pudsey. It looks busy; a couple of pharmacies have long queues, as does Sainsbury's, and judging by the number of people standing in a line smoking and playing with their phones outside, B&M is doing a roaring trade too. It's odd to see the queues with the social distancing measures in place, everyone standing as far apart as they can, avoiding everyone else's gaze.

The house at the drop is a mess. It's a typical estate street, semis with the now-familiar trashed gardens full of broken TVs and the like. Another thing I notice again and again is the furniture left to rot outside – armchairs, sofas, and quite often entire three-piece suites abandoned to the elements; I can see all of these things on this street. Rather than being red-brick like so many others, these houses have been rendered in an off-white colour, but this one is swimming with black and green ooze that seeps down the front of the house like water down the walls of a cave. The window frames are wooden, paint peeling off in flakes, and the front door looks like you could kick it in without too much effort. Next to the green and grey wheelie bins I count twelve black bin liners bulging with stuff, but I can't tell from here what's in them.

The streets on the way looked nice enough but there's a distinctly different atmosphere here. Two young lads in tracksuits sit in a white Golf outside the house, drinking Cokes from plastic bottles, smoking and giving me evils. They stare at me pulling up, and they're still staring long after I've got back into the car and driven away.

The door is answered by a stick-thin woman with terrible skin, her face pock-marked like the surface of an asteroid-peppered moon. When she opens her mouth to speak her voice is almost as deep as mine, and she sounds like she smokes about sixty a day. She's flanked by a skinny lad whose age is hard to judge – he looks too old for primary school but too young to be a teenager. Even though his hair is cropped short I can see it's thick with grease, and he has the beginnings of a couple of spots on his dirty chin.

Ta love, she says. Is all that for me?

Yeah. I hand her one of the bags and she takes it, the skin on the backs of her hands cracked and dry, nails black and encrusted with muck. It's heavy and she nearly drops it as the weight takes her by surprise.

I'll put these inside for you, shall I. It's more of a statement than a question because it's obvious she won't be able to carry them.

Yeah, that'd be good. She seems edgy, keeps glancing around nervously and shooting what she thinks are furtive looks at the lads in the car. She stands back so I can put the bags in the house for her. Inside the walls are feculent with black mould and there's a lingering smell of shit, as if the toilet or drain is blocked. Through the open living room door I can see part of the ceiling hanging down, great wounds in the plasterboard crumbling flakes of grey dandruff onto the threadbare carpet.

Can you manage them from there? I ask.

Yeah. She puffs on her fag. Tom'll help me. Come on, love, let's get these in t'kitchen. They take a bag each – both of them clearly struggling with the weight – and the door closes, the woman casting a final weary glance back over her shoulder at the lads in the car as she goes in.

The last drop on this list is a real heartbreaker, a woman in a tiny ground floor flat who must be ninety if she's a day, practically bent double with arthritis in her spine, shrivelling up like a salted slug. She's unbelievably grateful, tries to pay me and is stunned when I tell her there's no charge.

You mean it doesn't cost *anything*? she asks incredulously. Well I never. What a *wonderful* thing.

She's another one that leaves me with a lump in my throat. It's been a pretty heavy day so far, from the probable virus victim with the nosebleed in the first tower block to the drug-addled spectre in the third, then the two women in Harehills who clearly had at least one foot in the grave – I'm not even two weeks into the job but I'm already finding it affecting on an emotional level. This old woman reminds me of one of my grandmas, both of whom died aged ninety little more than a year ago, and it's devastating to think how tough it must be for the older generations – who've already lived through so much – having to deal with the current crisis.

Late in the day I'm given a job sheet with eight drops in LS10 and LS11 to get through before the end of the day. These postcodes include areas like Middleton, Belle Isle, Holbeck and Beeston. There are at least thirty libraries in the city and I've worked in all of them over the years, but I've not done much community-based work in South Leeds so these areas are nowhere near as familiar to me as some of the others I've been to – although I know by reputation that there are sizeable pockets of deprivation in all of them.

The first house is in a wide cul-de-sac in LS10. There's a massive gated enclosure round the front, half lawn and half yard. The other houses have similar spaces in various states of disrepair but this one is different. It's full of Christmas decorations, illuminated fairies, tree lights and child-sized garden gnomes, glowing with a sad neon fuzz in the afternoon sun.

The door's opened by a woman who reminds me of Barbara Cartland, complete with lapdog trailing behind her, the only difference being that she speaks with a South Leeds accent and has an asthmatic smoker's cough. She's wearing so much make-up it looks like she put it on with a shovel: pale foundation, thick red lipstick and broad sweeps of green eye shadow, set off by a flouncy dress and a black lace bonnet. Her hands are adorned with rings and her neck is draped with costume jewellery, bright against the blancmange pink of her dress.

She takes the bags with the traditional Loiner expression of thanks. Ta, love, she croaks, turning on her heel and carrying the bags to the door, the lapdog following her every step.

The next drop is on a street full of dirty white semis hemmed in by overgrown hedges so it's difficult to see what's in the gardens. I can see curtains twitching at the sight of the car though, and every neighbour I see glares at me until I leave. I get out and shove open the rickety gate. There's a clump of straggly grass with a couple of paving stones leading to the front door, empty beer cans, fag ends and broken children's garden toys strewn everywhere. A sign in the window, scrawled in biro, says to use the door round the back, so I pull the gate closed and go round the other side. There's a biggish garden, with an overturned pink pedal buggy blocking the path. A washing line stretches from the wall of the house next to the kitchen window to a rusty old pole near the top hedge, hung with tracksuit bottoms, some boxer shorts and a couple of thongs. There's no answer here, so I give the woman a call.

Hiya. It's Stu from Leeds City Council. I've got some food parcels for you.

Oh great, ta, love. When are you coming?

I'm standing on your doorstep. You're supposed to be in.

Oh, right, sorry. My partner's just brought me to work. He'll be back in fifteen minutes if you don't mind waiting.

I don't have time to wait, I'm afraid. I've got six more drops to do before five.

He won't be long. A hint of pleading in the voice.

Look, I've got two more drops to do in LS10 and then I'm going to Beeston. I'll call in here on my way there, ok?

That's great, ta love. It'll have to be before half four though cos he's going out again later.

I tell her apologetically that if there's no one there I'll have to take the parcels back to the FDC. According to the instructions I've been given, if there's no one in the house when I first visit I shouldn't attempt to redeliver the food at all, but I can't help thinking about whatever children she has and that she must have called the helpline for a reason. It's worth remembering a lot of working people live below the poverty line, so if they ask for help we should give it to them – it's not for me, or anyone else, to judge.

The next drop is on a street that's virtually identical, this particular semi standing out because it has a beaten-up caravan covered in football stickers parked on the driveway. The man sees me coming and opens the door without me even knocking. He's thick-set, probably about forty, a tad shorter than me at around six foot but with muscle to spare, tattoos all over both his arms and hands, and a great big Yorkshire Rose right on top of his bald head.

He seems like a nice guy, tells me that he feels bad requesting food but his freezer packed up and he lost everything in it.

I don't like asking for help, our kid. You know how it is. His eyes are cast down in embarrassment, his voice heavy and sad.

Don't worry about it. There's a lot of people need help at the moment.

It's my lad I worry about, yer see. He's only five and he's eating us out of house and home. I've not been working for a while and me money doesn't come through till next week. I'm fucked without that freezer – the stuff in there were gonna feed us till I get paid. Thanks so much for bringing this, love. Christ knows how we'd have managed without it.

Before I move on, I have another go at dropping off the parcels at the house of the woman I spoke to on the phone. Her partner is in his mid-twenties, peering at me from beneath the peak of his baseball cap. Considering how many bags of food I have for him, he doesn't look particularly pleased to see me.

Cheers, he says, without much sincerity. Yer just caught us. I were on me way out again then.

I say nothing and hand the parcels over. We've still got some Easter eggs left over from last week and there's one in every bag. Hopefully his children will enjoy them.

After that there are a couple in Beeston and Holbeck. Dewsbury Road, the main route through the centre of Beeston is thronged with people and makes Harehills look quiet by comparison. It's a diverse, multi-ethnic community here too, with similar houses to Harehills, an impenetrable tangle of decaying back-to-backs with dead ends and bollards blocking the ends of many of the streets. There are groups of people hanging around as usual, no social distancing, and to look at it you wouldn't think that the pandemic was going on at all. Maybe news of it hasn't got to this part of the city, or maybe the people simply don't care.

Beeston runs straight into Holbeck, another part of the city which is woefully deprived in places. It's also notable for being home to the only managed red-light district in the country, where sex work has been decriminalised and the workers are left to get on with it. According to reports, in light of the new social distancing rules, sex workers have been banned from soliciting for the time being, although the council are putting in extra support services to try to help them through the crisis.

Today some parts of Holbeck are deserted, but others are pretty hectic. I drive up one long terrace where three or four houses in a row have decided to have a party. Sofas and armchairs are arranged carelessly on the pavement, techno music thumps from an open front door, ten or twelve people hang around swigging from cans and smoking the ubiquitous bifters, just like the people in Richmond Hill on my first day. It strikes me as I drive past, steadfastly ignoring their glares, that maybe this is how all those gardens end up with living room furniture in them. Could it be that people bring them out for parties like this, then get so trashed they're incapable of taking them inside again?

The first drop is at the end of a nondescript row of terraces, a bit shabby but nowhere near as bad as some of the wrecks I've been driving past today. I'm greeted by a hard-faced woman of about twenty-five, who barely even says thanks when I give her the food. As I turn to leave I hear the sound of fingers rustling around in the bags, then a little boy's voice says, OH WOW! He must have found the Easter egg. I've been feeling a bit strained all day, and the sound of the his joyous voice tips me over the edge; for the first time, there are tears in the car as I'm driving away.

The last drop of the day is on a similar street, although this time the house is quite grubby and the front door has been kicked in. I can hear whispers behind the door when I knock and I think no one's going to come, but it opens a crack and they're delighted when they realise who I am. They are two ladies in their fifties, skinny as you like, with furrowed faces that tell of lives lived in the margins. Both of them are smoking greedily and look frightened, harried. I don't know who they were waiting for, but it seems like it was someone far less pleasant than me. There's a significant problem in some areas of the city with doorstep lending, so maybe they've been expecting someone round to collect a debt? Whoever it is, it doesn't seem like it's going to be a happy occasion when they arrive.

Bloody hell, love, you give us a shock there, didn't he, eh? one of them says, clutching onto the other's arm with a scrawny claw. They're both breathing heavily and they look nervous, laughing the kind of laughter that could easily tip into hysteria. It's clear that can't wait to get back inside, eyes darting round in panic.

On the way home I come through town, past the Central Library and the Art Gallery, then Millennium Square, the Civic Hall, Leeds General Infirmary and the University. These places are integral parts of the city centre, and there's not a soul to be seen. The feeling I get on seeing this recalls that of the first morning on the job when I was driving through the other end of town – it's extremely eerie and greatly unsettling, this desolate, dystopian wasteland like the aftermath of a neutron bomb. The buildings are still standing, but all of the people are gone.

Saturday 18th April

I'm dog-tired this morning, having had a rough night and being up with the kids since half past six so my wife could have a lie-in. In between getting them breakfast and trying to get myself organised for work – which basically consists of drinking as much coffee as I can – I knock up a swift half-gallon of thick veg soup for them to eat over the weekend. Whether they'll want it or not remains to be seen, but at least it's there if they do and it'll save my wife having to cook a couple of meals. I'm looking forward to work, curious as to what the day may bring, but I'm hoping that it won't pack the same kind of emotional gut-punch as yesterday.

When I get to the FDC, Sharon informs me that I'll have to start using a van for the drops because her bosses are adamant that no one should be doing this job in their own car. I'm not fussed – it's not like I haven't driven a van before. In any case, one thing I've learned from driving around the city is that years of austerity have left the roads in a horrific state, with potholes a couple of inches deep in places, and I'm worried about the battering my car's tyres, suspension and shock absorbers are getting.

There was a report on the news last night saying there's a worry that councils could fail financially due to the increased costs of the pandemic. Expenditure on adult social care has rocketed, but income has flatlined because of the closure of leisure centres, car parks and other essential revenue streams. The report said that the Government were keen to help and have offered 1.6 billion to help local authorities, but it's a drop in the ocean when councils have been asked to save tens of millions each over the years of austerity; it's an ominous sign of how the pandemic could affect local authorities and public services in the future.

There's no one in at the first two drops in Harehills; the third one is in the adjoining area of Gipton, a place I know well because of my visits to the food bank. I drive through Oakwood and past the library, which I always retain a soft spot for. It's a quaint little building, set back from the road in a beautiful garden full of tall blossom trees; it was the first library I ever worked at, and remains one of the nicest. It's an old-school library, full of nooks and crannies and it still has its original wooden shelves. It's the kind of branch that's dying out, a real focal point for the community, the sort of place where staff are on first name terms with all their customers and some of the older ladies bring in plates of shortbread when they've been baking.

When I get to the address, it's very possible the woman has the virus. She's corpse-faced, eyes half-shut, throat so sore she can't speak. I try not to get too near as she keeps coughing, but I make sure I leave the food inside the door for her so she can move it easily. In the instances I'm dealing with people who may have the virus, I'm so focussed on the task in hand that it never occurs to me I might catch it; as I've realised, the job comes with its own peculiar set of emotional strains, but becoming ill from being in contact with a carrier doesn't figure on my list of worries. I've always been in fairly rude health, physically; subconsciously I think my brain is convinced that even if I *do* catch the virus, I'll shake it off in no time, and that delivering food to the vulnerable overrides all other concerns.

The next couple of drops are for some Romanian families in the middle of Harehills. There's been a large Romanian community in the area for a while now, and we've worked with them in libraries and Community Hubs, providing free lunches and activities outside of term time with a Healthy Holidays programme at the Compton Centre. No one at either of the houses I visit can speak a word of English, but they're very grateful and try to convey their thanks as best they can.

There are a *lot* of police around in Harehills today. I see three pairs of bobbies on the beat in the space of a couple of minutes, more than I've seen anywhere else in the rest of the city. It's hard to see what they can do; even if they break up the groups of people that are congregating on street corners, there's nothing to stop them reconvening once they've gone on their way, and judging by the amount of *Fuck The Police* graffiti, it's a fair assumption that respect for the law isn't as high as it could be in this part of the city.

The streets here are swimming with litter, and there must be an unimaginable amount of rats. I've noticed that the council have taped bags around the tops of all the litter bins in the city to stop people using them during the pandemic, presumably to save over-stretched staff from having to empty them. That's not had any impact whatsoever on the litter situation around here though – Harehills always looks like this.

The last drop on this run is on the border of Harehills and Gipton. There are grubby houses on both sides of the street, sticks of furniture outside and all the other usual trash. I knock on the front door and a man opens the adjoining window, fag sticking out of the middle of his mouth. He has a craggy, weathered look, cracks in his skin so deep and dirty you could grow spuds in them, and the kind of scarred face that looks like Saturday night is *definitely* alright for fighting. I tell him who I am and why I'm there; he doesn't speak, just jerks his head and wiggles the fag, which I take to mean he wants me to leave the food outside. I put it down by the front door and leave.

I head straight out with another sheet, featuring a couple of meds drops. The first one is in LS13, collecting from Boots in Bramley shopping centre, although to call it a shopping centre makes it sound a lot grander than it is. Really it's a small estate full of the usual establishments – Greggs, Costa, Pizza Hut, a few charity shops, a Boots and another pharmacy – the same kind of complex found in little towns all over the country. There are a few people around but it's nowhere near what I'd normally expect to see on a Saturday. Fultons and Poundstretcher both have long queues but a lot of places are closed.

I have to wait a little while before I can get into Boots so I stand in the queue, taking it all in. A handful of people are wearing face masks, and it tickles me to see an old woman who must be knocking seventy take her mask off so she can stick a fag in her mouth and light up. One thing that really strikes me here is the silence. No one is talking, not even the couples who have come out together. I can hear engine sounds from a few cars, the click of doors opening every time someone enters or leaves Boots, but otherwise there is just a quiet, lingering unease.

I get the prescription and manage to find the delivery address, which is only a five-minute drive away. When I knock, the man comes to the window. He looks like a proper old Yorkshire lad, late sixties, hardly any teeth, flat cap on and a Leeds Rhinos tattoo on his left forearm. He sticks his thumb up, grins gummily and points to the letterbox, so I shove the meds through and get on my way.

The next pharmacy is in the middle of Pudsey. On the way there I see a garage with petrol for sale at £1.02 a litre, the cheapest I've seen in about a decade. I remember the shock when it first went to a quid a litre and I remarked to my wife at the time that once that psychological barrier was broken, it'd never come down below that level again. I'll be proved wrong before too long, but look what kind of global catastrophe it's taken to make it happen. It may seem like a minor concern in the grand scheme of things, but the plummeting price of oil and its resultant effect on petrol prices is another indication of how the pandemic has turned the world upside down.

The chemist is right opposite the library, another one I used to work at in the dim and distant past, running a troubleshooting drop-in for people who needed help with IT issues. The main drag is busy in a socially distanced kind of way; both B&M and Sainsbury's have big queues. As with Bramley, no one is talking and the silence is weird. The drop is in what would be a *gorgeous* estate, were it not for the fact that there's a huge electricity pylon plonked it the middle of it. There are some chippies and sandwich shops open on the way up here too; it looks like people are deciding to start bending the rules. According to regulations, premises that sell takeaway food can open; I saw a greetings card shop open in Pudsey with a sign outside advertising crisps, sweets and cold drinks.

I'm worn out when I get home, and my wife is too; she's had another tough day. Before lockdown started the kids were great friends, but now they're being forced to spend every waking moment together they're starting to get on each other's nerves. They miss me when I'm out at work too. It's hard to believe we're only four weeks into lockdown – it feels like an eternity already, and it shows how quickly people can acclimatise to such drastic changes in lifestyle and social circumstances. The idea of any kind of return to 'normal' seems laughably distant, as does the comfort and safety of the pre-viral world. Everyone is feeling the strain.

For my part, my mind is slowly overloading. The driving is tiring in itself, but I'm also frantically scribbling down detailed notes between jobs, then typing them up every night, as well as keeping a diary of other events – personal and national – so that hopefully I can write it all up into something concrete at the end. This is hugely time-consuming – not to mention emotionally challenging – so when combined with the struggle of trying to effectively parent two young children during lockdown, it seems inevitable that at some point the stress will start to take its toll.

Sunday 19th April

This morning I have to pick a van up from Leeds Building Services, which is on an industrial estate off the ring road near Seacroft. It's home to a variety of businesses including a JD gym, Tool Station, Doug

Cleghorn Bathrooms and the wonderfully named Well Stoned, which sells paving stones, flags and the like; LBS is a big builder's yard right at the top.

I introduce myself to Lee and Sarah, a super-friendly pair who are looking after the electric vans. We have a quick chat about the pandemic, then they say I need to have an induction. This consists of asking if I've driven a van before, taking my license details and getting me to sign a form saying – amongst other things – that I won't drive it drunk or high, and that if I get caught speeding it'll be me that gets fined and not the council. After that, I'm on my own.

We should take you out for an hour in it, really, Lee grins, but we haven't got time. Us number's on t'key fob if you have any bother.

And that's it.

The van is a Renault Kangoo, bigger than a standard Caddy but not a large van by any stretch of the imagination. The cab's quite spacious apart from the bit where I sit, and my long legs end up wedged a little uncomfortably under the steering wheel. Once I adopt my usual slouch, though, everything is fine. It's a funny thing to drive. I turn the key, it beeps, a green light comes on, and I'm all set. No vibrations, no engine noise, nothing, only the slightest hint of the buzz you might hear from a flying saucer in an Ed Wood film. I get as comfortable as I can, then head out to test it on the road.

The first thing that hits me is how keen the brakes are. I give them a gentle dab at some traffic lights and nearly put myself through the windscreen. Pretty soon I figure out that you barely need them. In a normal vehicle, you take your foot off the gas and the thing keeps going, at least for a little while; in the van, as soon as I ease off it feels like someone's caught the rear end with a fishing line and is reeling it backwards. The other thing is that because there's no engine noise and no internal motion caused by the engine, it's impossible to tell how fast I'm going without looking at the speedo, which is hidden completely from my eyeline by the top of the steering wheel. It's like a giant dodgem. There's no pleasure in driving it, but I'd rather be using this than hammering my own car on the cratered city roads.

At the FDC, Terry – Sharon's new right-hand man, who has come to help coordinate the deliveries – says he has a mission for me and a couple of the joiners. A local charity called The Real Junk Food Project is giving away milk, so we are to go down to Hunslet to get some. Three of us drive off in convoy. We know that this place is somewhere near

Thwaite Mill, the gigantic waterwheel built in 1825 which claims to be one of the best remaining examples of a working water-powered mill in the country, but there are a lot of industrial estates down there and we're not sure which one it is.

We drive round three or four of them before we find the one we're looking for, and at first they're not going to let us in. They've had a dispute of some sort with Fare Share, who've been working in partnership with the council on the food parcel project, but one of the joiners – a gruffly intimidating fella who is definitely not to be messed with – is extremely persuasive and they relent in the end. We get three pallets each, quite a heavy load when you lift them, and head back up to the FDC. As soon as we've unloaded them, someone calls from the Compton Centre to see if they can have some, so I have to load my van back up again and deliver it there.

In the afternoon I'm sent out to do a couple of food drops and one for meds. The first food drop is in Beeston. It's for a pretty young Polish woman, probably about twenty. She tells me that she's already had one food parcel today so she doesn't need this one, but I tell her it's her lucky day and make her keep it anyway.

From the poverty of the south to the affluence of the north, the meds pickup is from the Tesco in Oakwood, delivering to Shadwell. There's a horrendous queue when I get there, but I speak to the security guard, flash my LCC badge and he lets me straight in. The address I'm delivering to is on a road known to locals as Millionaire's Row. The houses round here are, frankly, fucking huge. Mansions – no two alike – line both sides of the street, stretching off into the distance as far as the eye can see. Most have ornate metal gates in front of them, and some have three, four and even five cars parked on forecourts around the front. It's crazy to think of all this wealth when there are people living in slum houses not too far away, and I find myself wondering what these people do to earn all the money they must have to be able to afford these places.

The place I'm delivering to is a case in point; the garage built onto the side of it probably occupies more floor space than the entire ground floor of my house. Two brand new Mercedes – a black family saloon and a silver SUV – sparkle opulently in the afternoon sun. I'm standing at the gates trying to work out how to get in when there's a faint humming sound and they slide open. Someone must have seen me.

I start to walk down the driveway when a man appears from inside the SUV with a cleaning cloth in his hand. He's a handsome gentleman in his fifties, immaculately dressed in pristine white robes and with a perfectly trimmed grey beard. He's pleased to see me.

Thank you to you and all your colleagues, his voice brims with sincerity as he indicates for me to leave the medication on a little wooden table next to the house, you're doing a wonderful job.

There are a few more drops to do before the end of the day, starting with one in East End Park. It's a ground floor flat in a small complex with the usual array of old roaches, fag ends and broken glass scattered around the floor. The lad who comes out is about twenty, head shaved to the bone, six feet tall and probably about nine stone. He has no front teeth, looks and smells like he's been sniffing glue, or maybe it's nitrous, looking at all the whippits on the ground at my feet. His eyes are glazed and his words come out in a breathless rush.

Nice one brother safe man thanks so much for this mate I'm fuckin starvin' like innit.

The next drop is in the Lingfield Estate in Alwoodley. It's part of one of the most affluent postcode areas in the city, but the Lingfields are its dirty little secret, a rundown mix of houses and flats where a sixteen-year-old girl had half her face sliced almost right off in a machete attack in 2015. I'm beginning to notice more and more these juxtapositions of extreme wealth and poverty; even the nicest parts of Leeds seem to have these pockets of deprivation festering within them.

This drop is for an oldish man in a ground floor flat, another proper Loiner with a broad accent and thick-framed bottle bottom specs.

I got one of these yesterday, love, he tells me.

What, from the council?

Aye.

I ask him if he got in touch with the council to order it, but he says that someone from the council phoned *him*. It must have been a massive task for them to identify who they thought was in need of help, not to mention contacting them all to establish the level of provisions that needed to be put in place. It's another example of how dedicated local authority workers are playing such an instrumental role in keeping everything going during this crisis.

You might as well take it, anyway. It'll all keep.

Nay, lad, can't you give it to someone else?

I'm not going back to the depot today, chief, you might as well have it now.

He's reluctant, says he doesn't want to take something someone else could have, but I insist. I'm expecting him to ask how much he owes me as I say goodbye, and right on cue, he does.

It's been a tiring day again. When I took this role on, I wasn't prepared for how exhausting the work would be. Physically it's not too bad – nowhere near as strenuous as the work the people in the warehouse are doing, although it *is* tiring carrying the heavy bags to some of the addresses, especially when there are multiple bags at each drop – but to drive for four or five hours a day and maintain the level of concentration needed to do it safely is a lot more difficult than I expected.

Later in the evening, after I've put the kids to bed, I sit down to write in my diary. The full entry for the day reads as follows:

Far too tired and fried and sick to death of having a head full of this fucking stuff to be arsed to write tonight. Was having nightmares about starving children in the larger hours of this morning and they woke me up early. Have written up some notes on today at work so that'll have to do for now. Will try to catch up tomorrow.

Week 3:
Testing times

Number of recorded deaths: 20,732

"Our goal is that everyone who could benefit from a test gets a test." – Health Secretary Matt Hancock's Downing Street briefing, Thursday 23rd April 2020

The week begins with the official opening of the Government's Coronavirus Job Retention Scheme; it receives 67,000 claims in the first half hour. Professor David Spiegelhalter of Cambridge University says figures for infection rates suggest the UK is past the peak of the virus. On the same day, the Office for National Statistic announces there were 18,500 deaths recorded in the UK for the week leading up to 10th April. This is 8,000 higher than would normally be expected for this time of year, and marks a twenty-year high.

Parliament reconvenes after the Easter recess, but most MPs choose to stay at home and attend via video link. Foreign Secretary Dominic Raab stands in for Prime Minister Boris Johnson at the first ever virtual Prime Minister's Questions, and promises that 100,000 tests per day will be available by the end of the month. Health Secretary Matt Hancock announces that current testing capacity has increased to 51,000 per day. He also says that the UK has reached the peak of the virus, but social distancing measures cannot be relaxed. Shadow Health Minister Justin Madders responds, saying, "The Government really needs to move away from making big announcements at its daily press conferences if it cannot be sure what it says will actually happen. Whether it is the number of tests per day, ventilator capacity, or deliveries of protective equipment, too often ministers' promises are not being delivered. The public need and deserve a candid, realistic appraisal of the situation, not spin and exaggeration."

According to the Health Secretary, all keyworkers and their families will be eligible for testing. The day after this announcement is made, the website for requesting virus tests crashes as it is unable to cope with the volume of traffic it is receiving. This prompts Shadow Health Secretary Jonathan Ashworth to say, "The fact that the website crashed within minutes reveals the extent of demand that ministers should have prepared for. Questions need answering as to why this happened, what mechanisms are in place to ensure everyone who needs a test gets one quickly and whether a workable tracing strategy is being prepared."

Chief Medical Officer for England Professor Chris Whitty says there will have to be some sort of social distancing measures in place for the rest of the year. On 25th April, the UK becomes the fifth country to register more than 20,000 Covid-19 deaths.

Monday 20th April

The day begins at a tower block in Seacroft. It's a beautiful clear morning and the view from the top of Ramshead Hill is spectacular, much of the city spreading out below like a map on a table, the turbine at the Knowsthorpe water treatment plant near the FDC spinning away silently in the distance.

The block is stark against the blue sky, sticking up like a rotten tooth in the splendour of the early morning. I park right outside. Stuck on the front door of the ground-floor flat is a handwritten sign, scribbled in pink marker pen, that says, *Please knock LOUDLY* ☺. I give the door a good wallop and it opens with a whiff of stale smoke. There's a tall woman standing there, probably in her mid-twenties, wrapped in a pink dressing gown which opens at the top to show tattoos all over her chest. She smiles when she sees me, eyes half-shut against the sun. I'm sure I recognise her from somewhere.

Thank yooooooooooooou love, she chimes in a sing-song tone.

I definitely know that voice. Later, it dawns on me that we'd met before at an outreach event on the estate, but I used to do so many I can't even remember the half of them now. It could have been practically anywhere round here at any point since 2015 when I first started working in the area. It annoys me all day like an unscratched itch but, no matter how hard I try, I can't put my finger on exactly where our paths crossed.

The next address is right over the road. I dump the van on the verge outside, crunching a couple of old Strongbow cans that have been left to disintegrate on the grass. It's a strange-looking house. There are crystals and pendants hanging in all of the windows, scintillating prettily in the sun, but they're set against a backdrop of nicotine yellow net curtains that look like they carry all the tar from the inside of a cancerous lung. Next to the step there's a small rockery filled with stone animals, which would be lovely if you like that sort of thing, but then I take a look at the scabby brown lawn and see that it's scattered with old bread crusts, thick with green mould, and bits of fruit that are putrefying slowly in the heat. Right in the middle of the front step there's a big pair of metal scissors with the blades open that are arranged just so, as if they've been put there deliberately like some sort of protection, or a curse. I knock at the door and wait, but there's no one here.

After this I have a trip out to Scholes, a tiny village a couple of miles off the main road as it heads out of Leeds towards the east coast. It's a picturesque drive and one to savour after the less than salubrious sights of the estate, including a burned-out camper van outside a block of flats just before I get to the ring road.

Driving down the main street in Scholes, I could be in middle England. It's full of quaint houses and cottages, lots of greenery, beautiful gardens with immaculate lawns and colourful flowerbeds, the air vibrant with bird song. It's only a stone's throw from one of the most deprived estates in the north, but you'd never know from here – it's like being in the heart of the countryside.

The drop is on a street near Scholes Library, one of the few remaining that are so small we used to call them chocolate box libraries. Sadly, most of them were closed about ten years ago to help with the library service's financial contribution for council savings in the early years of the Cameron Government. Scholes has held out for now but it's long been in the firing line for closure, and it wouldn't surprise me at all if it were never to open again after the pandemic. It's sad to think of these venues closing, libraries, pubs and post-offices disappearing from the map in places where community spaces are at such a premium, but it's the stark reality of modern Britain. Libraries – vital community resources – in outlying areas like Rawdon, Lofthouse, Shadwell, and less affluent places like Holbeck, Kirkstall, Ireland Wood, and Swinnow, all swallowed up by the twenty-first century, never to return.

The street is like something from a postcard. Instead of the chewed-up grass verges I'm used to parking on in the estates, there's a massive flowerbed full of primulas and pansies, with a miniature tree growing out of the middle. The woman I'm delivering to is about sixty and we have a little chat. She tells me she has underlying health conditions so she's classed as vulnerable and isn't allowed out. Her main worry initially was how she was going to feed her cats, but apparently one of her neighbours has bought a huge supply of food for them, so now she's ready for anything.

Duty calls, so I hop back into the van and head off. The afternoon turns out to be one of the toughest I'll have on the job. I drive along a lengthy thoroughfare that snakes from somewhere near the stadium in the middle of Headingley – site of some of England's greatest test cricket victories – out to where the top of Kirkstall meets West Park. Parts of Headingley are very well-to-do, but this bit is a little more run down, with lots of sheltered housing and little collections of grim and dingy flats. I know the area well because my children used to go to nursery not far from here. I wonder how the nursery is coping, and hope that it will manage to stay afloat. It's been in existence for years and is run on a not-for-profit basis, which is an admirable principle, but makes me fear the worst when faced with the harsh economic realities of 2020.

The drop is at some flats that used to be white but are now discoloured to varying degrees, depending on what kind of dirt is covering the outside. The first thing I see is a tall white gate, not quite six feet high because I can more or less see over the top of it, with one of those brass plaques screwed to the front of it that says, *Beware of the dog*. I'm pondering what to do when the dog shows itself. It's gigantic, a hulking, slobbering boxer that jumps up with both its paws on top of the gate. It's going ballistic and looks like it's trying to bite my face off, drenching me in drool and gassing me with toxic clouds of rancid, meaty breath.

I love big dogs but this catches me completely off-guard and I jump back, heart racing. Soon enough a young lad comes outside in tracky bottoms and an England football shirt, all scruffy hair and brown-blonde stubble, eyes narrowed against the sunshine and quite possibly stoned judging by the smell coming from inside the house. He tells the dog to get down and it stops barking immediately. Over the fence, I see it tilt its head towards him so he can scratch its ears before it pads away into the house, looking pleased with itself.

Scared the shit out of me, that, I tell him.

He's meant to, mate. He grins. He's my burglar alarm.

Looks like you've got him well trained.

Definitely. He does whatever I tell him.

It turns out I'm at the wrong house, but I'm only out by one so he goes inside, knocks on the wall and calls for his neighbour to come out. He's a heavyset man in a dressing gown who won't look me in the eye, never mind speak to me. I take the bags through the gate and into the yard but he doesn't acknowledge me once.

The next drops are in Armley, with the first two on the same estate. When I get there, I'm met with a tableau of smashed TVs, trashed cars, houses with plastic sheets for windows and boarded-up front doors. There are people sitting in the jungles that pass for gardens, giving me the evil eye. At the top end of the street, two lads who can't be older than twenty are openly selling drugs out of their Corsa. They sit tapping at their phones, eyes down; periodically, people walk past and there's a brief touch of hands through the open window as the deals are done.

I park the van and get out. Immediately a man comes bursting out of the front door of the house I'm parked outside, shirt off, arms and legs pumping. He's about fifteen years younger than me, in his mid-twenties, lean and mean, washboard stomach, biceps like cricket balls. He has a wild look in his eye.

Alright, what the fuck do *you* want, yer fuckin' cunt? he snarls from over the fence.

I wasn't expecting that and my heart starts pounding again, palms sweating, instant shakes as the adrenaline kicks in.

I've got a food parcel for next door, if she's in, I choke out.

Ah, yer dropped fuckin' lucky there, pal. I were gonna give yer a *proper* one then, I was.

He's laughing, but I don't think he's talking about a friendly handshake. I can't wait to get the fuck out of here, but I still have to do the drop, so I heave the food out of the van and carry it up to the door. The man is standing on his doorstep, chest out, arms folded, watching me with a sardonic curl of the lip. I'm tempted to dump the food and scarper; I've already decided that if this woman isn't in, I'm going to leave the parcels on the doorstep anyway so I can make a quick escape.

It turns out she's there, though; she's so thin that you'd probably lose sight of her if she turned sideways. She's got tattoos and track marks all over her arms, a skeleton held together by sinew and skin. She croaks a toothless thanks and I turn to leave, feeling the eyes of the man next door burning into my back, my body tensed and ready to turn round and lamp him one if he jumps me from behind. I wouldn't fancy my chances in a fight against him, though – he'd have me for breakfast.

Back in the relative safety of the van, I'm sweating buckets and feeling more than a bit panicky. The last few minutes are something I'd never have expected, but unpleasant as it was, there's a valuable lesson to be learned. Some of the people on these estates are so disenfranchised that they're suspicious of everyone, even those who are trying to help. They see the council livery and automatically think I'm there to chase unpaid rent, evict them, or any number of other unpleasant things. To them, I'm driving the van and wearing the badge of The Enemy; that's all they see.

The man's reaction is about as extreme as it will get during my time doing the job, but it's not the only time I'll feel threatened.

I'm keen to get away but the next drop is only a couple of streets over, so I try to get it done as quickly as I can. This street is the same, a devastated wreck, some of the houses so ramshackle they look like they're a strong breeze away from falling down. I park outside a house where two ladies – both smoking in their dressing gowns – are having a screaming row over the fence, voices so loud and shrill I can't understand what they're saying, apart from the odd *shithouse*, *fuckin'*, *bitch* and *cunt*. There are no tears, no sense of upset or hurt feelings in the voices, just pure, unadulterated rage. One of them has a tiny baby cradled in one arm, its head tucked up in the crook of her elbow, swinging it around as she shouts; the other has a child of maybe eighteen months crawling around her feet in the dirt. I'd like to think that there's no broken glass down there, but looking at the state of the place I wouldn't be too sure.

The woman at the drop is probably in her mid-seventies, and I've got to wonder what she must make of living here in the midst of the estate, surrounded by the constant shouting of angry voices, the perpetual smell of over-filled bins, alcohol fumes and weed smoke. There's violence in the air; you can almost reach out and touch it, as if the whole estate is a powder keg waiting for someone to drop their spliff end into it and set the whole thing off. She seems oblivious, though, chatting away about the weather and thanking me for the food. I've met people of her generation who've lived in Seacroft all their lives and watched as it's slid inexorably into crime and poverty. Their take on it is usually a shrug of the shoulders and, *It's a shame, in't it, love, but as long as they leave me alone I'm not bothered.* You can't help but admire their fortitude.

It's been an incredibly hard day and the incident in Armley has given me some cause for concern. It was probably naïve, but it never occurred to me that I might fear for my physical safety while out trying to feed the people of the city; when I get home, it takes a couple of hours and a six pack of cider before I start to calm down, but the bad feeling still lingers. The threat of violence came right out of the blue, and the shock will leave marks that cast a paranoid shadow over the rest of my time on the job.

Wednesday 22nd and Thursday 23rd April

After the stresses of Monday afternoon and a quiet Tuesday spent catching up on some work-related admin, I have another couple of welcome days off. The kids have been really missing me and my wife has been getting increasingly frazzled as the days roll by, so when I'm not working I try to take them off her hands as much as I can. We're hugely fortunate in that we live next to one of the biggest parks in Leeds, so we have a gentle wander round there on Wednesday morning, then have a barbecue in the afternoon and another couple of hours where daddy gets pelted with water bombs and sprayed with freezing cold water from the paddling pool while mummy sits at a safe distance with her feet up, snoozing in the sun.

Thursday follows a similar path – a pleasant morning spent walking with the kids in the park and rolling down grassy hills, then an afternoon of den-building and water-fighting in the garden. My wife enjoys having some time to herself while I'm out with the kids, I love spending time with them on my own for a while, and the kids enjoying having some daddy time too. This kind of family time is a world away from the sickness and poverty I'm being confronted with on a daily basis, and these two days off are a welcome respite for all of us from the monotonous drag of lockdown life.

Friday 24th April

It's a beautiful morning and for the first time, I'm not looking forward to work. The incident in Armley has got me rattled, and I'd rather stay at home and sort out some more admin stuff than have to head out onto the estates again. All I can do is try to focus on the good that the job is doing and hope that there are no repeats of Monday, but I'm consumed with a paranoid feeling of unease all day long.

I get an easy run for the start of the day: East Ardsley and Morley. East Ardsley is so far out of Leeds it actually has a Wakefield postcode, but it still falls within Leeds City Council's remit. It's quiet on the motorway today, but not the same kind of Ballardian desolation of Easter weekend. I wish I could have filmed it, but it wouldn't have been the same, the way no camera can capture the vertiginous sense of altitude at the top of a mountain or the loneliness in the heart of a desert.

The address is at a small complex of houses and one-up-one-down flats surrounded by green space and blossom trees, a stark contrast to the wreckage of Armley on Monday. I knock on the door and a man in his fifties sticks his shaved head out of the window. He shoots me a big smile, then comes downstairs in jeans and a white vest. He's got big, well-defined biceps, a broad chest and shoulders and patchy white stubble spattered all over his face. He tells me he's ex-army and says he can't go out due to "various disabilities", which I have to assume are psychological ones as physically he looks to be in pretty good shape. He's really appreciative, asks me to repeat my name, then asks how a librarian has come to be driving a van for a living. Nothing wrong with his eyes if he can read the job title on my name badge from where he's standing. We have a quick chat and I think he wants to shake my hand, but I don't offer mine and get back in the van instead. The first job on the next sheet is in Halton Moor. On the way there I see a woman who looks to be dressed in something like a steampunk fantasy of a nun's outfit and I do a comedy *what the fuck?!* kind of double take as I drive past. A little way up the road, I spy Corpus Christi Catholic Church and Primary School, so I assume she must have come from there. The habits have certainly changed from the old blue wimples I used to see shuffling out of St Stephen's in my hometown when I was growing up there in the 1980s.

When I arrive at Halton Moor, I get confused and find that I'm at completely the wrong end of a long street that cuts right across the estate. There are some nice places here, not necessarily what you'd expect to find in a place with the reputation that Halton Moor has – but the further up the road I go, the more it appears to deteriorate. The houses start to look age-worn, litter appears in the gutters and on the grass verges, broken TVs and armchairs start to jump out of gardens and there are a couple of St George's flags flying, something I only ever seem to see in the less affluent areas of the city.

On a corner, two shirtless young men with backs and shoulders that look like they've been scalded are poking around under the bonnet of a black VW Touran. The whole front end of it is caved in, so the engine is probably the least of their worries. Several pairs of eyes set in smoking faces glare malevolently at me as the van drives on up the road; an arid silence pervades the afternoon heat.

The woman at the drop is speaking to someone from another agency when I get there. I try to introduce myself but they both blank me completely, so I leave the bags on the lawn and depart without another word.

The next stop is in Rothwell. The air is bursting with pollen; you can actually *see* the stuff and the van is covered in it. There's a gorgeous smell of warm grass tinged with the faint sweet whiff of honey. The main road is lined with trees and fields, and I find myself thinking how amazingly green the city is. It's a sprawling place, but you never seem to have to drive very far to feel like you're in the countryside.

The man at the job is really pleased to see me. He's in his sixties with a gut so big it nearly touches his toes. He has no front teeth and his pale blue shirt looks like it's not been changed for a week; unidentifiable brown and yellow marks smudged all down the front make it look like a pair of shit-stained Y-fronts. He says he only phoned up the helpline this morning, so he can't believe I'm there already. I ask how he's doing and he says he's okay but his legs have gone and he's had to give up the car, so he's lost all his independence. Someone must be looking after him though; he asks me to leave the parcels in front of the open garage door, and when I look inside I can see five full cases of Carling sitting on top of a dirty wooden workbench.

The first one on the next sheet is in West Park. I don't recognise the address, but as I get closer I realise where it is. Halfway round the ring road between the affluent areas of Weetwood and Horsforth there are two large blocks of flats which appear out of nowhere; it looks like it's going to be one of those. When I get around the back, there's a relaxed vibe. A young lad grunts and sweats as he changes a tyre on his pushbike; not far away, a woman is playing a gentle game of badminton with a small child of indeterminate age and gender; by the garages, four men gaze in admiration at the gleaming bodywork of someone's pride and joy, a sleek blue and white Japanese motorbike.

I park outside the main entrance. As soon as I get out of the van, two vampiric creatures on the balcony above ask me if I'm looking for Dean. I tell them I am. He's not in, apparently, but he's asked them to come down and get the food for him. I shouldn't really give the food to anyone other than the named recipient, but seeing as though they seem to be expecting me, I tell them to come and get it. Only one of them comes down. She's a woman of about twenty, I think, but she's so strung out and emaciated that she looks more like a twelve-year-old boy. There's not a curve on her body; she's straight up and down, with a dirty face and black teeth – a couple missing, too. I bet there are track marks under the thin grey top she's wearing, and she smells like she's got half an ounce of weed in her pocket. She's smashed but polite and grateful, struggling to lift the parcel with her childlike arms while her spaced-out friend gazes bovinely down from the balcony.

Yeadon is next on the list. It's a beautiful drive up Rawdon Road with acres of open countryside out of the passenger window and some massive houses on the other side; the ambience is only spoiled by the crematorium and John Penny and Sons Slaughterhouse, just before you come into Rawdon itself.

There's a lot of traffic on this road; the flow seems to be creeping up with every day that passes. At this time on a Friday it would normally be pretty much at a standstill; it's a long way off that, but the volume of vehicles is noticeably increasing as time goes on and more people start venturing out in defiance of lockdown.

The address is right at the top of a street so narrow I can't get anywhere near it in the van. I wander up past the row of small, tumbledown houses to the one at the end and knock on the door, which rattles loosely in the frame. It's opened by an older woman wearing orange pyjama bottoms and a vest, riding on a stinking cloud of cigarette smoke, mildew and stale sweat.

I feel terrible asking for this, you know, she tells me. I've never asked for nowt in all my life, but I can't get out, you see.

It's alright, we're happy to help.

Thing is, I'm dying. I've got cancer, you see, love. It's amazing how dispassionate she is when she says it, as lightly as if she were making a comment on the weather or the colour of someone's hat. That and chronic airways disease so the doctors have told me I have to stay at home. I wouldn't mind going to t'shop, but my arthritis is bad so I can't walk there now. I've got my son here with me, but he needs looking after an all.

I tell I'm sorry to hear it.

He's got severe depression and anxiety, poor love. I can't send him to t'shop cos it's too much pressure for him and he panics, you see. I don't know what we'd do without people like you.

I pop the bags in the house for her, trying not to inhale the poisoned air. Inside is a maelstrom of dirt and clutter, an upended basket of laundry spilling its contents over the floor at the bottom of the stairs, a white swing bin liner full of kitchen waste reeking by the side of the door, the carpet silver with dust. I wish her all the best as I leave, inwardly sorry that I can't do more to help.

The last drop of the day is in Morley. I've done so much running around today that I'm worried I'm not going to be able to get there on the amount of charge left in the van, so I phone the man on the sheet to see if he's in, but he doesn't answer the phone. Fuck it, I'll have to chance it.

There are queues of traffic on the way, compounded by someone trying to steer a wooden cart pulled by two terrified horses round the ring road at what would normally be rush hour, surrounded by cars and HGVs. It takes ages to get to Morley through the hold-up and the general traffic, but when I arrive I find the house immediately. There are two huge men outside, with cast-iron biceps and flabby stomachs, soaking up the sun with their wives/partners/girlfriends/whatever. There's a massive Alsatian sitting with them too. They're all drinking. I call to him over the fence and he comes to give me a hand with the bags. He's some sort of tradesman, I think, judging by the van on the drive, but he tells me he's got health problems so he's stuck at home. It doesn't look like it's bothering him too much.

When I get home, I'm pleased that the day has passed by without much incident. The terminally ill woman in Yeadon was a desperately sad sight to behold and I find myself thinking about her more than once while I'm going about my daddy duties at bedtime, but the fact that there were no repeats of the Armley episode is about as much as I could have asked for, and for that alone I'm grateful.

Saturday 25th April

I'm tired this morning after an early start with the kids and to compound it I had another night of interrupted sleep. I've never been a good sleeper and I've been plagued with insomnia for prolonged periods at different times of my life so this is nothing new, but the tiredness certainly isn't helping my mental state and it makes driving tough.

I get a big job sheet to start the day, with drops all around the Bramley area. It turns out to be an interesting morning. To kick things off I'm delivering to a ground floor flat, one where the entrance is around the back. I buzz and am met with the sight of a corpulent man wearing nothing but his piss-stained pants, which I can smell from six feet away. He's has wiry black hair sprouting out of the white blubber that covers his bones, tattoos everywhere, a couple of gold rings on one of his giant paws and a big medallion dangling from his neck. I show him the name on the job sheet and he shakes his head.

No one of that name living here.

Are you sure? I ask. I've been to wrong addresses on occasion, but this time I'm convinced I'm in the right place.

Yeah, I'm sure, he nods.

From upstairs, a loud female voice calls down, Whoever it is, tell him to fuck off.

I take the hint, apologise for wasting his time and leave. As I'm sitting in the van tapping the next address into the satnav, I can hear muffled shouting from outside. I look up, and there's a woman standing on the balcony of the flat I've just visited, wrapped in a nighty that looks more like a pair of curtains, smoking and bellowing at me. I wind the window down and cup my hand to my ear.

Ere, have yer gorra food parcel? she shouts.

Yeah, that's right.

Sorry love. I thought yer were some fuckin' busybody sniffing around. Yer wanna be at that flat there. She jabs her fag in the direction of next door.

Ta.

Y'alright. She flicks her fag off the balcony and goes back inside.

It's good to get that one cleared up, but in the event the man is either not in or won't answer the door, so he doesn't get his parcel anyway.

If the remit of the service is to help those who can't get out, the next two people I meet are prime candidates. The first is a woman who is more or less completely deaf. I ring the bell to her bungalow and there's no answer, but when I bang on the door a little dog starts barking and she comes to open up. She's in her early sixties, wearing a dressing gown and smoking a roll-up, the dog still going crazy with its shrill yapping behind a door in the house. One of her ears is twice the size of the other one and is a bruised kind of scarlet colour, so sore you can practically see it throbbing and it almost hurts to look at it.

My name's Stu, I introduce myself. I rang the doorbell but you must not have heard me.

Sorry love, I'm deaf. She speaks with the flattened vowel sounds and slight lisp of someone with a lifelong hearing impediment. Can you speak up for us?

I said, I rang the doorbell. I enunciate as clearly as I can, looking directly at her in case she needs to read my lips. I don't think you heard me.

Ah, the doorbell. Never works, love. I've got my little helper to tell me when anyone's here. She jerks her head in the direction of the living room door, which her dog is still making a big deal of trying to get through.

I explain that I've brought her some food parcels and go get them from the van for her.

Ta, love. I've just had operations on my eyes and ears so I can't go out. The docs say my immune system is low so I can't risk it. I've still some more ops to have an' all. I've had medical problems all my life, me. This bloody virus thing is all I need.

I'm feeling a bit wobbly after that one, upset to think of someone undergoing repeated operations and having to recover on their own at home, and the next call does nothing to improve my mood. On the way I pass one of the more comical sights I've seen on my travels – a guy who looks like he could be a poster boy for the EDL: England football shirt, Union Jack tatt on his arm, built like a brick shithouse, walking down the road with two dog leads, a Doberman at the end of one and a Jack Russell on the end of the other. The levity soon goes when I get to the drop though.

It's one of a mucky little row of council houses inhabited by a man who tells me sadly, I'm sixty-nine and I'm knackered, kid. He's of average height, big boned but short on fat, his face gaunt and drawn.

I'm sorry to hear that, I say. It's a standard response bred into me from years of working with the general public. Experience leads me to intuit that I'm going to get this man's full medical history in a minute, and he gives it to me in pretty short order.

I've got angina, you see, he says. I've got a stent in my heart and type two diabetes, and that's not the end of it neither. I've got prostate cancer and bladder cancer an' all. Like the woman in Yeadon, he's impassive when he says it. I've just come out after a bladder op. They had a go but they couldn't get it all out – the cancer, I mean. I'm trying to get them to take me back in 'cos I'm pissing out half a pint of blood at a time, you know, but they won't have me cos of this virus.

It's difficult to know what to say, so I do what I usually do when confronted with this kind of information. I look at my boots and shake my head in sympathy. That's really tough, I mumble.

I were the head of security at a private bank once, yer know, he says. Good money an' that. But I fell asleep 'cos of me diabetes and they sacked me. I never got another job after that 'cos everywhere I went they said I were too old. That were a few year ago now. Then the cancer started and I've never been right since. I told you, love, I'm sixty-nine and I'm knackered. That's all there is to it. He shakes his head and trails off into silence.

There's a deep sorrow in his eyes and I'm nearly in tears at the quiet, dignified way he tells his story. He's another of the older generation that's truly grateful and tries to pay me before I leave; I feel desperately sorry for him.

The next house is thirty seconds away. The front door is made out of wood that's been painted red, but it has crude graffiti all over the front which looks like it's been gouged into it with a screwdriver. There are a few names, a crude drawing of a cock and balls, plus the words *FUCK OFF* in savagely angular letters. The parcel is for a middle-aged woman with fleshy arms the size of my legs, a big stomach and an ample bosom wobbling beneath her vest, her skin like old leather. She mumbles her thanks in a gravelly voice. She could be ill, she could be hungover, or she could have only just got out of bed – it's impossible to tell. It's clear that there are children in this house because there are NHS rainbows in the window, daubed in poster paint with childish slashes of the brush, but there's no sign of them anywhere.[15]

15 During the pandemic, the rainbow was adopted as a symbol of support for those who wanted to show solidarity with care workers and NHS staff. These were

After lunch I'm given a sheet with three drops in LS10 and 11. The first one is in Middleton so it doesn't take long to get there. It's on a wide avenue lined with grimy semis, not too shabby but not exactly easy on the eye either. There's a smell of barbecue smoke and cooking meat in the air which makes my mouth water – no weed smoke for a change. There are a few groups of teenagers milling around in threes and fours, not much social distancing.

An old lass in rollers answers the door, yelling chestily at someone called Jimmy to shut that bastard dog in t'living room! Like so many others, she's smoking. There's a loaf of bread in the top of the food parcel and she asks, That gluten-free, is it?

I wouldn't have thought so, I tell her.

Good. I told the council that I'm gluten-free. And I should be. But have you ever had that gluten-free bread? It's bloody 'orrible.

She tells me she had a neighbour who used to make delicious gluten-free bread for her but she moved away, so now she eats the normal stuff and puts up with the gut ache.

Gluten-free, she shakes her head, tuts in disgust. At my age, can you imagine? I don't bloody well think so.

The next drop is in Cottingley. It takes ages to find because it's on one of those strange estates wedged in between thr twin obelisks of Cottingley Towers and the back of the cemetery, where there are lots of ginnels going off in different directions and the numbering system doesn't make sense. I ask a couple of different people who are out in their gardens where the house is, and between us we manage to cobble together the location.

The drop is for a family of Asian origin, and it must be a large one because I have four dry bags for them, the biggest single drop I've had so far. There's been talk in the news of BAME communities being disproportionately affected by the virus and this could be one of the reasons why: with a relatively high proportion living as large families in small houses, once one person is infected it's easy to transmit the virus to everybody else in the house. Combine this with densely packed urban areas like Harehills and Beeston where many BAME families are concentrated, and it's not hard to see why these communities may

---

often – but not exclusively – painted on posters by children and were displayed in prominent places such as living room windows. A popular activity for parents during lockdown was "rainbow trails", which entailed taking children for a walk and counting how many rainbows they could spot along the way.

become hotspots. As Shadow Women and Equalities Secretary Marsha de Cordova said recently, "The devastating effects of Covid-19 on the BAME community cannot be overstated." The talk at the beginning of the outbreak was all about how the virus doesn't discriminate, but that's simply not true: as with everything else, the BAME community, the elderly and those on low incomes are bearing the brunt.

At the top of the street there's a lad in his late teens smoking a fag and supping a Stella. He's glaring at me, but I'm used to this kind of treatment by now so I ignore him. He's shouting at someone inside the house about a game of FIFA or something similar – it's hard to pick up on the details through all the profanity.

For fuck's sake, the cunt's about to fall off the fuckin' wall! yells a voice from inside. Maybe this is how all those flat screen TVs in gardens get broken?

On the way back to the van I see a couple of striking images in the cemetery next to the flats. There's a woman standing in the middle of the path with a mask on, talking on a mobile phone with not a single soul anywhere near her. As I'm driving away, a man in a suit sits on a grave covered in fresh flowers, eating a Subway sandwich and looking as serene as the Buddha under his tree. Two surreal Polaroids, freeze-framed in my mind forever.

A drop in Beeston finishes this run. On the way there I pass Middleton Railway. Founded in 1758 to carry coal from Middleton pits, it's the world's oldest continuously working railway, and in 1812 became the first commercial railway to use steam locomotives successfully. In 1960 it became the first standard gauge railway to be staffed by volunteers; passenger services were introduced in 1969 and have been operating ever since. Along with Thwaite Mills and Armley Mills, it's one of the jewels in the crown of the city's preserved industrial heritage.

The drop is uneventful and I'm hoping this will be the end of the day, but Sharon gives me a few final jobs, all of them in Beeston, including one on a street I've just driven down. It's annoying to have to go back to the same place, but on the plus side, all the drops are close together; the bad news is that they're in the rabbit warren of criss-crossing narrow streets that makes the area such a nightmare to drive around.

The first one is on a familiar street – a short, narrow cul-de-sac that never feels completely safe. There are groups of people hanging around, drinking and getting stoned, looking like they've been at it all day. Techno music plays from several different houses, and every voice I can hear is shouting. They're all having barbecues that stink like rubbish fires, the acrid smell of burning plastic undercut with that of strong weed and cheap booze. There's no one in at the drop though.

To get to the next address I have to drive past Holbeck cemetery, the setting and inspiration for one of my favourite poems: Tony Harrison's *V*, a savage condemnation of another era of Conservative government every bit as brutal and divisive as this one. The drop is at a house that's been split into flats but has nothing to indicate this from the outside, so it appears to be a normal house. It's a ploy used by slum landlords to make the most money they can from the houses they own – it's common in Beeston and Harehills, and in lots of the other more deprived areas of the city too. I'm looking for Flat 4 but I have no idea how to get to it, so I stand banging on the front door for a while and hoping that someone answers. There's definitely someone in because an upstairs window is open and I can smell the weed smoke curling out of it, but no one comes so I sack it off in the end.

The last one is up past Cross Flatts Park, a place that lives in my memory for all the wrong reasons. When I first started working for the library service we used to support a series of summer events called Breeze on Tour, which were one-day events aimed at children and young people. There were little fairground rides and a few stalls, plus people from different agencies to talk to the parents.

One of the first events I ever did was at Cross Flatts Park. I was standing behind the library stall watching a woman with four or five children having an argument with her eldest, a blonde girl of about twelve. All of a sudden, the mum lost her shit completely and smacked the little girl so hard around the face that she nearly took her head off her shoulders. You could hear the crack from halfway across the park. Everyone looked round for half a second, then carried on with what they were doing. To my eternal shame, I didn't step in, chiefly because I was scared the gargantuan fella she had with her would kick the fuck out of me if I did. I shudder at the memory and tears prick the back of my eyes even now, twelve or thirteen years later, whenever I think about it.

It's been another bruising day, physically tiring and mentally exhausting. The deaf woman this morning seemed to be making a good job of trying to put a brave face on her situation, but it must be terrifying to be in and out of hospital, especially when she's already vulnerable and is more likely to catch the virus in hospital than out of it. The old man after her was a real heartbreaker too – he spoke with the air of one who knew he didn't have long to live but had given up caring one way or another. It's hard being confronted with these lives of quiet desperation, hearing these kinds of stories day after day, alongside having to spend prolonged periods of time in places like Beeston where addiction, deprivation and hardship are everywhere. I've always been good at drawing a clear line between my work and home life – once I get home, it's *my* time and all thoughts of work are left at the front door. With the driving role this has been difficult from the outset, and at this point – only three weeks in – it's become practically impossible.

Sunday 26th April

Another rough night with little sleep. The kids sleep in for a change, but I'm up with the lark anyway, guzzling coffee to wake myself up before I set off. Everyone else in the house must be tired too, because they're all still in bed when I leave at half past eight.

I arrive early, but Sharon already has a couple of job sheets made up so I take one and head straight out. The first drop is at Brignall Croft in Burmantofts. I've never heard of it, but the satnav shows it's somewhere near the tower blocks by Jimmy's. I spin quickly through the empty city and there it is, a huge tower block piercing the blue sky. Even in the sunlight of a beautiful spring morning, it looks foreboding.

It's spookily silent while I'm waiting for the guy to come down, bits of birdsong cutting through the quiet – but other than that, nothing. It's oddly peaceful considering how many people must live in the building and the block next to it. Add that to all the blocks around this little square of the city and you have thousands upon thousands of people living in these crumbling streets in the sky. I can only imagine what's going on in there; I try to picture what it would look like if you sliced off the front so you could see inside every room, like those pictures of bombed-out houses in World War Two, bedrooms and bathrooms exposed to the gaze of the public, the lives of the residents on display for all to see.

He's youngish, about thirty, wearing a baseball cap and a couple of weeks' salt and pepper stubble on his chin. He's pencil thin, has terrible skin and an orange patch on his lip where he must glue his smokes; his fingers are carrot-coloured with nicotine too.

He's pleased to see me but doesn't hang around.

Cheers pal, this is fuckin' great is this. And with that, he scoops up the bags and goes inside.

Back to East End Park for the next one, behind the famous Irish Centre, the first purpose-built centre of its kind in the country which opened its doors in 1970 and has been a popular venue ever since. It takes a few knocks to get an answer.

Whaddyawant? A female voice, but deep and sonorous.

It's Stu from the council. I've got your food parcels.

She's a plump woman, hands, wrists and neck resplendent with gold jewellery despite the fact that she's wrapped in a towel from the chest down.

Sorry. I say, did I get you out of the bath?

What's that? Nah, can't sleep, she grunts as if that explains everything, towel flapping open over a quivering mass of belly flesh and her voluminous black and white striped knickers. I don't know where to look, apart from away. She either doesn't notice or doesn't care about the towel coming undone, simply drags the bags inside and closes the door, brushing her shoulder against a sheet of stiff, yellowed wallpaper that's hanging off the wall as she does.

The next set of drops are in Bramley and West Park. I take the inner ring road, coming off at the university and up through Headingley. It's been a few weeks now, but I still can't get used to seeing the Parkinson building deserted like this, even on a Sunday. Lockdown is still being observed pretty strictly by most of the public, and even though I'm accustomed to being out and about, the absence of people in such a busy city still feels strange. Hyde Park is the same, the odd couple walking hand-in-hand beneath the blossoms and a handful of skaters who've snuck into the skate park looping lazily round the ramps and half-pipes, but it's dead by usual standards.

Otley Road in Headingley is one of the busiest and most polluted roads in the country, and with its endless parade of bus stops and traffic lights it can be a tortuous experience to drive on; today I clear the whole lot in about three minutes without seeing another car, just the odd bus with no one on it.

Much of West Park is lovely. There are lots of new houses round here, plus some pretty big old ones. The address I'm delivering to is in a close tucked away in the middle of the estate. Most of it is well-presented, but there are a handful of places that stand out and look way more run down than I'd expect to find round here. There's no answer at the front door so I try the side; there's a broken armchair, a rocking chair and a bedside cabinet, all broken into splinters, piled on top of one another next to the fence, which is falling down. There's no answer here either; when I turn to leave, I notice a large fish tank smashed into three pieces underneath a privet hedge in the front of the house.

As I'm closing the gate, a young lad calls to me from the upstairs window. He's very, very thin when he comes down, unbelievably twitchy and completely paranoid, looking around him all the time, never still. There's a look in his eyes as if he may have some mental health issues, or it could be that he's wired on something, it's hard to say. He wants to know if it was me knocking on his door at seven o'clock this morning. I tell him we don't start till nine but he's insistent. Are you *sure*? he asks, looking spooked. I *definitely* heard someone...

I don't recognise the next address, which is somewhere towards the top of Bramley. It turns out to be a sheltered housing complex with signs all over the doors warning about the virus and the dangers of letting visitors in; there are also posters proclaiming that all communal areas are closed. It strikes me how alienating it must be for the residents to be living in such close proximity to so many other people, yet not to be allowed to mix with them.

I buzz the woman and she opens the door. The flat is at the end of a long dark corridor with a low ceiling that smells of fag smoke and cheap bleach, the kind you put down the toilet rather than the usual hospital disinfectant smell. She's a friendly woman in her early fifties with a deep suntan and a Leeds accent as broad as her smile, wearing a spaghetti-strap vest top and baggy jeans. At the top of her right arm is a huge purple bruise, fist-sized. I find myself wondering how she came by it.

Thank you so much love, you've no idea how much this means to me.

I smile and tell her to give the helpline a call when she needs some more food.

Them people on that helpline, they're saints, they are, love, she tells me. They've sorted me out someone to talk to and everything.

I say nothing and nod, inviting her to continue.

I don't like being on my own, you see, love. I've got a lot going on, you know? She taps her temple with her index finger. I've just come out of the hospital.

Sorry to hear that.

It's alright, love. I tried to kill myself again, is all. I took another overdose. I'll be okay though as long as I've someone to talk to.

She looks so lonely when she says it that I want to give her a massive hug, to stay to talk to her for half an hour myself. Obviously I can't and I have to leave, but she's on my mind for the rest of the day. Mental health services have been slashed as financial constraints bite for local authorities and there are a lot of people in desperate need of help who aren't getting any.

I notice a few homeless people as I pass through Headingley today. There have been more and more over the last couple of years since the police got their orders to start kicking them out of the town centre. They hang around in the atrium of the old Lounge Cinema which closed in 2005 and has been empty ever since. They seem to like it in Headingley because a lot of the students are a bit of a soft touch. It's fitting that I see them today; many of the homeless in Leeds have been put up in a hotel somewhere in town, but no one seems to know where it is. As it happens, I'm about to find out: my first drop of the afternoon takes me there.

I go in and speak to security who fetch me a support worker. It seems like a great opportunity to have the homeless under one roof – there are lots of support services here and it's to be hoped that they can try to help. The support worker is a bubbly lass, my age, all fag breath and tattoos with a massive mop of curly blonde hair and a wicked laugh. She brings out a young lad who can't be older than twenty, pitifully underweight and with ugly self-harm scars all over his arms, a mixture of deep red cuts and lurid purple scar tissue.

Come on, Sean, she's laughing, have a look at this stuff that Stu's brought you from t'foodbank, eh? What do you think of all this, then? She sounds like a mother talking to a young child, but there's no condescension in her tone.

He looks mortified, mumbles his thanks into his shoes, face so red that beads of sweat start to form on his forehead.

Looks like you'll have to be mekkin' a roast for me today then, Sean, eh? She's laughing, trying to jolly him along. Look, there's a cabbage in here and everything. Give us a shout later, love, and I'll show you how to cook it.

Well, enjoy, I say and leave them to it, her still trying to perk him up. He so wants to please her, lifts his head to try to look her in the eye but his whole body moves like his bones are made of lead and at the last minute he fails to meet her gaze. I don't quite catch the last thing she says to him as I turn to wave over my shoulder, but she laughs again, then from the corner of my eye I see him give her the weariest, saddest smile I've ever seen.

The next trip takes me into deepest Burley. En route I drive past the Royal Park pub and the legendary Brudenell Social Club, my drinking hole and gig venue of choice for the last twenty years. It's sad to see these places empty, and I really hope they can bounce back when the pandemic lifts. Grassroots music venues are another example of community spaces that have taken a devastating hit as a result of the pandemic and the whole industry looks to be in big trouble.

Opposite the pub is a patch of wasteland where Royal Park School used to be. It would have been an ideal place to turn into a community centre or something like that, but there were so many agencies involved that no one could agree what to do with the site after the school closed. In the end it became a hangout for skaters, stoners and street artists until the council got fed up and hauled the whole place down in 2014. There's still some tremendous artwork on the walls enclosing the area though, and happily work will soon be underway to transform the site into a multi-use games area for the local community.

After an uneventful drop, I head for Yeadon, past Hall Park in Horsforth, which looks beautiful in the sun. The address is on a grotty street full of run-down houses with paint peeling off the walls and cars with massive dents banged into them. There's nowhere to park. I walk up to the house and there's a big blank space where the garden should be – the whole lot has been dug out and is sitting in a skip that blocks the pavement. It looks like they were in the middle of having it paved when the virus hit.

There's an alleyway down the side that leads round to the back of the house with a delicious barbecue smell wafting out from it accompanied by some terrible cheesy Europop, all saccharine synths and autotuned vocals. I wait till the song finishes and call down the alley, hoping someone hears. The woman who comes round is a hearty-looking Loiner, bold as brass with a massive smile, all boobs and fright-wig hair, super chatty with reddish-brownish skin, like she's been spending a lot of time in the garden without sun cream.

I'm parked around the corner because I didn't fancy getting the van in and out of the cul-de-sac, so I have to walk back to get the food. It's a massive drop: three bags of dry food plus a fresh bag and some fruit and veg. I scoop it all up, hoping the handles on the bags hold out and trying not to burst any blood vessels as I hump it to the house.

Bloody hell love, you look knackered, she laughs, bending almost double when she sees me.

I'm sweating and out of breath, so I don't say much by way of reply.

I've got some nice cold beers in t'fridge love, but you're driving, aren't you?

I'm afraid so.

Never mind, love. You get yourself one when you get home, eh? She spins on her heel, grabs a few bags in each fist and heads off back to her barbecue.

The last drop of the day is in Tingley at the opposite end of the city. It's on a beautiful estate with more blossom trees than I can count, all of them in full bloom. There are so many of them around the city; in years to come, whenever I think of the pandemic, the pink and white blossom trees will be one of the first things I remember. Some of them have started to shed their petals and the road to the drop is carpeted with them, as if scattered in anticipation of a royal visit.

The man at the drop is extremely overweight, and it's easy to see why he can't get out. One of his thighs is about the same size as both of mine put together, and there's so much fat around his torso that it's a wonder he can breathe. It takes him a while to come to the door; when he gets there, he leans against the frame, sweating hard and wheezing like a broken squeezebox.

Today has been another day filled with extremely vulnerable people. The woman in Bramley recovering from another suicide attempt – she said she tried to kill herself *again* – put me on the back foot, and the state of the homeless lad at the hotel in the afternoon would have made a snake weep. It's shocking how many people there are around the city – and by extension, the country – who are living lives like this. On the plus side at least both of them today appeared to have access to some sort of support services, but one has to wonder how many more people there are in the same boat who aren't lucky enough to be receiving the help they so urgently need.

Yet again, I'm struggling to shift the images when I get home – the sadness in the first woman's voice, the lad's spindly arms that looked like a butcher had been at them with a carving knife, the wild eyes of the man hearing noises outside his house at 7 a.m.

My wife is in a real state this evening too. She's had another tough, tiring day with the kids and is feeling very anxious about a lot of things. We're supposed to be trying to do some sort of home schooling with the children, but neither of them will engage with any of the activities, so we've taken the approach that at that age anything can be educational. We've been doing lots of art, lots of music, lots of reading, and generally trying to let them learn through play rather than making them sit down to do structured learning. This is working well so far, but I think the strain is really starting to get to my wife; she's worried that the kids aren't happy and is wondering what we can do to change it. We have a good chat about it and eventually she calms down.

Delivering the food parcels has given me an enhanced sense of perspective: life is hard for us, as it is for everyone at the moment, but my wife and I are both still employed, we've got food in the cupboards and a roof over our heads. We don't have much money, but we have just about enough. Whatever problems we have are small fry compared to those of the people whom the pandemic has left out of work, whose businesses have been destroyed, who are unable to keep up rent or mortgage payments, who are now unable to support their families. And that's without mentioning the other people I've been delivering to, the many whose lives were a constant battle even before the ravages of the pandemic hit – the starving, impoverished underclass, wracked by unemployment, poor health and penury, hidden in plain sight amidst the chaotic mess of modern life. Compared to these people, my wife and I occupy a position of great privilege indeed.

Week 4:
Turning the tide

Number of recorded deaths: 28,446

*"I in no way minimise the problems we continue to face,
and yet it is true that we are also making progress. [...]
We are now beginning to turn the tide." – Prime Minister
Boris Johnson's statement, Monday 27th April 2020*

*It is announced at the beginning of the week that all families of NHS
staff who have died from Covid-19 will be entitled to a payment of sixty
thousand pounds. Health Secretary Matt Hancock also announces that
deaths in care homes will start to be included in official figures. On
28th April, testing capacity stands at 73,000, though only 43,000 were
completed on the previous day. A minute's silence is held for those who
have died from the virus.*

*Prime Minister Boris Johnson announces that the UK is past the
peak of the infections but that we cannot risk a second spike. He says
that detailed plans on how the Government intend to go about lifting
lockdown with be laid out next week. Facing questions about fears the
Government may look to make huge public spending cuts in the wake
of the pandemic, he states that "[Austerity] will certainly not be part
of our approach."*

*Responding to reports that Boris Johnson's chief adviser Dominic
Cummings is a member of the Governments SAGE[16] committee,
Shadow Health Secretary Jonathan Ashworth says, "These are very
serious revelations and raise significant questions about the credibility*

16 Scientific Advisory Group for Emergencies. This group "provides
scientific and technical advice to government decision makers during
emergencies." [https://www.gov.uk/government/publications/scientific-
advisory-group-for-emergencies-sage-coronavirus-covid-19-response-
membership/list-of-participants-of-sage-and-related-sub-groups]

of decisions taken by the Government on Coronavirus. [...] He is a political adviser, not a medical or scientific expert."

Also this week, care home deaths are retroactively added to the official figure, leading it to rise by 4,419. Acting Liberal Democrat Leader Sir Ed Davey responds to the announcement, saying, "As we finally see the Government's revised figures [...] the sheer scale of this human disaster is becoming clearer."

Monday 27th April

Today turns out to be the most frustrating day I've had on the job. There isn't much work to do in the morning, then at lunchtime I'm given a sheet full of medicine pickups. However, a lot of the chemists are closing for long lunches during the pandemic, so it's likely they won't be open.

The first one is in Stanningley. I go via the ring road, the gothic edifice of Armley gaol rising up on the left-hand side, a dark stain against the pristine blue of the sky. As I'm driving past, I see a policeman in a squad car coming down the road in the opposite direction to me; he's on his own, but he's wearing a mask. I understand the need to be cautious, but I wonder how people on their own in cars think they're going to catch anything.

I'm lucky. I get to the pharmacy five minutes before they're due to close for lunch and there's no queue so I head straight in and get the prescription, which I need to deliver to a place in Rodley. I've seen some startling levels of deprivation around the city these last few weeks, but this part of Rodley isn't like that at all. The address is in a cul-de-sac lined with massive houses, four or five bedrooms each by the look of things, double garages, loads of Mercs and a few Jaguars scattered around. A large man in glasses clocks me through the window when I knock on the door; he points to the doorstep and doesn't even say hello, never mind thank you.

The medical centre in Armley is right at the top of the main street, opposite an open patch of grassland with a couple of tower blocks down at the bottom of it. There are some desultory benches next to the low metal railing that separates the grass from the pavement; a young horse is chained to one of the benches and stands there with its head down, cropping the grass in silent mouthfuls. Dirty pigeons flap about the place, looking for scraps on the grass but finding none. The street is thronged as usual and it's noisy with voices, people having arguments, doing deals, shouting to make themselves heard over the steady flow of traffic. Super Savers and Poundland are both doing a roaring trade and their queues snake down the road in both directions. The whole road is caked with the dirt and grime common to these areas, scores of nitrous cans rolling around in the gutters.

It turns out that the chemist is closed for the next hour, so I head down to the next one in Morley, thinking that I'll come back to this one at the end of the run. It takes about twenty minutes to drive there. This chemist is closed too, and there's already a queue waiting for it to reopen. More people standing in silence, tapping their phones. I wait for forty-five minutes, at which point the woman behind the counter – who is lovely – sees my badge and tells me that council employees on medicine runs don't have to queue and that I should have come straight in. Unfortunately for me, a volunteer came in before lunch to pick this one up, and it's already been delivered.

It's another long drive to the next one which is at Killingbeck Asda, near Seacroft. There are long queues here too, as well as at the B&M next door. The security man lets me in when he sees my badge. There's only one person in front of me in the queue at the pharmacy but her order takes ages, and when she's gone the pharmacist disappears for ten minutes, leaving me twiddling my thumbs. Usually I'd be playing with my phone like everyone else, but I've left it in the van. When I realise this, I am worried that someone will smash the window and nick it – a very real possibility round here – but it's too late to do anything about it now.

I glance around the supermarket while I'm waiting. There are signs up about the virus and social distancing and there's a strange atmosphere. There are a fair few people about but the store is massive so there's plenty of room for them all. One or two people are wearing face masks, but mostly they're figure skating their way around each other with their trolleys in a silent form of retail ballet, like a piece of performance art.

When the chemist finally gets to me, he's wearing rubber gloves and a mask. I tell him whose prescription I'm there to pick up, and I swear I see him smirk beneath the face covering.

Sorry sir, he says. You're the *fourth* person today who's been in for that one. The woman collected it herself this morning.

I thank him, shake my head and walk out. I've heard from other drivers that this has been happening a lot. The council have been working in partnership with Voluntary Action Leeds to get people to help out with certain tasks such as delivering shopping or befriending people over the phone, and collecting prescriptions is one of them. It's a brilliant initiative and has recruited hundreds of volunteers. There's obviously a failure in communication somewhere though, and being sent out for prescriptions that have already been collected is to become one of the most annoying parts of the job.

It's well into the afternoon now; I've been driving for hours without achieving anything and I'm starting to feel frustrated. I *know* that the next pickup isn't going to be there either, but when I call the pharmacy to check the phone rings and rings without answer so I have to head back to Armley. I follow the same route as this morning. It's clouded over now and the gaol looks even more imposing – a great scab against the miserable grey skin of the sky. God only knows what's going on inside. For a time the place had the second highest rate of suicides of all the prisons in the county, with 25 inmates having taken their own lives between 1994 and 2003; since 2013, it's second only to Woodhill Prison in Milton Keynes as the prison with the highest number of inmate fatalities in the country. Completed in 1847, the gaol is one of Leeds's most infamous landmarks and one of the most visible remnants of the old city. I defy anyone to behold it without shuddering.

The street is as busy now as it was earlier; it'd look like business as usual if it weren't for all the people queueing to get into the shops. I've got the window down to let in a bit of fresh air, but all I can smell is fag smoke and engine fumes. As predicted, I get a sad-faced apology from the pharmacist, who tells me that someone came in for this prescription earlier today. I'm totally pissed off now. I decide enough's enough and go back to LBS to return the van. Thankfully, that's it for a few days and I'm looking forward to having the time off.

Wednesday 29th and Thursday 30th April

Wednesday and Thursday prove to be a couple of restful days that follow the usual pattern, with me taking the kids off my wife's hands to give her a bit of peace and quiet. She's been doing a sterling job bearing the full horrors of lockdown with them while I've been out in the van. On one of our walks in the park we bump into some acquaintances, parents of a child our son used to go to a pre-school group with. We get to talking about the pandemic – what else is there to talk about? The dad has an interesting take on the situation, and over the course of our chat, I find out that the virus isn't real, but if it is, it's no worse than a common cold and people are worrying about nothing; that numbers of deaths are greatly exaggerated; that a vaccination will kill more people than it saves – in fact, vaccinations generally are terrible because injecting bacteria into your body makes no sense; that the world has a plentiful supply of fossil fuels that we can use for hundreds of years, they're just being mismanaged to make a profit for energy companies; that green energy costs more to produce than fossil; that climate change isn't real either; and finally, that electric cars are more damaging to the environment than petrol ones because of the rock crystals used in their batteries. I get the feeling that if I ask him if he thinks the earth is round he might not be too sure.

It's a surreal quarter of an hour. It seems inconceivable under current circumstances that anyone could be of the opinion that Covid-19 isn't real, or that people aren't dying from it in huge numbers. The conversation is a timely reminder that we are living in the Age of Disinformation, where anything can become Fake News for no other reason than because someone says it is. I'm left wondering how many more people there are out there who share these views.

Friday 1st May

The time is out of joint. I'm tired as usual after another sleepless night, and I can't get my head around the fact that my working week now starts on a Friday. Everyone I know is celebrating the onset of the weekend – for what little that's worth during lockdown – but I'm staring down the barrel of five days at work.

It's overcast, grey, cold and damp; it feels like the sky could crack open and piss it down any time it wants to. I'm in an ugly, sluggish frame of mind; though I like driving and I'm enjoying the work, doing it on two hours sleep feels like a massive drag.

It's an uneventful morning, a drop up by the Holt Park leisure centre to a young lad in tartan pyjama bottoms and not much else, and then another around the corner where there's no one in. We've had some flyers printed to post through the letterboxes of addresses where we've tried to deliver food but the person wasn't there. More and more people are going out as lockdown goes on, and it's obvious now that the service we're delivering is moving away from its original intention to help people who were self-isolating and had no other means of accessing food shopping.

In the afternoon, I have a drop at Cottingley Towers that takes me past Elland Road. Outside the stadium is a site of mourning, scarves, flowers and football shirts strewn to mark the passing of two of the city's favourite sons, the iconic Norman "Bites Yer Legs" Hunter and Trevor Cherry, who have died within about a week of each other, the former being the city's most high-profile victim of the virus. There's so much memorabilia that the bronze statue of Billy Bremner is all but submerged.

Times have been tough for Leeds United of late. For a brief instant at the end of the '90s they were a real force under the management of David O'Leary, challenging for major honours and even reaching a Champions League semi-final in 2001. They paid the price for daring to dream with relegation in 2004, and have been in the wilderness ever since. They've had a few close shaves with promotion in recent years, but it's been looking like this may finally be the year they make it back to the big time. They were top of the league when the football season was suspended. Fans are already wary that the season will be declared null and void, thus depriving the team of promotion; typical, they say, of the club's bad fortune and the FA's hatred of them.[17]

It's always hard to park at the tower blocks so I dump the van on the pavement at the foot of Cottingley Towers. The postman is coming out of the front door, past the stinking heap of black bin bags that's piled four feet high against the wall. The food turns out to be for a youngish lad, early twenties probably, with a pierced eyebrow, an acne-scarred face and a Dallas Cowboys baseball cap. He doesn't say much in the way of thanks.

As I'm driving away, I pass an empty playground. A man in a face mask is standing on the grass right next to it, dick in hand, having a piss in broad daylight – another freeze-frame shot in my mind, never to be forgotten.

From here it's on to Beeston. The first drop is right in the heart of the labyrinth and takes some finding as I keep going down dead ends. In the end I park up on some waste ground and get out to look for the address. It's at another slum house; I'm looking for number 10a

---

17 They needn't have worried. Leeds were promoted as Champions and took the
    Premier League by storm, beguiling neutrals with their expansive, flowing style
    and involvement in many high-scoring games. They finished the season in 9th
    place with 59 points, the highest position for a promoted team since Ipswich
    Town in 2000-01. Their tally of 62 goals scored was also a record for a newly
    promoted side.

and there's no sign of it. Even by Beeston standards this place is dirty. There is broken glass everywhere, so much of the stuff it's impossible to fathom where it could have come from. All manner of other junk is scattered around – whippits, fag ends, bottles and cans; a brown leather suitcase with a big slash in the lid flops incongruously in the middle of the pavement. I keep my eyes down, wary of standing on a needle, glad to have my boots on. I brought my son to a school friend's birthday party at a soft play centre not far from this part of Beeston last year, and when I got out of the car and bent down to tie my shoes I found the arse end of a bag of heroin on the floor, gritty brown gak sticking to the inside of the tattered plastic.

In the end I have to phone the man, and he comes to meet me. He's a big lad with a Brummie twang, all gut and jowls, wearing baggy knee-length shorts and a heavy metal band t-shirt, grateful to receive the food. After this it's a regular afternoon in Beeston – a few people aren't in, and the ones that are are of a similar type, men in their fifties with missing teeth, tattoos and voices that sound like they smoke asbestos roll-ups. It's an afternoon of litter, fag smoke, broken glass, graffiti and overflowing bins, set against an aural backdrop of languages from all over the world. Everyone round here shouts all the time; it's impossible to tell whether they're angry or if that's just how they speak.

There are a couple of meds drops to finish the day. The first is a collection from Oakwood Lane pharmacy. The prescription is there for a change and I take it to the Parkway Court flats in Seacroft. When I buzz up, there's an old man on the phone who says he can't come down, so I go up to the flat. The inside of the building is identical to the other blocks I've been in, although the lift looks brand new. It still smells of fag smoke though, like the flat of the toothless old-timer I'm delivering to; ironically, he tells me the medication I've brought is an asthma inhaler. The second prescription, from a pharmacy in Moortown, has already been collected.

Saturday 2nd May

A couple of days of breeze with a touch of rain, and all of a sudden the blossom has gone. You can still see it on the roads and collecting in the gutters, but already it's starting to look like snow that's been melting and is turning into dirty brown slush. The trees are now a luminous, liquid green. It's cool but sunny this morning, breezy with a lot of cloud. It'd be a great day for the cricket in Headingley, if anyone was able to play.

I'm a bit groggy this morning. I took some pills to get to sleep last night and it always slows me down when I first wake up, like I've come to my senses in a pool of deep warm water and have to fight my way to the surface. I don't like taking sleeping pills, but sometimes it's the only way; with the stresses of lockdown, work and family life, restful nights are hard to come by and the amitriptyline – originally prescribed as a painkiller after a bout of shingles prior to lockdown – is a lifesaver.

The postcodes on the job sheet are the last thing I want to see. Six drops in LS8 – deepest Harehills. With its densely packed grid of narrow streets, it's not an ideal start when I've got a head full of cotton wool and feel like I'm still half-asleep.

The first drop turns out to be in Roundhay, which is usually a lot easier to drive around, but it's actually on a narrow street that's almost impassable because of the number of cars parked on both sides. I finally manage to park on the pavement at the top of some steps outside a row of maisonettes, which looks more like the kind of place you'd expect to find in Belle Isle or Middleton than Roundhay, another example of the pockets of deprivation that can be found even in the wealthiest areas of the city. There are broken doors and windows in lots of the flats, glass and rubbish everywhere. It doesn't take long to spot a broken TV a little way up the road.

There's a stench of butane in the air when the door opens, and the young woman who answers is quite clearly off her head. She's a skinny little thing, with short dark hair, hollow cheeks and piercings in her lip, eyebrow and nose, wearing a dirty white vest and army pants. I show her the name on the job sheet – which is male – and she jerks her head.

He's asleep on t'sofa innit. Shall I wake him up?

Nah. Got you some food parcels, that's all. Wait there.

The slack-jawed expression on her face doesn't change, but there's a glimmer of light in her eyes at the mention of food. I take it down the steps and watch her as she struggles to carry it in, then dumps it by the sofa before the door closes, fruit and veg spilling out over the black, carpetless floor.

Next up is a drop in the middle of Harehills. It's desolate; a lot of the houses look like they're about to collapse. Walls secreting damp, chunks of masonry simply missing from the sides of some properties, holes in roofs, doors and windows broken, gates hanging off, gutters coming away. The litter strewn everywhere is the usual mix of fag ends, whippits, glass and cans. The centrepiece is an old white minibus parked outside the drop, utterly trashed and completely unroadworthy. It has four flat tyres and it looks like the bodywork has been attacked with a baseball bat. There's graffiti scrawled all over it in black marker – *FUCK, SHIT, CUNT, FUCK THA POLICE* and right across the bonnet, in massive black letters, *SUCK YA MOM HIGH SCHOOL.*

It looks like an English man's name on the job sheet but the door is answered by a woman who appears to speak no English at all. I show her the number on the sheet to confirm the address, then point to the man's name and she nods. I get the bags and she does her best to convey her thanks. There's a heavy atmosphere akin to the one in Armley where I was threatened last week. Even though there's no one around, the silence of the morning is oppressive, pregnant with the threat of violence. Every now and again a loud voice cuts through the quiet. It's as if the people have forgotten how to speak at a normal volume and, as with Beeston, it's impossible to tell whether they're angry or if they always talk like that.

As I'm pulling away, a woman in a dressing gown and Converse walks past smoking a spliff, and shoots the van a glance like it's something nasty she's just stepped in. I'm getting so used to these kinds of looks that they barely register any more, and I'm long past wondering where she's going dressed like that. It seems like it's a perfectly normal way to dress for any occasion in some areas of the city.

The final drop of the morning is right behind the Mosque. It says in my notes that these people need baby products too, which can be troublesome because we very rarely have any, and when we do it's usually not the specific things that people need. All I have in the van are two bags of nappies, plus a few packs of wet wipes. The house is made of damp redbricks and has a tiny yard, but without the same amount of rubbish you find in a lot of them. A makeshift washing line made of red household twine has been strung up, with some toddler clothes and some tiny babygrows hanging from it too. It's devastating to think of a household with a baby needing assistance with food, but as I know from my visits to the food bank, it's not uncommon at all. According to the Shadow Environment, Food and Rural Affairs Secretary Luke Pollard, "This is not a crisis of food supply, it is a crisis of poverty. People simply do not have enough money to buy the food they need."[18]

They're a very young couple as it turns out. They can't be older than twenty, and I wonder how old they must have been when they had their first child. Possibly not even eighteen, looking at the size of the clothes on the line. The lad is so thin he's barely there, skin as pale as the white of his tracksuit, face shaded by a baseball cap, although unlike most of the other boys you see on the estates he isn't wearing a hood. He's trying to seem impassive but he looks shattered, bewildered, as if life has taken him completely by surprise and he has no idea how he's ended up where he is.

Y'alright, bud. I give him a nod.

Morning, pal. A small voice. He's trying to look confident, hands in pockets, chest out, but really he's shy. He can't stop looking at the food bags either, eyes swinging back and forth between them with the twitchy excitement of a small child. Behind the hard veneer he's trying to project, there's still something of the vulnerable little boy that he's unable to hide.

The mum looks completely exhausted but tries her best to greet me with a big smile. Her face is pale and panda-eyed, the pink top she's wearing spattered with white patches where the baby has either spit up or puked on her. She's wearing a bit of make-up but it looks hastily applied – the bright red lipstick not quite straight, mascara in clumps on her eyelashes.

Thanks you so, so much for this, she keeps saying, I don't know what we'd do without it.

There's a lump in my throat; I swallow hard. I've got you some nappies. Are these any good?

Let's have a look. Brilliant, size four, you're a total lifesaver, love, these are perfect.

I hand it over, feeling the supplies to be pitifully inadequate. There are about twenty nappies and a couple of fresh packs of wipes, probably enough to last for a week at the very most. I feel so sorry for these kids that it physically hurts, and if I had any more food in the back of the van, I would give them every last bag of it. The mum even waves as the van's driving away, and the sight of it in the side mirror breaks

18 The Labour Party (2020). Labour calls for urgent government action over Coronavirus food poverty [online]. Available from: https://labour.org.uk/press/labour-calls-for-urgent-government-action-over-coronavirus-food-poverty/

me in half. Through the mist of tears I'm trying hard to stem, I see a man and a woman walking past with a barrel-shaped barbecue that looks like it's been fished out of a skip. It's rusted all over, blackened to hell in a lot of places and is so full of holes it looks like it's been blasted with buckshot, but they seem over the moon with it.

The afternoon is even worse. The first drop is at an address in Middleton, which the satnav doesn't recognise at all. I don't know Middleton very well, so I give the number on the job sheet a call before I set off.

I just want to check your address, I say to the woman on the end of the phone.

D'yer know Miggie, do yer?

No. That's why I'm calling. I can't find you in my satnav.

Satnav? Fuckin' useless, love, yer won't find us with one of them. D'yer know where them white houses are down by Asda?

I don't, but I know where Asda is so I decide to head in that general direction and see if I can wing it from there. It turns out to be a monumental pain in the arse. I end up driving up and down Middleton Ring Road for half an hour, getting more and more pissed off by the minute. I try to use Google maps on my phone and that sends me in the wrong direction too. In the end I find it, more by accident than design, only to find that the street has bollards halfway down it and I'm at the wrong end. Cursing a blue streak, I head back onto the main road.

When I eventually arrive, the bloke who comes out is in his fifties, Leeds United tattoos on his arms, workman's hands and a deep, smoker's voice; a proper Loiner. I make a joke about what a pain the house was to find and he sympathises.

No one can ever find us here, kidder. Which bit of Leeds are yer from?

I tell him, and it turns out he works for a company about half a mile away from my house on the same industrial estate where my son has his drum lessons. He says some of the lads are going back to work next week and he's hoping he'll join them the week after, but he's not been paid while he's been off and they've run out of food. He seems embarrassed to take the bags, but I tell him that's what we're there for. It's obvious that whatever the initial remit of the service, we're now here to feed the poor and needy people of the city and I'm totally on board with that.

On my way to the last drop I pass an old woman in a winter coat with a mask on and her hood up, pulling a shopping cart behind her. It's boiling hot and she must be melting. How anxious must a person be to dress like that on a day like this?

The final drop of the day is near Cemetery Road in Holbeck, an apt name when you see the state of many of the residents. Here reside the people of the abyss. The drop is on a row of big old terraced houses, all of which seem to be split into flats; one on each floor, including the basement. In *The Road to Wigan Pier* there is a plate featuring a picture of the outside of a house, shot from a low angle so you can see the top of the cellar window, barely poking up above street level. The caption simply says "Poplar: the basement is lived in," as if that's sufficiently awful to speak for itself.[19] All the basements here are inhabited too, and it strikes me as odd that so little has changed in the near century since that book was written, with slum housing, unemployment and crippling poverty still rife. In some ways we live in a completely different world, but the age-old problem of wealth inequality is only getting worse as the years go by.

I park next to a bus stop a couple of doors down from where I'm meant to be delivering. As I get out of the van, a youngish lad in a tracksuit sways around the corner, clocks the van and starts running. He dives down the steps of the house I'm parked outside and starts banging on the boarded-up window of the basement flat, yelling at the top of his voice, Hughie! Hughie! It's me! It's me! You've got to get out mate! There's some cunt here in a Leeds City Council van and it's right outside your flat! Hughie!

He gives the board one last thump, scrambles up the steps and starts stumbling towards me. I'm remembering the man in Armley last week and my nerves are blazing. I can see him coming and I'm convinced he's going to attack me. Why else would he have been yelling at his mate in the flat to come out? I'm not close enough to the van to be able to get back in if he's coming for me. I weigh it up in my head; I think I might get away with it. He's on the left-hand side of the pavement, looking like he's angling towards me. If I shift my body slightly to the right he's going to be in the perfect position for me to swing and stick one right on him with my left hand. I'm visualising it, the arc of my fist curving through the air, the split second of impact,

19   Orwell, G., (1936). *The Road to Wigan Pier.* London: Penguin Modern Classics (1989), plate 29.

the crack of cartilage and snap of bone as his nose splatters all over his face and he falls to the ground while I hop in the van and get the fuck out of here. I'm not a violent man but I fancy my chances against this guy. He's obviously a drug user and looks like he'd weigh ten stone soaking wet; I'm nudging six foot two and about fourteen stone, so I'll only need to hit him with one good one and it'll be game over.

My heart's pounding as he comes swaying towards me. I've got my body in position, fist clenched and arm ready to launch it, but he veers away at the last second and staggers off, muttering to himself. In my paranoia he was gunning for me, but the reality was simply that he was so fucked he couldn't walk straight.

I let out a big sigh of relief and almost collapse against the side of the van. I nearly get in and drive away, before remembering I have a parcel to deliver. I walk closer to the door, breathing heavily. I'm about to walk up the front steps when a voice calls out from the basement flat down by my feet.

CanIhelpyerpal?

I jump out of my skin, take a deep breath, then I tell him I'm looking for Melanie.

Melanie? Ah, Melanie. Soundmate, yeah yeah yeah sound. I'lltellher yerhere. MELLLLLLLLLL!

She comes to the door in a dressing gown and pyjamas, possibly a similar age to me but looking at least twenty years older. She has a fag on the go and she's so thin she can barely lift the bags. Her face is drawn, weathered, worn, with huge black bags under her eyes and a few missing teeth. She's friendly and polite on the surface but her eyes are like glass beads and I get the impression that behind them she's not really there at all.

It's been a frazzling day. When I get home the kids are all over me – Daddy, daddy, can you take us for a walk in the woods? – and it's hard to say no when my wife's been looking after them all day, even though I'm so wiped out that all I really want to do is lie down on the sofa and sleep. There's no denying the fact that life at the moment is exhausting. Work is physically and mentally far more demanding than I ever expected it to be, and my wife and the kids are, like everyone else, suffering from being stuck at home. We have a lovely walk in the woods while my wife has a bit of respite, and although I'm zombified by the end of it, it helps me calm down after thinking I was going to have to fight the man on Cemetery Road. Even so, it takes a six pack of cider and a couple of pills to get me to sleep later on, and it's still not the most restful of nights.

Sunday 3rd May

It takes a while to wake up. I'm a little shaken again after the incident in Holbeck at the last drop yesterday. I'm feeling pretty jangled as it is and the sparodic threat of violence doesn't help at all.

I'm off to Harehills to kick things off this morning, an address on the street that's home to the *SUCK YA MOM HIGH SCHOOL* van.

Driving through Harehills at 9 a.m, the area is still asleep and I've never seen it so quiet. There are a couple of people drifting around smoking and two or three pairs of police officers surveying the scene, but other than that it's dead. Every single shop looks to be closed and I'm struck with the same end-of-the-world feeling I got on the motorways at Easter, which feels like a lifetime ago now. It's usually such a bustling, vibrant place even at this time of day, and you can guarantee that if I have to come back an hour later, the scene will be completely different.

The man next door to the drop is walking up the steps to his house, but he senses the van and as I get out he turns around and starts walking back down, eyeballing me. Fucking hell, not this again. He's a big, mean-looking man with scars all over his face, loads of piercings and shovel-shaped hands that look like they've been broken more than once, a thunderstruck grimace of rage snarling across his face. If the shit hits the fan, I don't stand a chance.

My heart's racing and I'm starting to panic again. I don't say anything, but point to the house next door and indicate I'm going there. He grunts, shrugs his shoulders, gives me one last glare and walks off, sticking a fag in his mouth and lighting up as he goes. It seems odd for him to be walking away when thirty seconds ago he looked like he was going to open his front door and go inside, but to be honest I'm just glad he's gone.

Like most of the other houses on the street, the place I'm delivering to is a wreck. The fence has fallen down and is lying in several pieces in the front yard on top of cracked, uneven flagstones that are strewn with glass. The bins are upended and there's rubbish seeping out, empty beer cans and rotting vegetable peelings, juice oozing from the split bags. The window frames are in a terrible state, and the hideous brown door, all its paint flaking off, looks like it's on the verge of disintegrating.

I knock and wait, knock and wait, knock and wait some more, but it's clear there's either no one in or they're all in bed. Not a single voice cuts through the silence, which is unusual and does little to help my nerves. In the end I'm happy to climb back into the van and drive away.

The next job is on a street I haven't been to before. There are even more nitrous cans here than usual – literally hundreds of them clogging the gutters. I drive up the street, turn round at the end and park outside the drop. Across the road, sitting atop a crumbling wall, an ancient, toothless woman peers in slack-lipped curiosity at me from underneath her multi-coloured headscarf, henna tattoos all over her wizened hands. Her milky eyes are deep and dark, set back in a weathered face that makes her look older than time itself. I wonder what she makes of everything that's going on?

A young woman answers the door, strikingly pretty with dark hair and eyes, although her face is practically fleshless. She's skeletally thin and doesn't look well – her skin pallid beneath what would normally be an olive complexion. I can see at least two young children in the house behind her; it must be a big family because I have three dry bags for her, plus the refrigerated stuff and some fruit and veg. Her English is non-existent, from which I infer that she's probably a recent immigrant to the country. So many new arrivals to the city end up in the cultural melting pot of Harehills, which is one of the reasons why the community is so diverse. She squints when I show her my ID and shakes her head, pauses for the slightest fraction of a second when she looks past me and clocks the council livery on the van, but brightens up when she sees the bags, points to herself as if to say, for *me*?, then breaks into a beautiful smile when I nod.

As I'm driving away another man stands on his doorstep glaring at me and smoking with vicious intent, as if he's trying to inhale the whole fag and not only the smoke coming from it. If looks could kill, I'd have died scores of times since I started this job.

Heading back up through the middle of Harehills I see a sight that nearly stops me in my tracks. Two old ladies who must be seventy at least, ragged sparrows with thin white hair, are grabbing onto each other, wheeling round in the street outside Greggs. It looks like they're fighting or that one is mugging the other, but a closer inspection shows that one of them is trying to fit her friend's surgical face mask and it keeps falling off. It really chokes me up, something that's happening with increasing regularity.

The last drop on my final sheet is another in the middle of Harehills. It's an ugly scene. The yards are full of people, weed and fag smoke hanging in a pall over the whole street. Two lads across from where I park are screaming at each other and squaring up for a fight; a multitude of loud voices fill the air, shrill, aggressive, loaded with threat. All eyes are on me and the van, none of them friendly. It's hugely intimidating and I don't plan on hanging around. The idea is to get out, knock three times at the drop, pause, then get back in the van, and that's exactly what I do. I'm about to give the man a call when he opens the front door and I beckon him out to the van. He's a heavyset lad, built like a boxer whose best years are behind him, a skinhead with circles under his eyes so big they seem like they cover half his cheeks. He's thankful to see me but he's on some powerful gear and when he tries to say thanks he's virtually incoherent. For my part, I just want to get the drop over with as quickly as possible so I can go home

On the way back to LBS to drop the van off I reflect on the weekend. At least half of the drops have been in Harehills, and it's noticeable how the same areas keep cropping up – Beeston, Harehills, Middleton, Belle Isle, Armley. By now, there's no escaping the fact that we're feeding the poorest of the city and that the virus isn't coming into the equation at all. The stark reality is that in the present economic climate there are huge swathes of the city's population – concentrated in, but not exclusively limited to the areas mentioned above – who are unable to feed themselves or their families properly, and the food parcels we are providing are vital to their survival.

Week 5:
Mixed messages

Number of recorded deaths: 31,855

"It has been enraging to see the difficulties we've had in supplying PPE to those that need it." – Prime Minister Boris Johnson, Prime Minister's Questions, Wednesday 6th May 2020

As of Tuesday 5th May, the UK has the highest death toll in Europe, with the official figure reaching 29,247. Shadow Health Secretary Jonathan Ashworth responds to the news, saying, "The public will rightly ask why our death rate is so high." Chief Scientific Adviser Sir Patrick Vallance tells the House of Commons Select Committee, "I think if we'd managed to ramp up testing capacity quicker it would have been beneficial [...] For all sorts of reasons, that didn't happen."

Deaths in hospitals are falling as deaths in care homes rise; 5,890 care home deaths are recorded up to 24th April. On 6th May, Prime Minister Boris Johnson says on Prime Minister's Questions that he "bitterly regrets" the crisis in care homes and that he is "working very hard" to rectify the situation. On the same day, deaths increase by 649, taking the death toll past the 30,000 mark.

The following day, the 400,000 gowns sourced by Communities Secretary Robert Jenrick from Turkey are deemed to be unusable as they do not meet the required safety standards. Shadow Health Minister Justin Madders responds by saying, "This is the latest in a number of mistakes by the Government during its response to the pandemic. It is vital that the Government produces a clear and credible plan for what comes next to avoid further serious missteps like this."

On the same day, the Bank of England warns that the UK economy will shrink by 14% in 2020. At the end of the week, the Government's official message on Covid-19 changes from "Stay at home. Protect the NHS. Save lives." to "Stay alert. Control the virus. Save lives."

A new five scale alert system ranging from green to red is announced; Acting Liberal Democrat Leader Sir Ed Davey warns, "Changing the message at this critical stage risks what people have fought so hard for. Boris Johnson has not provided the country with any evidence or justification for change. Instead, he risks creating more confusion than clarity by badly communicating his government's plans."

On Sunday 10th May, a recorded address from Boris Johnson is broadcast at 7 p.m. in which he outlines a conditional plan to reopen society, describing it as "the first careful steps to modify our measures". People who are able to go back to work are now encouraged to do so, although they must avoid public transport wherever possible. Schools may open no earlier than 1st June; shops, parts of the hospitality industry and other public places may open from 1st July. Keir Starmer responds by saying, "This statement raises more questions than it answers. [...] The Prime Minister appears to be effectively telling millions of people to go back to work without a clear plan for safety or clear guidance as to how to get there without using public transport. What the country wanted tonight was clarity and consensus, but we haven't got either of those."

Monday 4th May

I'm hoping for a better day than I had last Monday, with all the dud medicine pick-ups. It's hard to believe that was a week ago already. The passage of time feels warped. The days can feel like they last forever when there's nowhere to go and nothing to do, but the weeks are flying by at a terrifying pace as lockdown becomes accepted as the norm and everyone adjusts to this new way of living.

There are only two jobs on my first sheet. The first address is in Middleton, on an estate comprising of a mix of red-brick and stone houses; there are some expensive cars around and the properties look to be in reasonable order. They're not exactly newbuilds but they're a world away from the century-old back-to-backs of the slums.

The house is hemmed in by black metal gates that lead into a spacious yard, free from any mess other than a broken bed base, wood poking through foam like a bone protruding from a broken leg. A woman of about my age answers the door; her phone's glued to her ear, but she doesn't appear to be speaking to anyone. She has dyed blonde hair, wide brown eyes and a big smile. She's accompanied by a girl of about twelve and a boy of pre-school age. The little boy tries to run out to greet me, but she shoos him inside like a mother hen with a big scoop of her arm.

I've got a few bags for them; when I'm coming back with the second load, I can hear the little boy complaining that there are no mushrooms in the bags.

No mushrooms, what's he like? the mum says in a broad south Leeds brogue.

I tell her there might be some in the fruit and veg bag.

Come on, love, let's get these inside, she tells him. The mister says there might be some in here.

The boy grins happily and she shepherds him into the house. As the door closes, I hear him happily exclaim, look mummy, cupcakes! I smile as I'm walking back to the van, hoping that the buzz of finding the buns will offset any disappointment when he realises there are no mushrooms in the other bag after all.

The next drop is a more forbidding prospect at a tower block in Beeston, stuck up like a middle finger at the brooding sky. There's a patch of grass that has started to turn brown from the recent lack of rainfall right outside the main entrance. A couple of teens in trackies and surgical masks, perched on top of BMXs that look way too small for them, are doing a quick deal with the sleight of hand of a pair of accomplished stage magicians before they bump fists and go their separate ways. Closer to the side entrance some residents who look to be in their early sixties are grouped around a pair of benches, having a chat. An old man with a walking stick and opaque eyes squints myopically at me as I get out of the van. I wave at him and say good morning. He nods in reply and carries on his way.

The drop is on the top floor. I buzz the intercom but there's no answer, and I can't get through on the phone either. I'm uneasy. The tower blocks always seem faintly threatening and I don't feel quite as safe in some of these places as I did when I started first started delivering to them. As I'm leaving, the heavens open and it doesn't stop raining for the rest of the day.

The afternoon takes me to Yeadon for a food drop and a prescription collection. Cross Green looks desolate with the rain lashing down; there's a vast expanse of open ground that's technically a construction site where a new development of warehouses is in the early stages of being built, but for now it's a wasteland, nothing but dead space cluttered with rubble and heavy earth movers that have been in the same abandoned positions for weeks. On the way I drive through Kirkstall, past the ITV building and the *Emmerdale* set, also closed, the lives of the characters stuck on pause just like the lives of everyone else. It'll be interesting to see how they decide to kick-start the storylines again in the post-virus world.

At the Abbey there are a few people trudging disconsolately around the ruins in anoraks or beneath umbrellas, so desperate to get out of the house that they've decided to brave this sudden Yorkshire downpour.

The food is for a woman in her seventies, who tells me in a matter-of-fact manner that she has terminal cancer. You'd never know to look at her – in fact, she looks strangely well under the circumstances, full in the face and with a twinkle in her eyes. As with so many of her generation, she can't believe that the service is free and it takes me a few minutes to get her to put her purse away.

I'm not supposed to go out, love, she tells me. The doctors say I'm at risk, what with the cancer and everything. But what's it to me when I'm dying anyway?

I'm not really sure what to say to this.

Have you still been going out, then? I manage.

I've been trying, love. I used to like to get the bus into Yeadon so I could have a wander round there, but there aren't many running now.

It's nice in Yeadon, I tell her, my kids like visiting the tarn and watching the planes fly into the airport.

It's lovely, she says. Once of a day I'd've just walked up if I couldn't get the bus, but I'm not up to it now. I'm not as fit as I once was, you know. Her face falls for a split second, then she grins. Still, I like to try to be independent, there's no one can take that away from me. I go the butcher's up the road when I can, and I can get some little bits and pieces from the newsagent's if I need to. It gets me out the house, like.

I hand over the bags and she goggles. It'll take me ages to eat all this, love. I told 'em on the phone I didn't need any help but they said my name was on the list so I might as well take it, and in the end I couldn't really argue. Anyway, my mam always said it was rude to refuse a kindness. Are you *sure* you don't want paying?

I tell her I'm sure and bid her farewell. I almost can't believe she's dying. She seems so full of *life*. The question of how long she has left crosses my mind, but it's such a sad thought that I bury it as soon as it appears.

The pharmacist is on the high street, a narrow, crooked affair that should probably be pedestrianised. There's usually little point trying to get down it in a car, never mind a clunky van like the Kangoo, but it's quiet today and I even manage to find a parking spot. True to form, the woman behind the counter tells me that a volunteer came in to pick up the prescription about five minutes ago, so it's another wasted trip.

It's too late to go back for another job sheet, so I take the van back, hop in the car and head home. It's been a slow day but I keep telling myself that's it's worth it and the important thing is the good we're doing for the people of the city. It's been a tremendous experience so far; demand for the service is high and shows no sign of slackening off as the weeks pass.

Tuesday 5th, Wednesday 6th and Thursday 7th May

After a slow Monday I have a fairly sedate few days. Tuesday is spent catching up with work and attending a Zoom meeting with my manager, and my two days off are largely passed pottering around the garden, mowing lawns and pulling up weeds while the kids indulge in their favourite game of assailing me with waterbombs, shooting me with their water pistols and generally doing everything they can to make me cold and wet. With the weather as hot as it is, though, I don't mind. Tensions have been running a little high at home while I've been at work. My wife is finding it harder and harder to keep the kids happy under these incredibly difficult circumstances, and it's most welcome for the four of us to have a bit of quality time together, even if we don't do anything particularly exciting.

Friday 8th May

Today is a bank holiday, moved from next Monday, to celebrate the 75th anniversary of VE Day. I don't remember anyone ever caring about this before, save for the 50th anniversary in 1995, but it was a different world we were living in back then. Yes, there were Tories in power then too, but it was clear that their time was up and that soon the country would fall under the stewardship of Tony Blair. I think much of the celebration back then came from a sense of relief that a new day was dawning. It was all tied in with New Labour and Cool Britannia, although the latter phrase hadn't quite yet been coined; the end of a decade and a half of grim Conservative rule and the start of a bright new era. This year we have another Conservative government but the vibe is different – the jingoistic, flag-waving right-wing have hijacked the occasion, somehow turning an event marking the defeat of Fascism into a celebration of Brexit. Despite lockdown still being in full swing, plans are in the offing for socially distanced parties, bunting, barbecues, screenings of Churchill speeches and singalongs of *We'll Meet Again*.

It's supremely ironic that the generation we are told we're meant to be celebrating are now either isolated at home or stuck in care homes, and until about a week ago the Government weren't even counting their deaths.[20] It's also ironic that the zealots who are enthusing about VE Day are oblivious to the fact that their own views are heading well in the direction of Fascism and completely overlook the fact that World War Two was won, as the saying goes, with Russian blood and American money. No one's going to let that get in the way of a good piss-up, though.

At the moment people are still being told to stay at home, but there's talk in the news that some of the lockdown restrictions may be eased from next week. There's a lot of media speculation about what may be announced, but the consensus is that it won't be anything drastic. The majority of people just want to know when they can see their families again, but none of the official communication in the upcoming weeks will touch on this. The overwhelming feeling is that the Government are keen to get at least some shops open to pave the way for a proper restart of the economy, despite the fact that people are still dying in huge numbers. At the same time, Foreign Secretary Dominic Raab is saying that if measures are eased and the infection rate increases again, lockdown will have to be reintroduced. Chancellor of the Exchequer Rishi Sunak is on record as saying people are becoming "addicted" to being furloughed and that he is looking for a way to stop making payments already. The Liberal Democrats have responded immediately, saying, "Ending the furlough scheme now would be a disaster for millions of families and our economy."

At the FDC it's a slow start. I see a couple of vans go out but there's no sense of urgency. The only job on my sheet is in Morley so at least

---

20 Until 28th April, the official death toll only counted those who had died in hospitals and excluded anyone who had died in the community or a care home setting.

there will be a bit of a ride to pass the time, although once I'm on the motorway it never seems to take very long to get there. There is a lot of traffic on the motorways this morning. It's not the kind of rush you'd expect on a normal bank holiday, but for a time there are vehicles in front of me, behind me *and* blocking me in at the side, which has been unheard of in all the weeks I've been doing this, and for a few brief moments on the M1, life has a faint veneer of normality.

There aren't many people about in Morley, but it's still quite early. The drop is down a tight cul-de-sac full of mostly well-maintained properties, many with two cars parked on the driveways, but the house I'm delivering to looks a bit more run down. There's a white metal handrail bordering the path, rusted red in parts where the paint has flaked off. Through the glass on the front door it looks like a mattress has been propped up against it, so I wonder how I'm supposed to get the food in.

I give the door a bang, but no one answers. I try again, and a boy of about ten comes to the window, starts pointing next door but doesn't speak. I go to put the job list to the window so I can show him the name and address, but he turns on his heel and runs away. On the way back to the van a woman stops me. She's youngish, maybe thirty, slight and mousy in pyjama bottoms and a cut-off vest top, hand resting across her stomach in that unconscious way that women in the early, invisible stages of pregnancy sometimes do.

It turns out to be her that I'm looking for. She asks if I'm working with the police and I shake my head. She says they have just brought her some food, but I don't know anything about that. I know there are lots of other agencies in the city running food schemes, but I've not come across anything to do with the police. I ask if she contacted the council to get the food I've brought but she says it was all done through schools. Schools are another example of agencies working hard to identify need. Thousands of pupils from low-income families in the city are on free school meals, and there's a worry about what's come to be known as Holiday Hunger, where parents can't afford to feed their kids the extra meal a day when they're not at school. At a time when children are off school for what appears to be an indefinite period, this issue is more pressing than ever and it is to be hoped the service we're offering can do a little bit to help.[21]

21 The issue of Holiday Hunger was prescient during the pandemic. The government agreed that children eligible for free school meals should continue to get them

I give her the food I've brought anyway – she looks like she needs it. I'm curious as to how she's going to get into the house with that mattress pressed up against the door, but she must be lightning fast because by the time I get back in the van and look round, she's picked up the bags and vanished.

When I get back, I hang around for a bit talking to Sharon and Terry, before an urgent job comes in for a disabled woman in Alwoodley. I don't recognise the address, but it turns out it's only about five minutes away from my house. When I knock on the door, I hear her call. I think she says she's coming, but after five minutes of waiting she's still not there so I knock again and this time she tells me to come in.

She's an old woman, that's for sure, maybe around eighty with thinning wisps of grey hair beginning on her temples and straggling all the way down to her shoulders. She is deathly thin apart from her legs, which are swollen purple at the ankles and propped out horizontally in front of her, resting atop a pouffe of the type I haven't seen since I was a kid in the '80s. She's wearing a full-length house coat and the gas fire is on, even though it's about twenty degrees outside. The atmosphere is utterly oppressive. It's exactly the kind of house you'd expect an isolated old person to live in – curtains closed, faded carpets, some dusty shelves with their ancient books and a few trinkets scattered here and there. The TV is on but the sound is off, the air humming with the smell of dry heat and must. She asks me to bring the parcels into the living room, so I take them in and leave them in the spot she indicates in front of one of the bookcases.

Can you manage to move them from here? I ask.

I'll be alright later on, love, she tells me. Then – Are you standing far enough away from me?

I think so, I tell her.

Well. Do you mind standing outside the living room door if we're talking? I don't know what to make of all this, you know. It'd frighten the life out of anyone.

Am I okay here? I say, retreating and standing outside the room.

---

during the first lockdown, but initially was reluctant to make extra provisions during school holidays. Following a high-profile campaign by footballer Marcus Rashford, the decision was reversed, although the controversy over providing free meals during school holidays continued into 2021.

That's fine, love. She has to crane her neck nearly a hundred and eighty degrees to see me now, and I can almost hear it click when she does so.

She's polite and extremely grateful. She offers to pay, discombobulated like so many others that the service is free. We have a quick chat about the weather and the pandemic, then I make my excuses and leave. It's sweltering in the house and I'm grateful for a few gulps of fresh air when I get outside.

The first drop of the afternoon is an address I know in Harehills. I did a fair bit of work once upon a time at the community centre nearby, running some literacy schemes for the pre-school children that went to day care there. The staff were saints and did a brilliant job with the kids, but it was a difficult environment. The speech and language skills of many of the children were low – hence why I'd been asked to work with them – and the outside play area was out of bounds because the staff kept finding used needles there amongst all the broken glass.

The parcels are for a woman in beautiful traditional African dress, multi-coloured and vibrant, who's as tall as me and probably as heavy. There's a flowerbed and some bushes on the street outside that are bursting with beer cans, glass bottles, fag packets, carrier bags and nitrous cartridges. She doesn't have much English, but says God bless you, darling, as I'm walking back to the van. I head on up the road, ignoring the teenage BMX gang who are smoking outside the offie and flicking V signs at the van, on to the next address, which is over the road from Jimmy's.

I find a narrow cul-de-sac that branches off in two directions, one of those where the layout and numbering system are counter-intuitive, compounded by the fact that most of the houses and flats don't have numbers on the doors. I drive down to the bottom end of the close, where three teenagers are rolling a spliff on the bonnet of a Toyota Yaris. They eye me warily as I turn the van around; when I can't find the address at the top of the close either and come down for another pass, they've gone.

I'm wondering if the place I'm looking for might be in the little block of flats behind the rusty metal fence near where I've parked so I decide to have a look around. There's an old couple sitting outside their flat on the ground floor having a brew and smoking a fag apiece, so I decide to ask them. They greet me as soon as I get out of the van, friendly as you like, and it turns out the flat is directly above them.

The people upstairs must overhear our conversation, because a young lad, probably in his early twenties and built like a tank, walks through the open door onto the balcony and says he'll let me in. I go to the van and get the food, but I'm waiting for a while and in the end I have to buzz on the intercom to get him to come down. I can hear an angry female voice shouting indistinctly in the background and the sound of young children crying. He finally appears, mumbles his thanks as he takes the bags but won't look me in the eye. Meanwhile, the old woman is berating a Scottish fella who's stumbling past with a can of Special Brew; he's allowed his dog to do a massive shit outside their flat. He's pretending he can't see it but it's fucking *huge*, and I can smell it from all the way over here. I don't blame him for not wanting to clean it up, but it is his responsibility. They're still at it as I'm getting into the van; the man has finally admitted to being able to *see* the turd, but is now claiming that he's walking the dog for someone else and is telling the old woman he's going to go find his friend to get *them* to come back and shift the pile. I can still see them in the wing mirror as I'm heading off up the road: him slurring on in his thick accent, swigging from his can, the old lass waving her fag at him, having none of it.

I have one more drop to do today, back in Gipton. There are a few VE Day Parties in full swing next to East End Park when I pass, people with tipsy grins stumbling around their gardens, swigging from bottles and cans, toking on fags and spliffs, but it looks like a sad celebration from here.

The front garden of the house I park outside is about two feet high in dandelions and grass. The woman smoking a joint in the front garden next door is shrivelled up like all the life's been sucked out of her, covered in tattoos and without a single bit of flesh on her. Her skirt is short and the legs sticking out from under it are so thin it's a wonder they can bear her weight, however low that must be. It's impossible to gauge how old she is. The man at the drop seems startled to see me. He's jumpy, with the kind of darting, staring eyes that suggest mental health issues, possibly another lost soul in need of support yet getting none.

Everywhere seems busy today. I wonder if it's because there's talk of the lockdown easing, or maybe it's that chunks of the British public have decided that enough is enough and they're going to end it themselves. The calls to celebrate VE Day certainly haven't helped, that's for sure, and later the news and social media are filled with pictures of drunk people waving flags, trying to do socially distanced congas and singing popular songs from the Second World War.

I wonder if the term 'lockdown fatigue' has been coined yet? Whether it has or not, it appears to have set in and more and more people seem to be flouting the rules. This is confirmed later when I get home and go for a walk around the streets near my house. There are quite a few socially distanced gatherings on the streets and in gardens – not exactly parties, but people stretching the lockdown guidance to the absolute limit. It's a welcome change to hear the sound of people and the hubbub of happy voices again, however spurious the reasons for the celebrations may be. It's not natural for people to be isolated for long periods, and it feels as if, rightly or wrongly, the end is approaching.

Another thing that's really struck me about the last few weeks is how instinctively conservative many people in this country have proven themselves to be. Social media is awash with people posting such messages as, *I think my next-door neighbour has been having unauthorised visitors and I don't know what to do about it*, or uploading images of people in the park with scandalised comments about how many people there are about, as if they're not one of them. There is a lot of talk about how lockdown measures haven't gone far enough, but this seems like a dangerous road to go down. I understand the seriousness of the situation, but there's something deeply disturbing about a situation where people can complain that police haven't been given *enough* powers to make them stay at home.

Psychologically speaking, this is a very important point. The speed with which it was possible to implement lockdown and pass emergency legislation (such as The Coronavirus Act, which came into force on 25th March and created "a number of new criminal offences"[22]) – which is intrinsically repressive, no matter the circumstances – coupled with how quickly the population at large accepted it doesn't bode well for the future. It's a classic ploy used by totalitarian states: to introduce restrictive measures by telling the populace that it's for their own good, until "the normalisation of crisis produces a situation in which the repealing of measures brought in to deal with an emergency becomes

---

22 Full details relating to the act and its contents can be found at https://www.cps.gov.uk/legal-guidance/coronavirus-act-2020

unimaginable."[23] While I understand the need for measures to be put in place to control the spread of the virus, the precedent this sets is very worrying indeed.

Saturday 9th May

It's a glorious day again, set to be the last hot one for a while according to the forecast. It's been a tiring night – I'm too wired to sleep at the moment, but I'm trying to hold off taking the sleeping pills because of how they make me feel in the mornings. Work, combined with the constant pressure of having to keep the children occupied and happy is so draining – it's really become a drag and the pressure is getting to everyone. To make matters worse, it doesn't look like there's any chance of both kids going back to school before September, meaning that it's going to be an interminable summer as the poor things are going crazy with boredom already and are beside themselves at not being able to see their friends.

I barely see another car on the way to either LBS or the depot. It's all quiet in East End Park; the bunting and flags are still up, bins overflowing with beer bottles and cider cans, front yards trashed with the wreckage of yesterday's festivities. I bet there are some savage post-bank holiday hangovers this morning.

The day begins with prescription collections in Yeadon and Pudsey. As I drive into the top of Yeadon High Street, I see a house covered in bunting made from flags from all over the world. It's a beautiful sight and a refreshing change from the Union Jacks and St George's flags that have been decorating the city for the past week.

There are a few more people about on the High Street and there's a queue at the butchers, but I walk straight into the chemists to find that the medication has already been collected.

I have to queue a bit to get into Lloyds in Pudsey when I get there, but I enjoy sitting in the sun for a bit while I'm waiting. This prescription's here, thankfully. The drop is in Stanningley in a tidy complex of private flats. An oldish woman answers the intercom, lets me straight in and up I go to the top floor. She's waiting at the door. There's a smell of fresh fag smoke mixed with the cloying aroma of an aerosol air freshener wafting out. I can see a little decanter of pale sherry on table next to door, and a whatnot with loads of little glass ornaments on it.

---

23   Fisher, M., (2009). *Capitalist Realism – is there no alternative?*, Zero Books, p.1.

She's tiny and thin but she seems alert and looks relatively healthy compared to some of the other older people I've delivered to. She doesn't say much, just smiles her thanks and waves me on my way.

It's beer garden weather today, again. I keep passing pubs and thinking how busy they should have been while it's been so hot over the past few weeks; I ponder a game where I count how many pubs I pass while I'm out and about but count twelve in about four minutes and give up. How many of them are going to open again? The entire British hospitality industry is suffering horribly from the pandemic, and it's a legitimate question as to whether or not it will ever be the same again.

The Government today announced its intention to ask anyone flying into the UK to quarantine themselves for two weeks, a measure that has been in place for a couple of months in most other European countries, prompting Shadow Transport Secretary Jim McMahon to say, "Ill-thought-through proposals will fail as soon as they are rolled out. This sort of policy should have been worked through weeks ago."

Apparently garden centres are going to be allowed to open from Monday, the first steps towards opening up the economy again. Running alongside this, there has been word from the government this week that social distancing measures may be about to start being relaxed in some workplaces, another indication that they're slowly moving towards getting some people at least back into work. This, combined with constant references to what's become known as "the new normal" look to be a sure sign that change of some sort is on the way. There's talk of "putting the handbrake on" if necessary, but it's difficult to see this happening once the wheels start turning again unless circumstances take a real turn for the worse, which, given how bleak the situation is at the moment, is a scenario that doesn't bear thinking about.

The question of what to do in terms of the regulations is a sticky one and there isn't much middle ground – people either seem to have had enough and want an immediate end, or are advocating stricter controls. There's a case to be made for opening things up a little from an economic point of view, but from a public health point of view many people still don't think it's safe. The government, however, seem to be of the mind that the benefits outweigh the risks and that for the sake of the economy it's a gamble worth taking.

It's a deadly quiet afternoon, baking in the van outside the FDC with nothing to do. Eventually another meds drop comes in for me, just the one. I don't know why we're bothering given the abysmal record we have of being able to collect them, but I'm assured the place is open so off I go through town, past the new block of flats going up where the Yorkshire Post building, such a staple of the Leeds landscape for so many years, used to be. Now all that remains is old digital clock tower, the faded logo of the newspaper still adorning the top of it, another relic of old Leeds still standing defiantly as the city centre morphs around it.

When I arrive the pharmacy looks derelict, never mind closed. It's shuttered, bolted, graffiti tagged, lifeless in the shadow of the tower blocks around it.

Back at the FDC Terry comes out and asks if I had a look around the *back* of the chemist? He's been phoning but got an engaged tone, so he thinks someone might be there. Do I fancy having another ride out? I might as well do that as sit in the van so I retrace my steps and get there fairly quickly. I drive around the place, and it's determined to look like it's shut. It's sandwiched between Wortley Towers, Clyde Court and the Beech pub, surrounded by chickenwire on all sides and only accessible via a side road which takes a bit of finding. The whole thing is shuttered up apart from the front door, and even that looks like it's locked until I give it a shove and it swings open with a click.

I go inside and wander down a miniature maze of corridors that are more akin to the inside of a hospital than a chemist. Joy of joys, the meds are here so I pick them up, say my thanks and leave. The drop is on a street across the road and up under the railway bridge, still blackened with the soot of years gone by. It looks like there's not much housing amongst the wreckage and industrial sprawl but it becomes more residential the further I drive.

The house I'm after is on a small parade surrounded by a tall wooden fence that's falling down in several places. There are something like ten rubbish bags of household waste plus a load of old clothes, kids' toys and four or five pairs of trainers piled up by the bins in front of where I park. There are two shirtless men drinking in the garden, two women in jeans and t-shirts with them, all of them in their forties and shooting psychic bullets at the van. It looks like they're sitting round a rubbish fire, blazing in the afternoon heat, the thick black smoke giving off a toxic smell of melting plastic.

I ask if they know the address I'm after. They're not especially friendly but they tell me that it's next door. I open gate and there's a brand new Audi in the yard outside, glossy and black, not what I was expecting considering the state of the rest of the street. An older woman answers the door with a quick smile of thanks and closes it again without a word. It takes about ten seconds.

There are shouts of raucous laughter and the sound of breaking glass followed by cheering coming from over the street, slamming basslines, more parties in full swing. It's half past three and there's no point going back to the depot so I drive through Armley and head back to LBS.

It's a tough evening at home. My son has been getting more and more unsettled, so today my wife tried to cheer him up by arranging for him to have a Skype call with one of his best friends from school. They're still talking when I walk in and he's having a lovely time, chattering on about the *Beast Quest* books he's been reading and showing his friend the Lego spaceship set he's spent the morning building, but as soon as the call finishes the poor little man is in bits, crying and complaining about how much he misses his friends, and telling us that all he wants is to go back to school. My wife and I try to reassure him that it will all be over soon and that one day life will get back to normal, but the unpalatable truth is that none of us have any idea when this will be and all indications are that the kids will be stuck at home till September. He calms down for a little while, but he's crying for his friends again at bedtime and it takes me ages to get him to sleep.

Once the kids are in bed my wife and I have an uneasy chat about the children and how we're going to manage to keep them going if we have to have them at home until autumn. It's a muted, miserable, inconclusive conversation, full of the unspoken fear we're both feeling about the troubled times our children are being forced to endure. In the end we decide to get an early night, but I don't get a huge amount of sleep, and I don't think my wife does either.

Sunday 10th May

It's a cold start to the morning, the temperature having pretty much halved overnight. There's been a lot of rain and a blustery wind, the remnants of last month's blossom now nothing more than a soggy brown mulch clogging up the gutters.

My first job sheet has three drops, the first of which is in Middleton. As with other drops I've done here over the last few weeks, it's on a lovely street, long and wide with some big family cars parked by the sides of the road. About halfway down there are three or four houses in a row that have been converted into flats. They look ramshackle at best, and all are utterly filthy. The flat I need is upstairs and has an ugly, bad-tempered bull terrier pacing in moody circles on the tiny balcony beneath a ragged metal table that looks like it's been salvaged from the tip.

I have no idea which door to knock on, so I give them a call. A woman answers the phone sounding tense, muffled shouting in the background; she says she's going to send her partner down to meet me. He appears, a skinny guy in a dressing gown with a deep tan, eyes popping out of his head, gurning a little as he grinds his teeth, his body in constant unconscious motion. When he speaks his voice is a deep baritone, roughened by the smoke of thousands of cigarettes smoked over the course of his thirty or so years – or maybe he just had too many last night.

Sound mate, sound, yeah yeah, cheers mate, sound, yer an absolute legend, yeah?

As I'm getting back into the van I hear him laughing and shouting up to the woman in the flat, Fuckin' hell, Kelly, wait till yer see what they've sent us!

The reaction to what's in the parcels – teabags, biscuits, cereal, some beans, a bit of fruit and veg – is an indicator of how desperate some people are. To be excited by such mundane, everyday items shows how far below the poverty line some people live, and reinforces the importance of the service we are providing.

The next drop is in Belle Isle. From Miggie it's a couple of miles up Belle Isle Road, which is empty save for a lonely Strongbow can that clatters along in front of the van. The address is at a small block of low-rise flats, silent and grim in the cold of the morning. I park up and get out. As I'm looking around, a woman in a white dressing gown, smoking on the balcony shouts down to me.

Yer gorra food parcel, love?

That's right, I tell her. Come and meet us down here and I'll get it out the van.

This looks great, this, she says when I meet her with the food. I'm absolutely fuckin' starving. I was hoping yer'd come today. Been watching out fer yer.

Her dressing gown is flapping in the chill of the wind but she doesn't seem too bothered, even though she doesn't appear to be wearing anything underneath it. I take a sudden interest in my Doc Martens, noticing when I cast my eyes down that she has dainty pink and yellow flowers tattooed all over her bare feet, which must be freezing on a morning like this. She chucks her fag on the floor, takes the bags and turns on her heel, leaving me with a valedictory, Ta, love! called over her shoulder as she departs.

The next job Sharon sends my way is in Armley, on a street near where that man was going to chin me a couple of weeks ago. I laugh when I see the address and tell her what happened. Her face goes white.

You wanna swap, love?

Nah. I'm not fussed.

The other drivers ask where it is, and they laugh when I tell them. They all know it, and most of them aren't keen to go there either.

It's pissing it down and the gaol looks particularly sinister today under the rain-washed black of the sky. The house is in a messy cul-de-sac and I'm paranoid, wondering how I'm going to get the van out of here if I have to leave in a hurry. At the top of the street there are two men approaching the top end of middle age. They're wearing faded jeans and hoodies, fags in mouths, oblivious to the rain, tinkering about with the engine of a knackered blue Fiesta, laughing when one of them gets up too quickly and bangs his head on the bonnet.

I squeeze the van down the street and park on the pavement as there's nowhere else to leave it without blocking the road. As far as streets go, this is one of the most visibly deprived I've visited. All of the houses here are in terrible states of repair; the brickwork is stained and damp, the gardens are overgrown and filled with splinters of furniture, TVs, washing machines; shattered windows and broken fences abound; a lot of properties have roof tiles missing. There are bags and bags of rubbish spilling their contents into gardens, onto the pavement and into the road.

As soon as I get out of the van, a bloke comes out of a nearby house, looking every bit as hard as the man who threatened me last time I was on the estate. He's only wearing a vest and shorts but he stands there ignoring the rain, concentrating on the fag he's smoking and the look of pure poison he's shooting at me. He has a blonde boy of about three at his side, who is tapping him and saying, Daddy, daddy, who's that man? but he ignores him. My heart's racing and my palms are clammy with sweat despite the cold of the morning.

The house I'm delivering to is every bit as trashed as the others; it has a boarded front door and the living room window's been smashed in too, half-boarded over and half-covered with a black bin bag.

In the end there's no one in so I get back in the van. The man next door is still staring, lighting a fresh fag off the old one and chucking the tab end onto the step, continuing to ignore the boy, who's still pulling on his arms and asking him questions about me.

I stop off at home for a quick coffee on the way back to the FDC and find myself in the middle of World War Three. The door to the back garden is open and there's a tremendous noise coming from outside. My wife is standing in the middle of the lawn in floods of tears, while my son stands laughing and dousing her with the hosepipe. We have a slide in our back garden that they'd tried to turn into a waterslide, but when it didn't work, my son grabbed the hosepipe and turned it on his mum. She's been exhausted recently, and this is the final straw. She doesn't like getting wet at the best of times and she's inconsolable, caught between crying her eyes out and trying to get our son to stop spraying her.

My first instinct is to laugh, but I think better of it and grab the hose from my son's hand. I switch it off, although not before I've given him a good spraying. He thinks it's hilarious and his sister does too; my wife goes inside to dry off while my son tells me the story of the failed waterslide and how he came to be drenching his mum. She's fuming when she comes downstairs; in the end I manage to defuse the situation before I go back to work, but I'm wary that the armistice may not last long and all afternoon I'm fearful of what might be going on when I get back home.

In the afternoon a single job comes through for Garforth so I volunteer before anyone else has the chance. I'm delivering to a row of bungalows that have been adapted for older and disabled people, with wheelchair ramps and handrails. An old-timer answers the door, but I can't get a proper look at his face because he's tied a scarf around the lower half of it. If he's wearing a mask because he's worried about catching something from me, I think he needs to look a bit closer to home; there's an immediate smell of damp and the floor is crawling with black mould. There are mushrooms of black on the walls too, the wallpaper hanging down in limp strips in places. He's twitchy and paranoid, doesn't want to talk, so I leave the food on the doorstep and get on my way.

There's a drop in Burmantofts as soon as I get back, and it turns out to be a real heartbreaker. I can't park near the address so I ditch the van and set off to investigate. I head past a row of houses, up a couple of dirty steps and find a two-storey building filled with little flats. It must be in here. I go inside and climb the stairs, trying to follow the numbering sequence. I'm feeling a little nervous; I'm not keen on the vibe in this place – dark, claustrophobic, edgy – and there's no way to make a rapid getaway if anything untoward happens. It's amazing how paranoid I've become in the last couple of weeks.

When I find the flat, it is, in a word, fucked. The door has been kicked in and boarded so many times there isn't much of it left. The plaster around it is in an atrocious state where it's been cracked and shaken by the blows to the timber; it looks like someone's taken hold of the frame and tried to rip the whole thing out of the wall.

I knock, and a timid voice calls from within – Who's there?

It's Stu from Leeds City Council. I've got your food parcel for you.

The door opens slowly to reveal a woman who's probably in her thirties, wearing leopard print leggings and a baggy t-shirt, pipe-cleaner arms blighted by a mixture of deep, fresh cuts, dried blood, angry scars and track marks. The leggings should be tight, but she's so thin they're hanging off her and slipping down a little around her waist. She sees me and bursts into tears.

Thanks Christ you're here, love, I'm absolutely starving. I haven't eaten for *days*.

She bends over double and starts crying into her hands – huge, heaving, body-shaking sobs, and it's difficult to stop myself from stepping forward and giving her a hug. I've got a lump in my throat, tears welling and I excuse myself, telling her I need to get the food from the van. I stand outside for a minute and take a few deep breaths, trying to compose myself.

When I go back in with the parcels she's closed the door. I knock again.

Who is it?

I tell her and the door opens. Behind her, I can't see the floor for rubbish – dirty clothes, broken dishes, a couple of crusty plates, empty plastic water bottles, junk mail spread out all over.

Oh, it's you, thank you *so* much for coming back...

I pop the bags down on the floor and she launches into a spiel about how terrible it is for everyone who's living through this war – and I *know* it's a nuclear one, she says – and how angels like me have restored her faith in humanity and given her a completely new outlook on life.

I've no idea what she's talking about but she's so sincere that I can tell she believes every word she's saying. I let her talk, nodding and smiling. I infer from the track marks that she's a drug user and it would appear she's got some severe mental health problems as well. She seems so sad and unbelievably lonely. I let her talk for a little while longer then make my excuses, tell her to ring the helpline again as soon as she starts to run out of food, and leave.

Back in the van, I'm in bits. This woman needs more than food, but there's so little help available. So many support services have been lost as a result of brutal cuts to local authority budgets, and many people have been allowed to fall through the net. It started with Care in the Community in the 1980s, a programme of deinstitutionalisation which aimed to have more people with physical and mental health issues looked after at home rather than in hospitals, thereby shifting the burden of care from the state to local authorities; as budgets have been decimated in the intervening years, more and more people in need have been left without access to support services, which are oversubscribed and chronically under-funded. The decade of austerity has seen further cuts as local authorities have had to make tough decisions around budgeting, so it looks like this problem is only going to get worse.

When I get home the patio is in ruins but my family are all smiles. They've spent the afternoon chalking murals onto the floor and the garage wall which borders the garden. It looks like the pictures were beautiful, but the kids have got hold of their water guns and have started spraying it so the whole area is awash with mingled colours. My first thought is that there's no way I can be bothered to clean this up after the day I've had, but it's immediately overridden by a buzz of pleasure that at least they're happy and lunchtime's events have been forgotten.

I have another uneasy night. I swallow a couple of tablets at bedtime but tonight even they don't help and I might as well have not bothered going to bed for all the sleep I get. The emotional toll the job is taking seems to be getting worse as the weeks roll on. The poverty on some of the estates is horrific, and to see so many people suffering its ravages on a daily basis is hard, although it goes without saying that my main focus has to be trying to help the recipients of the food parcels rather than worrying about any adverse effects the job may have on my mental health. The cumulative effects are that I get home wiped out from driving but wired from processing the things I've seen; I can't stop thinking about the people I've met and I'm finding it impossible to sleep as a result. It's a vicious circle that shows no sign of ending soon.

Week 6:
The Disadvantage Gap

Death toll: 34,636

"It is now very likely that the UK economy will face a significant recession this year, and we're already in the middle of that as we speak." – Chancellor of the Exchequer Rishi Sunak speaking to the BBC, Wednesday 13th May 2020

Following Sunday's televised address, the week begins with the publication of a fifty-page document setting out detailed plans for lifting lockdown restrictions. Prime Minister Boris Johnson tells companies that they will have to make their working environments safe before staff are allowed back. The Government advises – but does not mandate – that people wear face masks in places where social distancing is not possible, such as in shops and on public transport.

The chair of the UK Statistics Authority writes to Health Secretary Matt Hancock to ask for clarification on targets for the number of tests available and how stats for the number of tests completed are compiled.

Also this week, care home deaths in England and Wales now number 8,312, with a total of around 11,000 including the devolved administrations. The government furlough scheme is extended until October; somewhere in the region of 7.5 million people are currently using the scheme, at a cost of fourteen billion pounds per month. Gardening and recycling centres are allowed to reopen, while figures show that the economy contracted by 2% up until the end of March.[24]

24 Office for National Statistics (2020), GDP monthly estimate, UK: March 2020 [online]. Available from: https://www.ons.gov.uk/economy/ grossdomesticproductgdp/bulletins/gdpmonthlyestimateuk/march2020

On 15th May, the British Medical Association announces its support for teaching unions who claim that reopening schools on 1st June is unsafe. The Children's Commissioner for England says the Government and teaching unions should "stop squabbling and agree a plan" to get children back to school, claiming that disadvantaged children are suffering as a result of schools being closed.[25]

The week ends with an increase in deaths of 170 – the lowest daily total since lockdown began.

Monday 11th May

I'm totally burned out this morning. Yesterday was a tough one, and after spending the night tossing and turning, haunted by thoughts of the woman yesterday, it's a real effort to drag myself out of bed and get myself in the mood for driving.

It's freezing cold again, grey skies seeping the kind of mizzling drizzle that soaks you to the skin. The Prime Minister made a big announcement last night about easing some of the lockdown restrictions. The main message is that people who are able to go to work are now being encouraged to do so, although they're still being told to avoid public transport wherever possible. People are encouraged to wear face masks, but as of yet these aren't mandatory. The most glaring omission, and one of the biggest talking points, is that there wasn't a word about whether or not people can see their families, which is really what everyone wants to know.

Following the Prime Minister's address, the signs by the sides of the road have changed already. Instead of *STAY AT HOME. PROTECT THE NHS. SAVE LIVES.*, the one on the corner of Roundhay Park Road says *RECYCLING SITES NOW OPEN – APPOINTMENTS ONLY.* That was quick; it strikes me that the council have been waiting for a cue to start getting essential services up and running again.

25 According to the Commissioner's website, "There are also real dangers of a 'disadvantage gap' – the disparity in learning and education outcomes between disadvantaged children and their more affluent peers. Disadvantaged children, already behind in terms of attainment, slip further behind during school holidays. It has previously been found that summer holidays already account for as much as two-thirds of the attainment gap between rich and poor children at age 14. The implication is clear that keeping schools closed will worsen social mobility and the future costs to the education system of attempting to rectify this may also be substantial." [https://www.childrenscommissioner.gov.uk/2020/05/16/government-and-teaching-unions-should-stop-squabbling-and-agree-a-plan-to-get-kids-back-into-school/]

There's a lot more traffic about this morning, that much is certain. I even have to wait for other vehicles at the Seacroft Roundabout. There are more wagons, vans, artics, tankers and HGVs driving through Cross Green too. Heavy industry has been waiting for the green light, and now they've got it, it's all systems go. There are queues at the Amazon warehouse too, although this has been pretty much constant throughout as the pandemic continues to work to Bezos's advantage and the money keeps pouring in.

Social media is full of pictures of packed tube trains this morning too, the horrified users questioning what the hell all those people are doing when they've been told to avoid public transport. This is to miss a pretty big point, I think. It's clear that the Government have no idea how most people live and work; London's entire infrastructure is built around public transport, and a huge number of people in the city – and others all over the country – rely on it to get around. I have a lot of friends who've lived there over the years, and not a single one of them ever used a car.

The first drop on the list today is in Lower Wortley. The house is at an address on top of a big hill, with all of Wortley spreading out below it. There are some large houses up here and the gardens are well-tended; people have had plenty of time on their hands these last few weeks. The woman I'm delivering to is about sixty and wears a blue patterned dressing gown; she spies me from the upstairs window.

Are you from Armley Helping Hands, love? she asks, when she comes down.

Nah. I'm from the council.

It's just, I haven't sent you a shopping list?

You don't send us a list, I tell her. We've just got bags of stuff down at the depot. Everyone gets the same.

She tells me she's been in touch with a community group to discuss getting a food parcel delivered, and they told her someone would contact her to ask for a shopping list. I don't know the remit of the organisation, but it would seem impractical to let people give them lists – though I don't say so. I advise her to take what I've got for now, and if someone gets in touch from the community group to make sure she gets what she wants from there as well.

I'm embarrassed to be asking for help, really, love, she tells me. All my life I've never asked for nowt, but I'm stuck now. My son's been doing my shopping but he can't anymore.

That's a shame. I shake my head.

It'd be alright, but I've got asthma so I'm frightened to death of going out. I went up to Aldi yesterday but it was the first time I'd been out for weeks and I came over all queer, like. There were too many people in there for me and I couldn't cope. So I came home.

It sounds like you had a panic attack, I tell her.

Panic attack? I dunno about them, love. All I know's I had a funny turn in that shop and I'm not going back until all this is done and I feel like it's safe again.

Our conversation makes me think about what the long-term psychological effects of the pandemic are going to be. When this is all over, are people going to revert to old behaviour patterns and start packing out pubs, clubs and stadia every weekend, rammed in like sardines? It's hard to envisage. People have been drip-fed fear for a long time, been told to stay at home and cross the street to avoid their neighbours; surely, that is going to cause the kind of changes in behaviour that will be hard to reverse. There will be those who can't wait to get back to normal – as evidenced by some of the scenes on the news on VE Day – but for a lot of people, life may genuinely never be the same again. People with anxiety issues have had their fears exacerbated; those who had milder problems may have found they've got worse; people with no previous mental health issues might have developed some. The effects on the nation's collective mental health could be catastrophic, especially for the children who are missing out on invaluable social interaction during their crucial formative years.

The next house is at the other side of Bramley. The drive takes me through the top of the area, along some roads with potholes so deep it's possible to see the old cobbled streets at the bottom of them. The drop is set back on a long road opposite the rain-washed greenery of Fall Park, another one where the numbering system makes no sense, and I get the feeling it could turn out to be one of those days. I hop out of the van in the pissing rain, coatless in a thin jumper, and get drenched immediately. I ask for directions from a man who's just come out of a house with a number that should be more or less right next door to the place I'm after. Surely he must know?

No idea, our kid, comes the answer. Mebbe try t'flats over there.

I phone the number on the job sheet and speak to a lad who's obviously stoned out of his tree. I tell him which house number I'm parked outside; he tells me he doesn't know where that is, but that he can see a Sky TV van when he looks out of the window of his flat. I spy it myself maybe two hundred and fifty yards up the road, and we manage to suss it out from there. He's young, possibly not even out of his teens, red-eyed and mashed beneath a tight afro. It's barely half-past eleven, so it must have been a wake and bake job this morning. A haze of weed smoke billows out when he opens the door; he takes the food with mumbled thanks, then I get on my way.

When I get back in the van I'm shivering so much my teeth are chattering. I'm freezing cold, piss-wet through and utterly sick of this stupid fucking job. I bang the heater on and try to get warm but it doesn't work and all the tension of the last few weeks explodes. I lose my shit completely, banging on the steering wheel and shouting FUCK IT! FUCK IT! FUCK IT! at the top of my voice, still shouting as I drive away, water streaming down my face. I can't tell whether it's tears or rain or both.

Driving back to the FDC, I manage to pull myself together but I'm wobbly for the rest of the day. I pass an artic blocking the road outside the recycling centre near my house, which already has huge signs on the gates saying *PLEASE MAINTAIN SOCIAL DISTANCING* (with a diagram in case anyone has been living under a rock and doesn't know what social distancing is), and *PLEASE DO NOT GET OUT OF YOUR VEHICLE UNLESS ASKED TO DO SO*. There are a couple of smaller ones about staff not being able to help with heavy lifting. The council must have had these signs ready to go for a while; like all authorities, they have their critics, but my view is that they've dealt with the crisis very well so far, even if the Government hasn't.

I get stuck behind another artic as I'm heading to the middle of Beeston for my next job. A homeless man huddled wearily under a blanket on the pavement outside the news-and-booze shop nearby nods his thanks as someone drops a few coins into his cup. He is soaked to the skin.

It takes me ages to get to the first address. If there is a hell, it could be driving in squares around this infuriating grid system, knowing full well where I need to be but not being able to get there due to the mass of dead ends, bollards and packed streets with virtually identical names.

Beeston blurs into Holbeck; there's a lone man playing with a little boy in Holbeck Moor Park – a patch of grass with a few trees, really – and a young mum holding onto a toddler's bum as he slips and slides his way up the half-pipe in the skate park next to it. It looks like finding this drop is going to be a nightmare too, but when I get to a little car park at the top of one of the streets I can see the house right in front of me.

There are two overflowing bins in a tiny yard, black bags bulging like haemorrhoids out of the top. On the floor next to them there are a couple of empty Carling cases, some used glo-sticks and a broken ironing board, all drenched from the hailstorms and downpours of the morning. There are a couple of broken vases too, split into several pieces each, water droplets quivering on the colourful glass. The woman who answers the door is about sixty, with a crimson lipstick gash for a mouth, carved into a face that's orange with trowelled-on make-up; she must use a year's supply of hairspray every morning to keep her '80s rock hairdo in place. There's not much else to report here though.

I get back to the FDC and am sent straight back out on a meds run, picking up a prescription from Tesco in Seacroft. The queue outside is considerable, snaking out around the rest of the shops in the centre, a few people in dressing gowns, everyone smoking and playing with their phones.

After a quick chat with security, I go straight in. I used to come here all the time when I worked at the old Seacroft Library but I'd forgotten quite how big the supermarket is – it's like being in an aircraft hangar. There are arrows all over the floor where a one-way system has been implemented to guide people round and there are lots of signs about social distancing and how best to observe the rules. What strikes me, though, is how few people there are in here. Security are implementing the now commonplace one in, one out rule, but the shop is practically deserted. Looking at the queue outside the supermarket, you could comfortably fit every single one of those people in the building and there'd still be plenty of space for everyone. I understand the urge to be cautious, but there's no way it can be economically sustainable to run shops this size on this model.

I have to wait a little while to get the prescription but I'm not bothered. The address is a two-minute hop away. It's halfway up a narrow hill with cars parked on both sides, but there's a big patch of grass where some of the houses are set back from the road so I ditch the van there.

The meds are for an affable man, tall and thin in shorts and a vest despite the cold. There's a big dog woofing somewhere but it's taken heed of his instructions to fuck off in there, which I hear him bellow before he opens the door. He's all smiles, says thanks in a broad Yorkshire twang, and then it's the end of my shift.

The atmosphere is much calmer at home than it was yesterday. The kids have been treated to a duvet day; they're sitting on the sofa in their pyjamas watching the *Captain Underpants* movie for the umpteenth time, stuffing their faces with popcorn, all hugs and smiles as soon as I walk through the door. We manage to get them to bed early and have a chilled night in. My wife's shattered – she's been on the go for weeks, and now that she's had a quiet day it's hit her all at once. She's snoring on the sofa by nine o'clock and I have to wake her up to get her to bed. I'm not anticipating getting much sleep, and true to form, I don't.

Friday 15th May

The right-wing press is full of screaming headlines this morning about "hero" teachers who want to get back to work and trouble-making union bosses who don't want them to. This is disingenuous, to say the least. If schools are to return, the current model says that social distancing would be in place for pupils which seems impossible for very young children; it would also mean splitting children up into smaller classes, which in turn would mean doubling or even tripling not only schools' physical space but also staff numbers overnight. Shadow Education Secretary Rebecca Long-Bailey has already queried the plans to reopen schools, saying, "There is no information about how social distancing will work in schools, how teaching and support staff, pupils and parents will be protected from the virus, how small classes will be achieved, and no evidence behind the decision to select some year groups above others."

The consensus among head teachers and unions seems to be that under current circumstances, any attempt to fully open schools would be unworkable. The Government, however, still seem keen to try to do it as soon as they can, presumably as a measure running alongside the drive to get the majority of people back to work.

My wife called into school on Wednesday to collect some reading books for the kids, and she had a chat with the head while she was there. She told my wife that head teachers have been instructed to prepare their schools to get Reception and Year 6 back on 1st June and asked how we feel about it. My wife said we'd like to get our kids back if the school can provide a near-normal environment, but if they're going to try to make children as young as five socially distance and wear masks, we're not interested. The school is usually a caring, nurturing environment – to send them back into a cold, sterile place where staff aren't allowed to cuddle them if they hurt themselves seems almost cruel to us, so if that's going to be the case, our kids will definitely be staying at home. The head fully understands our concerns – which are similar to those voiced by a lot of other parents we've spoken to – and she's of the same opinion. She doesn't want to open the school unless she's one hundred percent certain it's the right thing to do, and right now she's far from sure.

The media fetishisation of the word 'hero' is disturbing – NHS heroes, teaching heroes. It's an easy label to attach to people who then become expendable as it adds validity to their deaths, as if they've died for some glorious cause. It's a typically reactionary stance and only one step away from the old lie: *dulce et decorum est pro patria mori*.

On my way to the first drop of the day, I look at the site near the FDC where seven new warehouse developments of 6,000 to 105,000 square feet are being erected. It has been at a standstill since I started this job, but in the few days since I was last here the metal skeletons of two units have now been covered, and a third smaller unit has sprung up. This is the end of the first week since restrictions on working were lifted, and the traffic has visibly increased again since I was last here on Monday.

The first drop in Oakwood is in a grimy close, two small rows of terraces in a cul-de-sac with a patch of waste ground separating the opposite sides of the street, choked with long grass, weeds and some unruly bushes. There are a couple of rows of garages down at the bottom, damp and dingy, with a mixture of grungy white metal doors and rotten wooden ones. There must be a big family at this address because they're down for three dry bags, and they have two black wheelie bins outside instead of the usual one; both of them are full to the top. Propped up against the bins is an ancient mountain bike, chain unoiled and bright orange with rust.

The woman who answers the door is about thirty, wearing purple pyjama bottoms and a dressing gown, talking over her shoulder to some kids that I can't see. She's pretty, with tangled brown hair and dark eyes, but she looks worn out, pasty-faced and with dark circles under her big green eyes. Through the door I can see into the kitchen where there are toys on the floor for children of varying ages, everything from a baby walker to a Nerf gun and a scattering of bullets covering the cracked lino. The sink's piled high with dishes, there's a basket of dirty laundry on the table and a clothes horse draped with baby clothes in one corner. The smell is one of gas, burnt toast and baked beans sticking to the bottom of a pan.

Morning love, she sighs. What you after?

Hiya. It's Stu from the council. I've got you some food parcels.

Brilliant, thanks so much. Her mouth smiles but the rest of her face is sad.

Here, look, you take these two, and I'll go get the rest from the van.

It takes me a couple of minutes to hoof the rest of the bags up from where I'm parked. When I get back she's talking to the kids again, but stops when she sees me coming.

Thank you so much for this, she says again. It's a proper lifesaver.

The next job is in Gipton, not far from the food bank but on a street whose name I don't recognise. I park the van somewhere near where I think the house should be and decide to explore on foot. Across the street I can see four people – all of whom are extremely overweight – standing around the open boot of a twenty-year-old Ford Focus, swigging from bottles of Pepsi and staring at a mound of broken wooden furniture on the pavement. They clock the van and pause to give it the side-eye, but stop paying attention as soon as they see me get out and walk the other way.

I find the house fairly quickly once I start walking. It's a bit run-down, white rendering coated in the same black dirt and green slime I've seen in so many other places. There's a tumbledown fence at the bottom of the front garden, with five footballs in various stages of deflation lined up against it; there's also a rusty child's bike that looks like it's been left out through the winter and will never turn a wheel again. On the parched brown lawn sits the broken nozzle from the end of a garden hose, and next to that there's a clump of bloody feathers and a few bones from where a cat or possibly an urban fox has eviscerated what looks to have been a gull of some description.

The food is for a young woman, maybe about twenty, wearing floral pyjama bottoms and a white t-shirt that has something that looks like bloodstains spotted across the front. She has dark eyes, wild hair and braces; she thanks me quickly in a broad Leeds accent before shutting the door in my face.

I have a look at the list and see the next job is in the middle of Harehills, on one of the kind of bollarded streets that are horrific to get around. Even if I can find somewhere to park – which is so rare as to be barely worth mentioning – the streets are so tight that I can't turn the van round and have to reverse back up them; not an easy task when people keep crossing the road behind the van without looking where they're going.

There's always a lot of noise on these streets, loud voices from open windows. The houses are small and they're packed with large families. The front yard of this address is full of fag ends, a few beer bottles, some empty coffee cups dotted around and a load of mangled children's toys. As usual, there's plenty of broken glass too and the bins are full to bursting. The kid who answers the door has dark skin, hair and eyes. He looks to be about fourteen, gangly and awkward, all arms and legs and big buck teeth.

I hand him the bags, then get lost as I try to navigate my way out through the impossible grid. I pass one house with a red leather armchair plonked in the yard, huge slits in the covering like it's been mauled by a tiger. A house nearby has a broken bed and enough old furniture to make a bonfire piled up on the pavement right outside the front door. Round another corner I pass a group of six mucky-faced children, none of whom can be older than eight or nine, playing unsupervised in the middle of the road.

As I find my way back onto a road I know, I pass the lad I've just delivered the food to, walking along with his family. There's a woman who must be his mum, plus three children tumbling along around her feet. He's carrying a fourth child, a beautiful pre-school girl who's probably his youngest sister, on his shoulders. He clocks the van, waves, sticks his thumb up and shoots me a toothy smile. I was extremely frustrated a minute ago, but this has made my morning.

The next drop is in Little London. Little London is in the inner city, squashed between Woodhouse and town, but it has nothing in common with its capital city namesake other than an ethnically diverse population and pockets of grinding poverty. There's a boarded-up pub at the top of the street – someone has drawn a tombstone with *RIP* written on it underneath the John Smith's sign. There's loads of street art on the walls, some featuring slogans – *STAY STRONG, TALK MORE, DIRECT ACTION AGAINST POVERTY ABROAD* – but a lot of it is the usual dense wash of neon bubble letters and hastily sprayed tags.

About ten years ago when my wife worked for Shelter, I dropped her off near here to meet a client one morning. The client was facing eviction because, amongst other things, she kept throwing dog shit out of the window onto her neighbour's head. The final straw was when she got caught walking down the street with the boiler she'd torn off the wall of her own flat, hoping to sell it so she could buy some heroin. With this in mind, I'm not really sure what to expect at this drop.

The food is for a woman who wears traditional African dress and doesn't have any English. She looks tired and unhealthy, a malarial yellow sheen to her skin, and her eyes look glazed and sad. She thanks me and takes the bags inside.

As I'm leaving I spot something shining on the road and stoop to pick it up. It's a tiny metal pendant in the shape of a skull. It's a curious little thing, no bigger than the nail on my little finger, so I stick it in my pocket as a keepsake. When I get home and inspect it properly, it has the word *POLICE* etched on the back. I've no idea what it means, but it raises a portentous shiver.

The afternoon run takes me up to Moortown to pick up a prescription. Driving up Meanwood Road, I'm presented with a truly surreal sight at the recycling centre. The gates are flanked by four ShowSec security guards in high-vis vests with lanyards, clipboards, walkie talkies and sunglasses who look like they're on the door at Leeds Arena. They're having a barney with a man in a Merc who's trying to access the site but obviously hasn't got the message about booking a timeslot. His name's not down and he's not getting in, that much is obvious, but the back end of his car is blocking the road in one direction and a few people are starting to beep their horns.

I park on the double yellow lines on a side street next to the pharmacy and give them a call to see if the prescription is there. Thankfully it turns out the medication hasn't been collected by anyone else, so I hang around outside waiting for someone to bring it out. There are a few other people waiting too, a couple of them in masks, socially distanced to the nth degree; they're standing so far apart you can't tell who's waiting and who isn't.

The address isn't far away, in an unassuming estate full of bog-standard semis with dormer fronts. The drop is at one of the bungalows that punctuate the rows of houses. It has paving at the front and a small raised flowerbed full of weeds, but no distinguishing features apart from that. No one comes to the door when I knock, but then a voice comes out of nowhere and tells me to leave the meds on the step. I look to my left and see a small black box on the wall – there must be a speaker in there. I do as I'm told and go back to the van, where I watch and wait for the meds to be picked up. The door opens the tiniest crack, a hand comes out and drags the box in, then it closes again, and that's the end of the day.

Saturday 16th May

I had a horrible night last night, plagued with the sweaty shakes and the screaming horrors. I got a little bit of troubled sleep, but I woke myself at one point flailing under the duvet with clenched fists, shouting, I fucking hate you, you cunt, although I've no idea who I was talking to. These kind of nightmares are usually the precursor to a dramatic deterioration in my mental health, but I tell myself it's a one-off and try to push it out of my mind.

The day begins on the edge of Hunslet. I pass Thwaite Mill and turn left off the main road at the Crooked Clock pub, passing an idling police van that looks like it's waiting for something, or someone.

When I get to the house I can barely squeeze past the SUV that's occupying the driveway. There's no access to the side door, which is blocked by a gate with a *Beware of the Dog* sign on it. I'm a bit nervous after the incident with the boxer in Headingley, so I don't want to go through the gate if I don't have to. I give them a call from outside, but they don't pick up. Maybe I'll have to try the gate after all. I take a deep breath and just as I'm about to open it a little mongrel, about the size of a spaniel, comes flying out barking like mad. It makes me jump for a second and then I crack out laughing. It's leaping with all four feet off the ground, getting nearly as high as my chest, as if it's bouncing on a trampoline. I stand there chuckling and waiting to see if its owners are going to come out.

A woman appears eventually, curses the dog affectionately and tries to get it to shut up, but it ignores her. She's in her fifties and wearing a dressing gown, but even at this time of day her neck is wreathed in gold chains, hands bedecked in matching rings; there are a couple of gigantic hoops dangling from her ears and she's wearing full make-up. We try to have a chat but neither of us can hear a thing over the sound of the dog, so in the end we mouth our goodbyes and part with a cheery wave.

I move on to Belle Isle. On the long drive up Belle Isle Road I pass a couple of squad cars and a police van pulling up outside a house on the right-hand side. It looks like someone's getting busted this morning. Two pre-teen lads in trackies and hoodies pass by on electric scooters, looking uneasily at the police and giving them a wide berth.

I turn off the main road and find the drop in the middle of three sets of semis, opposite a parade featuring a Chinese takeaway and a St Vincent's charity shop, both closed. There's a news-and-booze place right at the end which looks like it's closed too. A man in dirty, baggy grey shorts and a Jack Daniels vest answers the door. He has a nicotine yellow beard and both his front teeth missing. He rubs his bleary eyes with hairy hands.

Sorry it's so early, I laugh.

No fuckin' idea what time it is, mate, he says as he drags the wheelie bin wearily from the pavement to the front of the house. I leave the bags on the step and notice that this is another house with no carpets or wallpaper, and that everything is suffused with the smell of fag smoke.

A job in Morley is the first one on the next sheet. Coming into Morley I pass a transport café adorned with the slogan *Munching On Together* painted in the white, gold and blue of Leeds United, its name taken from one of the fans' favourite terrace anthems. The route also takes me past the Gardner's Arms pub. I have to pause for a second at the traffic lights outside it and see a sign that reads, *Save pub life. Buy vouchers to spend in our pub when it re-opens, and it will*, a reminder what's at stake for so many of these establishments. A good friend of my brother-in-law owns a couple of pubs in the Dales; the amount of money he's been losing on a monthly basis is more than I earn in a year.

This drop is in a cul-de-sac of flats and adapted properties. There are lots of little gardens in tubs, lines of washing hanging out in front of some of the houses, cobbled parking bays harking back to a time when all the streets were made from them. Near to where I park, a pair of old couples are having a brew in front of their house.

The wheelchair ramp at the drop is lined with pots full of colourful flowers. The man inside comes down on a stairlift; he's in his sixties, wearing shorts and a Rhinos top. I ask him if he wants me to carry the bags up but he shakes his head.

Leave it there, kid, I'll sort it.

I have a real job finding the next one. I get lost in a tight complex of low-rise flats with a confusing numbering system. At the top of the street I find a flat with the number I'm looking for; the building is enclosed behind a big metal fence and the ground within is swamped with every kind of junk imaginable in a blanket so thick I can't see the ground beneath. I wade through the mess and bang on the door, but no one answers. When I ring the number on the sheet, it turns out I'm in the wrong place. He's actually in the low-risers, and when I get back down there he's waiting on the doorstep for me. He's about sixty, with a shaved head, piercings in each eyebrow and two in his lip, and messy, fading tattoos all over his scrawny arms.

We have a good old chat in the end. He tells me that he suffers from depression, anxiety and panic attacks, and that his girlfriend ordered the food parcels for him because he was too nervous to use the phone himself.

Have y'heard all this shit about people cleaning out t'shops? he asks. Fuckin' mental. They started wi' t'bogroll, then it were pasta, then t'freezer stuff. What the 'ell are folks thinking?

I shake my head in sympathy. The panic buying early on in the pandemic that left supermarkets looking like they'd been looted was a real sour point. To me, it exemplified the selfishness of certain sections of the middle class in this country; after all, you can only panic buy in bulk if you've got the money to do so, and those on low-incomes don't.

Our lass even said, he goes on, that some of these fuckers were buying so much stuff they had to buy an extra *freezer* to put it in. I ask yer. Could yer fit an extra fuckin' freezer in *your* house?

Not a chance, chief. And even if I could, I couldn't afford to buy one and fill it.

Tell yer what I thought when she told us about that, kid, I thought, I hope there's a power cut yer fuckin' greedy cunts.

He tells me he's never known anything like this. He's too young to have grown up during the Second World War but he says he can't imagine even that would compare. I heartily agree. All the invocations of Blitz spirit are, to my mind, a reflection of the awful English national trait of couching everything, from times of adversity to international football tournaments, in the imagery of the Second World War. The analogy makes zero sense in any case. How can people pull together when they've been ordered to stay apart and tell the police if they think their neighbours are having unauthorised visitors? And during the War you could still go to a café or a pub.

I were a bad drinker, kid, he tells me, when I mention the pub. But I stopped. I don't miss nowt, me. If I want a coffee and a bun, I'll have one at home, I don't need no caff. I like me brass in me pocket and the second-best stuff, that's all. I don't need nowt else.

I could talk to this guy all day; he really brightens up my morning. I have to go, though, this time to East Ardsley. Driving through Morley, there are a couple of people playing with their kids in the skatepark. Petrol is 99.7p/litre at Morrisons, which draws my attention briefly until I look over the road and see what looks like a drive-through testing centre in the car park of the leisure centre. There are lots of people in hazmat suits and some police marshalling a queue of traffic. It's a dystopian sight and I wonder if it's going to become a permanent fixture, but by the next time I pass through here, it will have gone.

I arrive at the address. Last time I was on this street the blossom was in full bloom and it was absolutely beautiful; it's still pretty now, but as I've seen in some other areas, about halfway down there are some shabbier places. It's one of these I'm delivering to. A bald man in his forties comes out, flanked by a staffy. I ask it it's friendly.

She's alright mate, she's lovely.

I put my hand down and the dog gives my fingertips a cursory sniff, then waddles off; it's a fat, docile thing, probably closer to the end of its life than the beginning.

People like you are a blessing, mate, he waves as I go back to the van.

I still can't get used to people saying things like that and when they do, I have nothing to say in reply. Their gratitude is touching, but as far as I'm concerned I'm just doing the best I can to help out.

The last run of the day starts in Beeston. It's the usual job, a street up near the park, a house that's been turned into flats but with nothing to indicate it from the outside. There's a smashed TV and a moped on the pavement outside, the usual trash stinking in the gutters next to it.

I give the woman a call and she comes down. She speaks with a thick Irish accent, and if I had a quid for every time she says the word 'love' I could have skipped work for the day and taken that as payment instead. She sits on the front step in her pink dressing gown, smoking a fag, demurely pressing her knees together underneath the towelling. She could be about fifty but it's hard to tell. She's raven haired, dark eyed, looks like she could have been a beauty once but her face is etched with the grooves of a hard life.

On the way to the next drop, I pass a couple of homeless-looking men who are raving at each other outside a derelict shop on the main road, arms windmilling enthusiastically as they try to reinforce whatever point they're making. Last time I was on this street all of the barbecues smelled like rubbish fires. There are no barbecues today but the residents are out in force again, the air thick with the usual miasmic fug of weed and booze. There's a party atmosphere; loud voices, harsh laughter and banging music bleeding together from all the different yards. There are little gatherings in most of them, often spilling out onto the street, lots of shirtless men and half-naked women, tattoos, sunburned skin, gold chains gleaming.

The house is at the opposite end of the cul-de-sac to where I'm parked – there are too many cars for me to get anywhere near it. The front gate has fallen off and there's a huge amount of shattered glass covering the stone, plus some broken plastic toys. I walk up the steps and bang on the back door, but there's no answer. The neighbour smiles at me, a peroxide blonde woman of about fifty in a pink tracksuit who's sitting on her step smoking a fag.

She'll be at her daughter's if she's not in, love. She exhales a cloud of smoke at me. JAAAAAAAAANICE! she bellows a couple of times at an open window, fit to wake the dead. Nah, she shakes her head, she's definitely out.

The last one is in Seacroft in a back-to-back flat; the one around the front has a rabbit hutch with a couple of floppy-eared things twitching their noses miserably inside. I go round the back to a familiar sight: a smashed telly, an eviscerated mattress and piles of black bin bags. The woman who answers the door is of indeterminate age and cadaverous appearance, wearing an open dressing gown with a washed-out towel wrapped around her lower half. She has barely an ounce of flesh on her and no front teeth on either the top or bottom. Inside the flat there are no carpets or wall coverings, just filthy floorboards and bare plaster; the ceiling crawls with black mould. When she speaks, her words are so slurred I can't understand a thing she's saying.

It's another difficult evening at home. My daughter has found some photographs from when she was at nursery and spends a couple of hours crying her eyes out and telling us she misses it and wants to go back. I don't blame her. It's not even a year since she made the transition from nursery to school and to her it'll be representative of a really simple time before she was locked in the house, away from her friends. I'm heartbroken for her, and angry that it looks like she's going to be cheated out of half a year of reception, which she'd settled into really well and had been loving. If school can come up with a plan to get the children back to school safely and with a sense of normality, we'll definitely ask her if she wants to go back. It'd be incredibly beneficial for her to see her friends, and it'd be good for the whole family to get some semblance of structure back into our weeks. Whether or not that's going to happen, however, isn't clear at all.

My son is upset again too. I think it's seeing his sister crying that sets him off, and he complains again about how he misses his friends. He's always loved school too; when lockdown started, he claimed to be delighted about not having to go but he changed his tune as soon as he realised that not going to school meant spending days and weeks on end stuck in the house with no one but his mum and sister for company.

It's a sad, snotty bedtime, and my wife and I are both pretty bummed out afterwards. People always talk about how adaptable children are and in some ways it's true, but both of ours are struggling and it's a real concern.

It's been another challenging day – relentlessly busy at work and emotionally battering at home. Every day feels like climbing a mountain at the moment, and I'm going to have to do it all over again tomorrow.

Sunday 17th May

The first job of the morning is to try to redeliver the parcel in Beeston that I failed to drop off yesterday afternoon. On the way to the house I pass the two men I saw gesticulating at each other on the street yesterday. They're still wearing the same unwashed trackies, wobbling out of a news-and-booze joint with a bag of cans and looking very pleased with themselves.

Beeston is comparatively quiet, probably because everyone's in bed sleeping off the effects of yesterday. There are a couple of people smoking in their yards, but other than that it's unusually peaceful. Now that there are no people I can properly see into the yards, and a lot of them look like rubbish dumps. The one I'm parked outside is full of carpets, a telly, two broken pushchairs, a knackered office chair, a whole pile of splintered wood, plus at least five black bin bags that are hanging over the wall and spilling their guts onto the pavement.

The woman I'm after is sitting on the step smoking a fag, wearing her dressing gown and slurping a brew from a chipped mug, orange with tannin. She's in her fifties with leathery skin and a voice so smoky you could barbecue a steak on it. She says she was in the bath when I came yesterday and that she hasn't left the house for weeks. I don't believe her, especially given that her neighbour said she'll have been at her daughter's house, but it's not for me to judge so I give her the bags and say my goodbyes.

Just after I get in the van, an emaciated man stops his bike and bangs on the window. It's impossible to say how old he is. He looks like he could be seventy, but really there's no way he could be as old as that and he may well still be of working age. He has waxy white skin with dirt in all the creases and jet black sacks under his eyes. He has nicotine fingers and white stubble, missing teeth and a washed-out bobble hat pulled down loosely over his forehead. He smells of stale smoke and weeks-old sweat.

You got a parcel for me, kid? he wants to know.

Don't think so, bud. Just delivered one to the end of the street. What's your address?

He tells me the number, but it's not on the list. He goes on to say that he called the number a couple of days ago, so I tell him it should be coming through to us soon.

Bet yer fuckin' rushed off your feet, like, eh?

Yeah man. There's a lot of people need our help.

We do that, kid, you're not wrong there. He shakes his head. His voice drops a couple of levels, and there's a lifetime of sadness in his eyes when he says it.

I tell him to give us a call if he's not got one by the end of the day to make sure he's definitely on the list. If I had anything spare in the van I'd give him it, but I've only got enough for this drop.

Cheers, kid, I'll bell 'em later, he says, and with that he gets on his bike and rides off.

The second sheet of the day only has a couple of drops on it. The first is in Richmond Hill on a litter-strewn street. A couple of pensioners with massive white beards are having a chat over the front wall of one of their houses; the house next door to them has NHS rainbows and hand-painted signs in support of key workers plastered all over the outside. A surly woman out the front shows her support for *this* key worker by fixing me with a Gorgon glare that doesn't waver until I'm driving away.

When the door opens, the first thing that hits me is the smell of weed. Not smoke, but the actual stuff itself, wafting out in a fragrant blast that nearly knocks me over. The occupants are either growing it or else have a living room full of the stuff for sale. There's no carpet and the walls are bare. The young lad who opens the door is in his early twenties, wearing tracky bottoms and an LA Lakers basketball vest, a few tribal tattoos on his arms, a pierced lip and eyebrow.

As soon as he sees me, his face cracks into a big smile. Amazing mate, cheers man, absolute fucking lifesaver you are, right, fucking brilliant, you stay safe out there man, yeah?

From here I move onto Chapeltown, an area of Leeds that used to have a bad reputation, chiefly because of the red-light district that was here in the 1970s and '80s and was infamously haunted by the Yorkshire Ripper. These days it's nowhere near as bad as legend would suggest and it's more famous for its annual West Indian Carnival, which began in 1941 and is the oldest of its kind in the country. Like so many other events, it's unlikely to be held this year. At first there's no answer at the drop and I'm getting ready to leave when a woman of about forty sticks her head out of the window and calls down; next to her is a little lad of about four, sticky faced with a thick mop of jet-black hair, waving cheerfully and grinning at me.

There are quite a few bags so it takes a couple of trips to unload it all. The mum now has two girls in their early teens at her side, plus the little boy, who keeps pointing at the bags going, For me? For me? For me? with a thick accent. I nod and give him the thumbs-up and he grins in amazement. His mum has little English but manages, You help me so much, council, clasping her hands as if in prayer while the two girls smile shyly at me, both of them blushing and looking away when I smile back.

The afternoon gets under way with a drop on a familiar street. Even by its usual standards, Harehills is filthy today. The strong wind has ripped the top off all the overflowing bins and there's trash blowing around the street like there's been an explosion at a landfill site. I can't get down in the van so I have to park a street away, watching curiously as two men walk past with what looks to be either a washing machine or tumble dryer mounted on top of a baby's pram.

I lug the bags all the way down the street. There are loads of houses with washing hanging out round the front, but the air is filled with the acrid smoke of rubbish fires, so I can't imagine any of it will smell great when it's dry. The lad at the drop is in his early teens and doesn't seem to speak much English. I point to the name on the sheet.

Your mum? I ask.

He nods, so I give him the thumbs up and put the bags down in the yard for him. Back in the van I see a black BMW crawling down the road with a squad car pressed right up against its bumper, both of them turning left and heading down another side-street. When I drive through Harehills it's as busy as usual with lots of groups of people handshaking, hugging, sharing food. There are a few people in masks, but they're a tiny minority.

The last drop of the day is an infinitely frustrating one in Hunslet. The playground opposite The Prospect pub has some families playing in it and I think of my own kids with a twinge. I can't wait for the playgrounds near us to open again, but I bet they'll be packed when they do. When I knock on the door, I know there's someone in because I can hear at least three voices coming from the upstairs window, which is wide open. I knock again, but no one comes. After a couple of minutes, a little boy of about four or five appears in the living room window, waves at me, grins, then disappears. I knock one last time, but no one answers, and my phone call is duly ignored. I'm not allowed to leave the food outside even if I know there are people in, so in the end I have to go back to LBS with the food still in the back. It's frustrating that I haven't been able to make the delivery and it's sad, too, as it means a family who need food are going to have to go without for another day.

I get home and have a shower, and when I get out I have seven missed calls plus several texts from an unknown number.

Why didn't you leave the food? I was in the bath.

I'm sorry. I waited outside for five minutes. No one came to the door, no one answered the phone and I'm not allowed to leave the food outside. Someone will be back tomorrow.

I need food now. You need to come back.

I'm sorry. The food centre is closed. We'll get some food out to you as soon as we can tomorrow.

Why won't you come back now.

I'm very sorry but the food centre is closed. All the drivers have gone home. There's nothing else we can do to help today, but we'll bring you some food tomorrow. Look out for the van and check your phone so you don't miss us when we come.

What will I eat tonight?

The conversation goes on a while; I offer apologies, the person on the other end refuses to take no for an answer, and in the end I switch my phone off. It's a miserable end to the day. They clearly need help, but what can we do if they won't open the door or answer the phone? The only course of action is make sure someone sorts it out first thing. I can't help but wonder about the untold horrors have these people must have endured to make them frightened to come to the door or answer the phone even when they know that emergency food is on the way.

The big news at home is that my son's lost his first tooth, which has been wobbly since before the beginning of lockdown. It's almost a champagne moment after the unrelenting bleakness of recent weeks. He's so excited that he doesn't want to go to bed, but he does eventually. It's a welcome end to the day and a happy start to the week when we awake tomorrow to find the tooth fairy has paid a visit, leaving a shiny two-pound coin and a handwritten note in a little pink envelope under his pillow.

Week 7:
An Insult to the British People

Recorded death toll: 36,793

"In every respect, he has acted legally, responsibly, and with integrity." – Prime Minister Boris Johnson referring to his chief adviser Dominic Cummings following media reports of his trip to Durham during lockdown, Sunday 24th May 2020

According to figures released by the Office for National Statistics on 19th May, claims for Jobseekers Allowance rose by 856,500, in April giving a total unemployment figure of 2.1 million, an overall rise of 69% in a single month. In response to the figures, Chancellor of the Exchequer Rishi Sunak says, "It is not obvious that there will be an immediate bounce-back" for the economy in the wake of the virus, and that "All economic forecasters and economists would agree the longer the recession is, it is likely the degree of that scarring [to the economy] will be greater." Shadow Work and Pensions Secretary Jonathan Reynolds says, "These figures show the severity of the crisis we are facing. Unfortunately, these claimants will now discover that the UK has one of the weakest out-of-work safety nets in the developed world."

Total care home deaths now stand at 11,600, leading the chair of Care UK to criticise the Government for not prioritising care homes from the outset when the risk to the elderly was apparent. On the same day, security researchers find major issues with the contact tracing app being piloted on the Isle of Wight and express fears over the security of users' data. The following day, councils and teaching unions ask the Government to reconsider their decision to allow schools to reopen on 1st June. Also that day, a study published by NHS England reveals that from 1st March to 11th May, a third of Covid-19 deaths were linked to people suffering from diabetes. Diabetics are not currently among the groups of people being told to shield by the Government.

On 21ˢᵗ May, the NHS Federation warns the Government that an effective test, track and trace system needs to be in place soon if a second wave of the virus is to be avoided. Shadow Health Secretary Jonathan Ashworth says, "The UK decision to abandon tracing on 12ᵗʰ March is widely viewed as one of the most serious mistakes of this crisis," before asking for confirmation that a testing, tracing and isolating system will be in place by 1ˢᵗ June.

At the weekend, the media report that chief adviser to the Prime Minister Dominic Cummings broke lockdown rules by travelling to see his family in Durham with his wife and child when his wife was displaying symptoms of the virus. The following day on 24ᵗʰ May, the media reveal that Cummings made a second trip to Durham. The Prime Minister insists that his adviser had "no alternative". On the same day, he confirms that schools will be allowed to reopen on 1ˢᵗ June as set out in plans detailed earlier in the month.

Leader of the Labour Party Keir Starmer responds to the Prime Minister's Press Conference about the Cummings incident immediately, saying, "This was a test for the Prime Minister, and he failed it. It is an insult to the sacrifices made by the British people that Prime Minister Boris Johnson has taken no action against Dominic Cummings. The public will be forgiven for thinking that there is one rule for the Prime Minister's closest adviser and another for the British people. The Prime Minister's actions have undermined confidence in his own public health message at this crucial time."

Acting Liberal Democrat Leader Sir Ed Davey echoes these sentiments, stating, "The Code of Conduct for Special Advisers makes it clear they must be truthful, honest and open. The buck stops with the Prime Minister. He should open an investigation, and if it finds Dominic Cummings has broken the guidelines then he will have to sack him."

Monday 18ᵗʰ May

It was another bad night last night – I've got too much on the brain as usual so I kept waking up and taking ages to get back off to sleep. I can't stop thinking about driving, about the places I've been visiting and the people I've been seeing; the few dreams I have are filled with graphic violence, starving children, toothless zombies and skeletons shooting up heroin into their bleached and desiccated bones.

There's much more traffic on the roads this morning on the way to LBS. In the pre-virus world, the traffic on this stretch of the ring road would be at a total standstill and we're not back at that level yet, but it's getting there. There are more buses around too, although they're still sparsely populated. York Road is busier than it has been, but it's nowhere near its maximum capacity. At Cross Green, cranes are swinging ominously and earth moving machines are crawling over the vast wasteland of the construction site as the giant wind turbine spins ceaselessly above.

It's half past ten before a job sheet arrives, but they come thick and fast after that. The first job is in Middleton. The street is a long, wide affair, over three hundred houses made from the usual dirty red bricks stretching into the distance in both directions. There are cars parked all over and a few vans. It's quiet, without many signs of activity in any of the houses or outside them. As with so many other places there seems to be a gap in the numbering system, but I'm used to this by now. I quickly suss out that the place I'm looking for is a house that's been converted into flats, and I need to go to the door at the side where I find a rough, brown lawn with a trashed caravan occupying most of it. It probably started out white, but now it's a pissy yellow colour, streaked with damp and dirt. Both tyres are flat, and all the windows are cracked.

The woman at the drop is probably about twenty and painfully thin. She's wearing a navy blue dressing gown and is barefoot on the bare floorboards, an orange clipper lighter by the side of her little toe. When she opens her mouth to speak I can smell stale fag smoke, and I notice that one of her front teeth has a big chip taken out of it. She doesn't say much, but gives a girlish giggle when I put the bags down on the floor. I've got a spare bag of veg in the back of the van that was left over from yesterday, so I tell her she can have that too as long as she doesn't tell anyone, and she giggles again. She looks like she needs feeding immediately.

The next one is in Holbeck. I drive round the ring road, past Middleton Children's Centre and the Community Centre with its adverts for Middleton Elderly Aid in the window. I've worked a lot with children's centres and community centres over the past decade. Their services are essential but they've been suffering from huge funding cuts in recent years and staffing is a state of constant flux. The kind of services they provide could be a real lifeline to people during this pandemic, but all the doors are closed and bolted, without much indication of when they may open again.

Tilbury Road and environs is an estate of back-to-backs down by the M621 with ugly metal flyovers at the top of the street so residents can walk across the motorway. The gable end of the house at the end of the street has a full-size Leeds United mural covering the entire surface area, a sign of affection for the club in this heartland of their support.

I park outside the address and the man's out before I've even opened the front gate. He introduces himself and looks like he wants to shake my hand, but mine are full. He's in his fifties, stubble all over his face, wearing torn jeans and a white Leeds United strip which looks like it hasn't been washed in a while. He talks as if he's half-cut and there's a strong smell of weed coming from inside the house. I mention the *Beware of the Dog* sign on his gate and tell him the story about the boxer dog trying to bite my face off.

Mine's a miniature boxer, love, but he's in the house. He's not big enough to get yer face, like, but he might get yer a bit lower down, know what I mean? He laughs good-naturedly, his whole face smiling.

The house has a big yard which is fairly tidy, save for the old washing machine that's propped up against the fence. The council used to have a collection service to remove items like that for free, but given all the cuts they've faced they've had to introduce a charge, which is probably why there are so many appliances like that rusting outside the houses I'm visiting; most people simply can't afford to pay. Over to one side of the yard he's lifted some flags and dug out a big patch of ground; it looks like he's growing veg in it.

The next drop is a couple of streets away and I drive there in under a minute. The house adjacent to the one I'm visiting has three huge dogs outside that have a wolfish look about them. They start going crazy when they see me. The owner has his front door open and gives me evils but, like so many others, he looks away as soon as he sees I'm going elsewhere.

I go to knock next door and again it's answered before I have the chance. Strange that these people keep seeing me coming when all their curtains are closed. She's a woman in her forties who doesn't speak much English, but makes it known how grateful she is and gives me a cheery wave as I'm leaving.

I'm so tired that I miss a turning on the motorway on the way to the FDC, so it takes me longer to get back than it should. This has been happening more and more recently. I know the city pretty well and the satnav's great for helping to get around the places I'm not quite as familiar with, but the mental strain of doing the job combined with the constant lack of sleep means I'm making more and more mistakes.

As soon as I walk into the depot I'm sent out again with some lunches for the homeless. The FDC has been providing 200 packed lunches a day for the homeless of the city, distributed by third sector organisations out of Knowsthorpe Gate, a few hundred yards up the road, opposite the incinerator. The homeless are going to need all the help they can get now, as it was reported this week that the government funding used to shelter them in hotels during the pandemic has quietly been pulled. It takes two trips to deliver all the lunches, and then it's straight back out into the community again.

At the FDC, Sharon gives me a sheet with a few jobs on it.

Sorry, Stu, there's one at Parkway Towers on there. It's urgent.

No worries. I'll do that one first.

Everyone's laughing as I'm on my way out – Parkway Towers has a formidable reputation and most drivers don't like going there, but I'm not bothered. Once you've been to one tower block, you've been to them all, and I'm so familiar with Seacroft that no part of the estate holds any fear for me.

I drive straight there and park on some grass outside the fence that hems the tower block into a dingy corner of the estate. As soon as I get out of the van I can hear loud music pumping from multiple open windows, and even from a hundred yards away the stench of weed is overpowering. I get out of the van and walk round the fence, through the gate into the main compound and start looking for the intercom system. Down by one of the side doors, I pass a young lad and two women leaning against the wall, smoking a massive joint.

You wanna get in, man? he asks. His accent is an eastern European but with the slight creep of a Leeds twang.

You can use our fob, one of the women offers, pulling on the spliff and blowing smoke in my direction. She's probably about nineteen, wearing jeans and a black vest top; she's one of the few people I've seen round the estates with no tattoos or piercings. She holds the spliff almost tenderly with long, slender fingers topped with bright red nails.

It's okay, thanks. I need to buzz up first to see if they're in.

You sure? the lad asks. We can let you in if you want.

It's cool. Thanks though. Could you tell us where the intercom is?

No worries, man. Just round there. He takes the spliff back and indicates which way I should go.

Ok dude, thanks.

No problem.

I walk around in the direction he said until I get around the front side of the building. The door is being held open by a youngish guy in the usual estate outfit of tracksuit and baseball cap. He's small and wiry, probably only about five and a half feet tall, puffing on a fag and peering inside like he's waiting for someone.

Yer going in are yer, bud? his voice is friendly. Ere y'are, I'll get t'door for yer.

Before I answer, another lad comes out. He's pushing a baby's pram piled high with black bin bags, stuffed to bursting point. I think I can see some clothes sticking out of the top of one of them; looks like someone is moving out.

Yer going in, then, or what? the first one asks.

You're alright mate, I need to buzz up to see if they're in first.

Yer not here to see me, are yer? the lad pushing the pram the door asks. He has a cheeky grin on his face when he says it.

Don't think so, pal. I smile back. Unless your name's Chelsea?

Chelsea? Ah, I bet yer mean Chelsea and Dave. He gives me the room number and I nod. They're next door to me, bud, gizza minute and I'll bell 'em on me mobile for yer, save yer going up.

Nice one.

He gives them a call, and while I'm waiting for them to come down he asks, 'Ere, how do I get one of these food parcels, then? I've not been able to work for eight fuckin' weeks with all this virus shit.

I give him the helpline number. There's no point trying to explain that the service was set up for people who couldn't get out due to the virus. We're way past that point now and I think everyone knows it. I tell him I don't know how long it will take to get anything out to him though, because we're mad busy.

Fuckin' bet y'are, pal. All these dossers spending their benefits and looking for handouts, bet yer rushed off yer feet.

He thanks me anyway and they head off, puffing on their fags and waving over their shoulders as they push the pram out of the complex and into the street, headed for pastures new. I stand for a couple of minutes waiting, assailed from all sides by the sound of urban music and the pungent smell of weed. There are used johnnies all over the floor with the broken glass, empty baggies and fag butts; I keep an eye out for needles too, but I don't see any.

Chelsea and Dave are a sorry sight when they come down. They're off their heads on something, that's for sure, pupils so small their eyes look to be all sclera, bloodshot and raw. Neither of them will look directly at me, and they're both swaying unsteadily. Neither of them is possessed of the power of speech, so I point them to where I've put the bags by the door, then leave them to it and get back in the van.

Across the way I can see something that looks like a traveller site on the playing fields. There have been travellers in this area for a long time, moving between the area around the Dennis Healey Centre and the waste ground that runs the length of South Parkway. They've been moved from both places and now the former site is fenced off, ready to be cleared for yet more housing as soon as the pandemic lifts and work can begin again; it would be interesting to know what kind of effect the pandemic has had on this marginalised and most-maligned of groups.

The next job is literally across the road. Halfway up the street is a patch of waste ground on which I can see the remains of what must have been a huge bonfire. There's a charred black circle of at least ten feet across, bits of burnt wood and the disfigured remains of some plastic toys scattered around it, loads of half-burnt cans and broken beer bottles. Someone must have had a hell of a party.

The drop is at a detached house – or possibly two semis, it's hard to tell – that's been turned into four flats. The front door is open but it's covered with a rusty metal gate that's been locked and bolted. I call from the van and manage to get hold of the woman who lives at the address.

I can see ya, love, I'll come on down, she says. It's a female voice but it's so deep she sounds almost masculine. She's tiny when she comes out, barely five feet tall in her slippers, smoking a fag and wearing a yellow dressing gown. She has brown hair that looks like it's not been brushed for weeks, dark eyes rimmed with green eyeshadow, chipped teeth and orange fingers; she's another one with hollow cheeks who looks to be in desperate need of feeding.

To get to the next drop I have to drive right across the estate. On the way I pass two of the local children's centres and two of the many local schools. I've done a lot of work with all the schools in the area over the years. The children they educate – particularly at these two schools – are often from extremely disadvantaged backgrounds, and

I love working with them. It's challenging in the extreme but can be very rewarding. I've done song-writing workshops, theatre projects, creative writing sessions, book groups, and I've had every class from every school into the library at one time or other. The kids in Key Stage 1 are still fresh – I can get through to them and fire their enthusiasm – but by the time I get to years 5 and 6, I can tell from the body language and the burned out eyes that many of them are *gone*. It doesn't stop me from trying though. When the Government talk about needing to get children back to school because it's a safer environment for them than home can be, these are the kind of children they're talking about.

The last one of this run isn't far away. There are shopping trolleys pranged into several gardens, and the houses are in a catastrophic state. There's definitely something untoward about this drop. It's a house-cum-flat and I need to get down the side, but access is impossible. There's a padlocked wooden gate blocking access to the side of the building; it has a second metal gate with big spikes on the top, also locked. There's also a metal grill across the side door.

I get in the van and give him a call. It rings twice, then the call is rejected. I'm about to leave when he calls back. He sounds like he's smashed but says he's two minutes away so I decide to wait. I see him coming up the street soon enough, a man in a white Adidas tracksuit, not too steady on his feet, his skinhead and little tache making his face bear more than a passing resemblance to the Monday Man from *Tina Goes Shopping.*[26]

Sorry, like, yer came yesterday an all and I weren't in, were I?

Dunno, mate. Someone might have been, but it wasn't me.

Ah well. Ta for coming.

I give him the bags and try not to look as he goes through whatever process he has to undertake to get the gates opened. I'm still sitting in the van outside checking some messages on my phone when he comes back and bangs on the window, which makes me jump out of my skin; something about this place has made me nervous. I wind down the window.

We alright, bud? he asks, eyes rolling.

Sure.

26 Penny Woolcock's seminal 1999 film about the English underclass was shot in the Beeston and Holbeck areas of Leeds described in these pages using a cast of non-actors who lived on the estates. From my experiences of delivering to these areas, in the 21 years since the film was made, it doesn't appear that much has changed.

All done, I mean?

Yeah man. Give us a shout when you need some more.

Ah, ok.

He wobbles off, but stays leaning on the fence, watching, waiting, until I drive away.

Tuesday 19th May

A quieter day, doing some work-related admin at home. It's a welcome break from driving round in the van all day. In the evening my wife and I, plus some other parents, have a Zoom meeting with the headteacher from our children's school to discuss plans for the school reopening on 1st June. This will only affect our daughter at this stage, because she's in reception and in the first instance it will only be her class and year 6 that can go back. Some of the measures that will have to be in place include:

- Parents will not be allowed in the playground. We will get a time slot to drop the kids off, and we will have to leave them at the gate, even if they are upset.
- Children will have their temperatures taken periodically throughout the day.
- Children will have to wash their hands at regular intervals.
- If a child injures themselves, staff will have to wear full PPE when patching them up.
- Staff can have no physical contact – e.g. cuddles – with the children at all, even if they are distressed or have hurt themselves.
- Children will not be allowed to play games involving physical contact at break time.

The school's hands are tied. These restrictions seem so contrary to their hands-on, caring ethos that the kids won't know what's hit them. It's such a warm, welcoming, homely environment and all that's going to be ripped away and replaced with a sterile imitation of how the school should be. The head is brilliant and has left the decision entirely up to parents: we can send our children in if we want to, but if we don't like the extra precautions, we can take them out; we can wait to see what happens and then send them in; they can even attend for half days or half weeks, but there's no chance of us doing any of that. My wife is going to be furloughed for at least another month, and as long as she's at home, we don't want to put our daughter through that kind of experience. Even worse than keeping her at home would be for her to re-start school and have to be pulled out again because she wasn't comfortable with the new ways of working. As parents, we have to think of the long-term psychological damage it's going to do and as things stand, we think it will be kinder to keep her at home.

I thought it was going to be a hard decision, but we listen to what the head had to say and it takes us about two minutes to agree that it's a non-starter. It's unbelievably weird for us, as fully grown adults, to walk down the street and have people body-swerve into the road to avoid walking past us, or to trek round empty supermarkets in total silence with everyone jumping around like scalded cats; imagine the shock for a child of five who loves their school to go in and find it transformed beyond recognition. It's hard in that the boredom and lack of social contact is getting to be a huge problem – my son was in tears again at bedtime because all he wants to do is play with his friends. It seems to us that for children to be kept in houses for months on end without proper social contact or being able to exercise properly is bordering on abuse.

Obviously, the children know things are strange, but they've not had to go to shops and see people in masks yet – we've tried to protect them from that as far as possible. Our daughter keeps talking about "when everything's back to normal" or "when Coronavirus is finished" in that beautiful blithe five-year-old way. It's devastating to think she's being robbed of her first year at school when she was enjoying it so much, but keeping her home is definitely the right thing to do for the time being. Under the current circumstances, nothing is going to change our thinking on the issue.

Friday 22nd May

Yesterday was tough. We had a chilled time hanging round the garden and had a walk to the park, but then my daughter got it into her head that she wanted to go swimming and was distraught when we told her that we couldn't go. It's impossible to reassure the children about anything at the moment, and one of the worst parts of parenting through the pandemic is the uncertainty and helplessness in the face of it. We can tell the children that one day things will be back to normal, but who knows when? She was crying for about two hours, which set her brother off as well because he realised swimming was another thing he's been missing out on. I hope that when they grow up they don't remember any of this, but it feels like it's been going on for a long time already even for us, so to the children it must feel like an eternity. It's bound to leave a mark.

The day begins with a few drops in LS6, starting in Burley. I drive up past the uni, past the Fenton and the Packhorse, past the Library Pub, a beautiful old building that was built in 1902 as a combined police/fire station and library. It still looks glorious from the outside, but it was converted into the Feast and Firkin pub in 1994 before being renamed The Library shortly afterwards. They're all Leeds institutions, these pubs, and keystones of the local DIY music scene. It's to be hoped that they live to gig another day.

Every single wall in Burley is covered with graffiti. I worked around here for a long time, but I don't remember it ever being as dirty as it is now. With the endless maze of back-to-backs, bollarded street ends and carpet of litter, it has a lot more in common with areas like Harehills and Beeston than I've ever realised before. There is no one in at the drop though.

Driving through Headingley on the way to the next one, I do a double take when I see the fancy dress shop looks to be open; I can't imagine how it counts as an essential business, but a lot of places are trying their luck now, I think.

The woman at the next drop is super-paranoid. It's at a tiny ground floor flat off the main road and she speaks to me through the window.

Just leave it there, love, I won't open the door till you've gone.

I do as she says and wait in the van, watching as an overweight woman in a green dressing gown opens the door enough to grab the parcels and pull them inside, looking around fearfully all the time. I can see she's desperate not to step outside if she can help it. The older generations, like this woman, seem to be the ones who are most afraid; statistics clearly show that older people are much more at risk of serious harm from the virus, and I can see the psychological effects of this when I'm delivering to them. It must be horrendous for the elderly to be told to stay at home with no visitors, especially when all the newspapers and TV channels are awash with stories about this mystery virus that could kill them.

The last address is right behind the stadium, a small complex of flats behind the Tetley's South Stand. There's a large group of people hanging around in masks, but they disperse when they see the van. The flats must be some sort of supported housing, as there's a tin hut with a security guard manning it. I speak to him and he knows the woman at the address, says he can see her through her window so he calls up and she comes down. She's a big, beautiful woman in African dress, all purple, pink and green, with golden hoops in her ears and wooden bangles clattering on her wrists. She smiles her thanks and the security guard helps her carry the food up the stairs, chatting away affably to her the whole time even though she looks like she doesn't understand a word he's saying.

Driving back through Headingley, I see two Police Community Support Officers walking into the fancy dress shop. If they were trying to open on the sly, it looks like they've been busted already.

It's a strange run in the afternoon. It's a long ride to Farsley round the ring road, and it's amazing how many expensive car dealerships there are round here – Mazda, Porsche and BMW on one side, then Ferrari, Maserati, Aston Martin and Rolls Royce. The placing is interesting – the amount of money some of these cars cost is conceivably more than most people around here will earn in a decade.

The drop in Farsely is uneventful. From there, on the way to the next job in Morley, I pass a parade of houses with a couple of families sitting on a communal area of grass. They've a picnic blanket and a table full of lemonade, coke, cherryade and orangeade, a few sandwiches and some buns. There's a child of about one year old sitting on the blanket and a couple of high-chairs around the table. It must be a birthday party and I find it a touching scene, the children oblivious to the carnage of the pandemic, the grown-ups keeping up the appearance of normality for them in the same way my wife and I are struggling to do with our own kids.

I can't find the house. First the satnav takes me to a road with no houses, then it tries to send me into the pedestrianised bit of the town centre. No one answers the phone when I call and time's knocking on, so I bin it and head off. Someone who knows where they're going will have to pick this one up tomorrow.

Cottingley Springs is the next address on the sheet. It rings a bell for some reason, but I can't think why. En route I pass the chemist where I need to pick up a prescription. I call in, and for a change I manage to get the medication without any trouble.

I drive out towards the rural enclave of Gildersome, then down a big hill and left onto a dirt road pitted with potholes, dust blurring up from beneath the tyres even though I'm driving slowly to avoid the numerous large stones that litter the track. I realise I'm on the travellers' site and my heart sinks. Many moons ago the mobile library service used to visit here with books for the children, and not everyone had a good experience; a colleague found a group of kids jumping up and down on her car after one of her visits and it cost a fortune to get it repaired; another had his vehicle pelted with glass bottles. It was a well-intentioned but short-lived enterprise that was pulled due to concerns over staff safety – hence my wariness.

As soon as I drive into the narrow complex I see three surly lads of about twenty swagger past, shirtless and sunburned, stacked and dripping testosterone. I'm feeling pretty nervous. Given the way some people on the estates have reacted to my presence, there's no telling how the sight of the council van may go down here and I'm really on edge.

There are cars and caravans everywhere, lots of wooden gates, and there doesn't seem to be much sense to any of it in terms of layout. The site office nearby is derelict, covered in muck and graffiti, and there are hundreds of nitrous cans littering the floor. I've no idea how I'm going to find the place I'm looking for, but in the end I spy a number that's close to the one I want, so I turn round in a tight gateway and park outside. There's a young girl in front of one of the caravans, fourteen going on forty, bright orange tan, blindingly pink top, chest out, with a made-up face that looks like she keeps it in a jar by the side of the bed. I ask her if she knows the number I'm delivering to.

It's this one, she mumbles, then bellows, MAAAAAAAAAA!

A plump blonde woman comes out, clocks the van, scowls. She's the girl's double, probably about forty, wearing the same kind of slathered-on make-up, jeans and a frilly blouse. Her ears, hands and neck are covered in gold jewellery. At a glance they could be taken for sisters.

I've got your food parcels, I tell her.

Wha'? she says, narrowing her eyes.

I said, I've got your food parcels. They're in the back.

Ah, cheers darlin'. Her face relaxes into a smile as I hand the bags over

After a quick meds drop, I head back to the FDC to unload the undelivered stuff. There are plenty more jobs to do, but Sharon doesn't think we're going to get them done because time's knocking on. I say I'll do some local ones, so she hands me a sheet.

The first address is at the bottom end of Seacroft, almost in the shadow of Parkway Towers. The road is so narrow I have to dump the whole van on the pavement outside to avoid blocking it when I park. There's a boy of about ten on a bike in the front yard with a little girl probably half his age. The lad's wearing a tracksuit and baseball cap, a miniature facsimile of so many of the adults I've seen around the estates. His sister is wearing snot-green cycling shorts and a grubby white Hello Kitty t-shirt; both of them look like they haven't had a bath for a fortnight. She smiles and waves when I get out of the van, but the lad looks at me warily, suspicious even at his age.

This number 28? I ask him.

He nods.

Is your mam in?

Hearing my voice, a man of about my age comes outside. He has an unopened Stella in hand but he walks like he's had a few already and I can smell ale on him from twenty feet away.

Got your food parcels, bud, I tell him.

Yeah, nice one, sound.

He comes out to help get the bags, still holding his beer. He reeks of the stuff, a stale, sour smell seeping from every pore of his sweaty, clammy skin. I have three dry bags for them so they must be in dire need. The lad, who's been practicing his impassive stare on me until now, lets it slip when he sees what's in the bags and he starts shouting Mam! MAM! There's food! There's food! beaming all over his little face.

His mum comes out in tattered pink dressing gown. Her skin is grey and she's unbelievably thin, hollow-eyed, cheekbones practically poking out through her skin. She thanks me in a rough voice with a strong Leeds accent, eyes shining with gratitude. She has a go at hefting one of the bags but she's so slight she can't do it, and in the end the lad takes it off her and carries it inside himself. I can see his skinny arm struggling to take the weight and it makes him walk lopsidedly, but he gets it in eventually and his mum shuffles in behind him, so weary it looks as if she's moving in slow-motion.

The next address is on a hill at the top end of the estate. There are loads of tiny flats here arranged like terraces but on different levels, joined together by steep, narrow stairways. There are shopping trolleys full of junk everywhere, litter and fag ends, lots of whippits too. Two older ladies on the top level near where I'm parked are speaking to some people down below, all of them smoking. I walk down the stairs and start looking round, knowing this might take a while. One of them calls down, 'Ey, yer need some help, love? It's 'ard to find places round 'ere.

I tell her which number I'm after and she points with her fag. Follow that fence round the corner and down, love, yer'll see it then.

I go down two more lots of steps, dodging all the mess on the ground and keeping my eyes open for needles. I find the flat quickly with the woman's directions, so I knock on the door. For a while there's no answer, then a little girl of about six opens it, smiles cheekily for a second then shuts it in my face. After a few seconds her mum comes out, face hard and tense, all red Adidas casuals and attitude, ready for a row.

Hi. It's Stu from Leeds City Council. I've got your food parcels for you.

Oh! Ta love. Instant smile.

Hang fire, I'll get them.

There's a woman in the stairwell when I'm on my way back down, fag in hand, with two kids, a boy and a girl of about ten and eight. She gets them to move out of my way because I'm struggling with five heavy bags, shooing them affectionately with her smoking hand.

Sorry love, she says. If I'd known you were coming down here I'd've carried one for you.

The little girl who shut the door on me before is a twenty-first-century urchin: spindly limbs, flowered purple leggings, dirty pink top, tangled blonde hair, sticky face, a couple of gaps in her crooked little teeth, and a bright orange blob of wax clogged around her right earhole.

Is that FOOD? she asks when she sees the bags.

I nod.

ALL of it?

I nod again.

For US? She points to herself, eyes wide.

Yep, all for you.

YAYTHANKYOUTHANKYOUTHANKYOU!

She starts dancing, jumping up and down and twirling around, clapping her hands like I'm Father Christmas giving her the gift she's always wanted. I think she'd have hugged me if her mum hadn't moved between us.

I've got tears streaming down my face on the way back to the van. The little girl can't be much older than my own daughter and her reaction to the food is so sad it's unbearable. Months later, I still won't be able to recall the event without welling up. It's a moment I'll remember for as long as I live.

The visit must have left an impression on all of us. When I visit this address again three weeks later, the little girl is overjoyed to see me, while her mum greets me with a broad smile and calls me by my first name, even though I've forgotten to wear my badge.

It's a five-minute drive back to LBS and I'm crying all the way. The idea of children in this country starving seems absurd, and yet I've seen it with my own eyes. I can't stop thinking about them – the little girl at the last drop in particular – for the rest of the day. When I get home, I go through the motions of being a good daddy, playing with the kids, swilling them in the bath and putting them to bed, but my mind's still at work and it's as if I'm watching a video of someone else doing these things. I'm utterly drained. When the kids have gone to bed, my wife remarks that I seem quiet and distant and asks if something's happened at work? I can't think about the last two drops without choking on the lump that immediately appears in my throat, so I shake my head, mumble something about being tired and tell her everything's fine before shuffling off to bed and another haunted, sleepless night.

Saturday 23rd May

I'm up at six while everyone else lingers in bed, and they're all still asleep when I leave for work. I could do with a quiet one with the way I'm feeling, but Sharon said yesterday she was anticipating a busy day today.

The first drop is near Hunslet Carr Primary School in Middleton, and I park outside, surveying the scene. It's an old-fashioned building with *Leeds School Board 1875* carved into the stone at the top of the gable end, emanating austere Victorian dread against the gunmetal grey of the sky. Red bricks, dark roof, blue fence. From where I'm sitting I can see a tradesman outside his house, washing his white van, whistling cheerfully to himself as he scrubs at the front wheels with a wire brush. Out of nowhere a ghostly figure materialises, a shade so slight it appears that an empty dressing gown has floated past, smoking a fag and holding a brew. It's a sexless, ageless spectre, head and face enshrouded within the cavernous hood, gone in an instant.

I get out and start to look for the drop, walking up and down the snickets in the usual aimless fashion and trying to make sense of the numbering. I don't have much luck and I'm thinking about going back to the van to regroup when I turn a dark corner and find myself in front of a flat with a door that's been booted in so many times it's a wonder there's any of it left. It turns out to be the place I'm looking for.

When I knock, I'm answered by a disembodied voice, a barely audible, Who's that? drifting from behind the door.

I introduce myself and the remains of the door open a crack. There on the steps is the wraith I saw walking past the van. She's sitting at the bottom of a carpetless flight of steps, junk mail and rubbish piled up twelve inches deep all over the floor around her. Her lips are puckered and sagging around toothless gums, she has a skull for a head and bones for hands – the nightmare death-in-life is she. Her dressing gown looks like it might have been white once, but now it's practically charcoal, so dirty that it looks soaking wet. Sticking out from under it are her rotten legs, mottled purple and black, and I can smell the suppurating flesh of her abscesses from here.

I go to the van to get the parcels and she's still sitting there when I return, staring into space and smoking. She looks a hundred years old. I leave the food at the bottom of the stairs, squashing down some of the multi-coloured junk on the floor. I've no idea how she's going to get it up the stairs – she's so thin it's a wonder she can even lift her cigarette. It's a doomy start to the day, and right on cue it starts to piss down as I'm walking back to the van.

When I get to the next address there are a mix of houses and flats on both sides of a wide cul-de-sac. The numbering system isn't great here either, so I decide to look for flats with kicked-in doors as they're so often the ones I'm delivering to. I manage to identify which block the drop is on, but my strategy is no good as every single window and door has been busted so I don't know which entrance to go to. There's a broken sofa puking its guts out into the yard, plus a ruined wooden table and something that looks like it used to be a CD rack. I sit in the van, call the number, and am answered by a voice with a heavy Irish accent that tells me to go round the back.

I sidle down the side of the house with the bags, crunching over an unavoidable spread of broken glass that lines the whole path. The door is opened by a woman of about thirty in black Adidas tracky bottoms and top, tangerine tan and a full face of make-up.

Ah god bless ye darlin', we'd be proper fucked without people like you, so we would.

The first job from the next sheet is in Little London. This place is in the crowded inner city, but it's desolate and a disconcertingly peaceful atmosphere prevails today. I park near the bottom of some tower blocks and have a look around, but I can't see the address from here. The only thing of any note to report is the strange sight of a battered wooden chair standing next to a metal bench with litter all around it, the kind of knackered old tat that hipsters would buy as shabby chic for seventy five quid from Ebay.

I find the address a little further away and manage to squeeze the van into the car park outside a little block of flats right at the bottom of the hill. I buzz up and a youngish sounding female voice answers.

Could you give us a minute to get ready? I'm not dressed.

Sure. You'll see the van when you come out. Just give us a wave.

She comes down not long afterwards. She's about twenty, dressed in black leggings and a grey vest top, still wearing last night's make-up and with the remains of yesterday's hair-do splattered ruinously over her head.

Sorry, she smiles sheepishly. Had a late night.

You're alright, I tell her. Most people don't even bother getting dressed for me at this time of day.

She smiles happily when I give her the bags and breezes inside with one in each hand, calling out Hey Karen, wait till you see this lot here!

A non-drop comes next, at Spenser Place on the border of Chapeltown and Harehills. There's a sign on the door when I get there that reads, *Prayer time. Please knock two or three times and wait.* I do as it says, but no one answers so I decide to come back to this one later on. It's the start of Eid al-Fitr today so I don't want to disturb anyone who's preparing for it.

The next drop is in Chapel Allerton, not a place I thought I'd ever be visiting to deliver food. It's an affluent, bohemian suburb in the north of the city, renowned for its thriving arts scene. I have a base at the library here and one of the highlights of my working year is always hosting a week's worth of literary events as part of Chapel Allerton's annual arts festival. I don't think I'll be able to do that this year, though.

Chapel Allerton is teeming with life. There are big queues at Lidl, Aldi and the Post Office, as you'd expect. At the top of Chapel Allerton High Street is a parade of shops where you can find a butcher, a greengrocer, a cheesemonger and a fishmonger; all of them have queues down the street, too. Chapel Allerton has always been a tightly-knit community with a focus on local businesses, so it's no surprise to see this and it's great to see these places thriving under such difficult circumstances, when there are fears that many smaller retailers may fold while supermarket profits rocket due to massive increases in online shopping.

There's no one in at the address so I go back to Spenser Place. The prayer sign is still on the door, but the woman sees me through the living room window.

Is food? she asks.

Food parcels, yeah.

No come out. Leave there? She says, pointing to the step.

Sure.

Need mask and gloves. God bless you.

I leave the bags and go to sit in the van, watching as an old woman comes out in a mask and gloves to pick up the food parcels from her doorstep, and I think again about how terrifying the pandemic must be for the older generation in particular.

The afternoon takes me back to Harehills, which seems to be the area we've delivered the most parcels to over the past weeks. I have to drive past Harehills Park to get to the job, thinking how important green spaces must have been to the city planners all those years ago. Even parts of the city that are now among the most deprived such as Beeston, Harehills, Richmond Hill and Armley all have beautiful parks in them.

The street is trashed; there are lots of shopping trolleys in gardens, there's litter everywhere and many fences are falling down. The house has a massive yard but I can barely get in as there's a long wheelbase Transit van taking up most of the room. It has the words *Security Dog Section* embossed all over it in large red letters. There are a few knackered mountain bikes piled messily against a wall, some broken plastic toys lying around, plus the usual carpet of fag ends and a few splinters of green glass. The wooden door nearly falls off its hinges when I knock. I wait for a bit, then knock again but there's no answer. They must be desperate because I have four dry bags for them, but there's no phone number on the sheet so there's nothing more to be done.

The next job isn't too far away. At first I think there's no one in again, but eventually a woman answers. She opens the door a sliver and I smell the mould before I see it, a viscous shimmer on the floorboards inside. She looks like she may be in her sixties, but it's hard to tell because she really doesn't want to come outside, apparently frightened out of her wits. As I leave the parcels, a fat black cat squeezes through the crack in the door and heads off into the overgrown tangle of grass and weeds that passes for a lawn, waving its tail disdainfully at me as it goes.

From here it's onto an address right in the middle of Harehills, a terraced house with no front yard – it's all been dug up and there are wooden pallets stacked in an unruly pile to the side, giving it the appearance of an abandoned building site. I climb the steep steps to the door, knock and wait.

A gaunt face with wild grey hair appears out of the upstairs window and greets me in a throaty Irish burr.

Keepin' busy, are ye? I fuckin' bet ye are. I'll come down.

The man is probably about sixty, drawn and thin, tattoos all over both his arms and on the backs of his rough, work-worn hands. When he opens the door I can see he has tufts of white hair growing out of his ears and nose, little whiskers on his chin. I leave the bags on the steps and watch as he picks them up with the gnarled, calloused hands of one who's spent his whole life doing manual labour. Maybe he's been digging out the yard himself but has been scared inside by the virus.

It's a grand job yer doing, so it is, he beams when he sees how much stuff there is in the bags. God bless ye, son, youse stay fuckin' safe out there, right? He gives me a cheerful wave as I leave.

The next drop is behind the Mosque, on a street which looks like the aftermath of a tornado, and it's even more miserable today for the fact that all the stuff blowing round the streets is slick and soggy with rain. As usual, there's rubbish everywhere and there's a broken bed outside the house opposite the drop. The front door has been kicked off and its replacement is flimsy in the extreme, which is putting it kindly. It's an Irish woman who comes to the door, blonde and in her thirties, wearing tartan pyjama bottoms and a vest. She has a lot of facial piercings and a deep smoker's voice. I have a spare bag of chilled stuff in the back of the van so I tell her she can have it as long as she doesn't tell anyone.

Thanks, love, are you sure? she smiles.

Yeah, no bother. I can't take it back once it's out, you might as well have it.

You're a star, love, she says, eyes popping out of her head as she looks into the top of the bag. Fuckin' hell, I can't *wait* to get stuck into this. I'm starvin'. And with that, she turns on her heel and disappears inside.

Later in the day, I get home to find that a scandal has erupted in the media about Dominic Cummings, chief adviser to the Prime Minister, who has been revealed to have driven 250 miles to Durham to stay with his family when he believed his wife may have had the virus, claiming he was worried that he'd catch it himself and not be able to look after his child. The Government says he was being a good, responsible man, trying to look after his family, but everything he did clearly flies in the face of every single lockdown guideline that has been issued so far.

There are lots of stories on social media from people who have not seen parents or close relatives for weeks because of lockdown rules and then that relative has died; stories of people missing the funerals of loved ones because of the rules and so on. It seems grossly unfair when the public are being asked to sacrifice so much for them to see an unelected official and close confidante of the Prime Minister behaving in such a way with apparent impunity. In an astonishing display of hubris, Cummings even told journalists outside his house that they weren't standing far enough away from each other and were breaching social distancing rules.

There's been no word yet from the Prime Minister. He's been conspicuously invisible for a long time, an endless parade of ministers being trotted out to do the press briefings every night in his place, although the reasons for this are unclear. The Government's handling of the Cummings story will become a real turning point in the story of the virus in the UK; the ill-feeling bred in the public consciousness as a result will never go away. With hindsight, the scandal seems to me to mark the point where the majority of the public really begin to lose their faith in the Government's ability to handle the crisis.

Sunday 24th May

It was another difficult day at home yesterday. I got home after work to find my wife at the end of her tether. Lockdown is really starting to get to the kids and because there's no one else around they're taking all their boredom and frustration out on each other; they'd been fighting all day again. I had a bit of patching up to do when I got back in, both of them keen to tell me why everything was the other one's fault, but I got them to make friends in the end and everything was sorted out by bedtime.

I'm a wreck this morning. The bits of sleep I snatched were beset with claustrophobic, creeping nightmares; in the end I came downstairs at 5 a.m. with a feeling of crippling dread and didn't bother going back to bed. It's a cold, grey morning which reflects my mood, with lead skies, drizzle and a strong wind rattling ominously through the chain-link fence all around the yard at the FDC.

The traffic is typical of a Sunday for the moment – light. There aren't many people around either, save for the lone figure on the corner of a street in Richmond Hill, grey hoody up over his baseball cap, smoking a fag and looking around nervously as if he's waiting for someone who might not turn up. East End Park is dead too – no dog walkers or joggers today, only a sole lad doing chin-ups on one of the kids' climbing frames.

There are only four drivers in today, and no job sheets to start with. Sundays have been quiet for the last few weeks so it could be another slow day. While we're waiting around talking, I look out the window to see another massive line of vans forming outside the Amazon warehouse across the way. You can see the livery on the sides of the warehouse from miles around – like the abbeys of old, these new temples of commerce like to advertise themselves from a long way away. A security guard patrols the fence, his Alsatian sniffing keenly at the ground and barking mournfully into the wind.

The morning is taken up with some trips around Kirkstall and Burley. On the way up Burley Road I see flashing blue lights in the distance. When I get closer there are two police vans and a squad car half-blocking the road, one policeman directing the traffic while a couple of others search through the back of a battered black Meriva. The way the police are ransacking it, pulling up the seats and peering under the mats tells me it's probably a drugs bust, but an officer waves me through before I can get much more of a closer look.

It's an old boy at the drop, well-spoken and in his early seventies. He wants me to leave the food outside and not come near him – another one of the older generation paranoid out of his mind. I do as he says and crack on.

The next job on the list is in Kirkstall. When I get there I find a big bungalow raised high up above the street, meaning I have to go through a small metal gate and climb up about ten steps to get to it. There's a spacious patio at the front, which is in the process of being re-laid. There are lots of plants, scores of ferns, heathers, shrubs and flowers scattered around in tubs and pots of various descriptions, as well as several imitation Graeco-Roman statues. Through the window I can see a TV the size of my patio windows mounted on the wall.

The woman who answers the door is about fifty, wearing a deep red dressing gown, blonde hair to her shoulders and a severe fringe. She's wearing bright red lipstick and has scarlet nails. She looks like she might have been quite stylish once but now has the appearance of an heiress who's fallen on hard times. The passage behind her has a gaudy carpet with a thin grey coating of dust on top of it; a grandfather clock stands at the end of the hallway with the hands pointing to the wrong time, and there are shelves all over weighed down with knick-knacks and coloured ornaments. If it wasn't for the smell of fag smoke, it'd be like the inside of an antique shop. She smiles her thanks, but doesn't say much.

I drive back the way I've just come and see the police have finished searching the Meriva. They have an old guy with grey hair and stubble, wearing jogging bottoms, a black t-shirt and a baseball cap in handcuffs as they stick him in the back of the car. Two more policemen are talking to a younger lad in the back of the van, but I only get a fleeting glimpse as I pass by.

The afternoon starts in Beeston. The first job is on a red-brick terrace of the kind that hardly needs describing any more. On the job sheet I have the address down as Flat 4 but there's only one front door – kicked in and boarded up – with nothing to demarcate there's more than one flat inside. I knock and wait a couple of minutes, but no one comes out. There's no contact number on the job list either, so it looks like a lost cause. As I'm about to get back into van I say hello to a woman walking past, smoking, pushing a toddler in a buggy.

Who're yer looking for, like, love? I know everyone in that house.

Martin.

He's in t'bottom flat, love, she tells me. Just bang on t'window. Yeah, that one there.

She points to the bay window to the right-hand side of the door, which has also been repeatedly broken and boarded up. I say my thanks, then bang on the board a couple of times, hard enough to rouse whoever's inside. A dog barks gruffly, then the man comes out. He's about thirty, wearing threadbare black joggers and nothing else, paunch spilling flabbily over the waistband. At first I think he's got a cleft lip, but closer inspection reveals his face is battered and covered with scars, yet another visage that tells the story of a hard life.

Fuckin' nice one, man, this is top. He's pleased when he sees what's in the bags. 'Ere, do yer smoke weed, our kid, like?

I can smell the stuff – loads of it – inside the flat but I shake my head and laugh. Not when I'm driving a Leeds City Council van, bud.

Ah, fuck it. No worries then.

The next address is at the other end of Beeston on a meandering little estate with numbers spidering off in all directions. The houses are small around here but it's cleaner and neater than a lot of the places I've visited.

I walk past a couple doing some sort of DIY in their garden, measuring and cutting something with a Stanley knife in silent concentration, and find the flat behind a rusty metal fence. I'm about to knock on the door when I spot a man hanging around on the corner eyeballing me. I'm hesitant for a minute, not wanting to get stuck inside the fence if he follows me in and jumps me, but I tell myself to stop being paranoid and get on with it. The job has made me incredibly twitchy – in some of these places the threat of violence is tangible. The PVC door nearly falls off when I knock, but no one answers.

The next three are on streets that are next to each other. The first is just around the corner. It's a house split into flats with a temporary door; whoever is fitting these things must make an absolute fortune. There's a pickled onion jar full of spliff ends and rollies on the back step, the usual mosaic of glass and fag ends ornamenting the yard. I call the number on the sheet; the woman who answers sounds inebriated. She starts telling me to leave the food, then asks if I can wait and says she'll be there in two minutes. I wait for ten, then leave.

The second is one street over, another terrace with litter everywhere, music pumping out of open windows, the air thick with the smell of rubbish and weed. Here's yet another house with a temporary door.

The word *KERMIT* is scrawled in yellow chalk on the wall next to the door; all the bins are overflowing, and for some reason there are pieces of charred wood scattered over the pavement. There's no one in at this drop either.

The third on this estate is a house on a street like all the others, with a kicked-in door and every downstairs window boarded up. A dog snarls angrily through the door when I knock. I wait a minute, knock again and then a head comes out of the upstairs window.

What do you want, like?

When he comes down, he's wrecked. He's a big lad, baggy boxers and a massive Red Dwarf t-shirt of the kind I haven't seen since the mid-90s. He's running to fat around the middle and fucked on something powerful. He can barely open his eyes, and when he speaks he slurs the words together like he's had a stroke.

There are more jobs when I get back.

Please, Terry, not Beeston again, I implore.

He laughs and looks for another sheet. Okay then – how about Garforth way?

That suits me fine. The next drop is on a wide street with lots of lush front gardens and a few luxury cars dotted around. I meet a well-spoken man in his seventies who says he wasn't expecting any food but *is* waiting for a prescription. He ordered it on Friday but it hasn't come through to us yet. I try to get him to take the food anyway, reasoning that he might as well have it seeing as though it's been allocated and his name is on the list, but he won't hear of it and I end up having to take it back.

It's not too far to the next drop. When I get there it's the kind of street you probably wouldn't expect to see in the relatively affluent area of Garforth. It looks more like the kind of place you'd see in a Lancashire mill town, a quiet row of small terraces without much room for parking outside. There's a tiny yard out the front with an overflowing wheelie bin in it and a small flowerbed that's massively overgrown. Through the front window I can see a brown slatted blind, thick with dust, and a wooden carving that spells out the word *HOME*. There's no one it at this address either.

The wind has dropped now; there's still a lot of cloud around, the air heavy and humid and pregnant with the scent of impending rain. Now I'm headed to the hamlet of Woodlesford; the drop is past the village train station and on a big cul-de-sac with some lovely houses at the top of it. On the job sheet under "notes" it says "dog walking service" and "befriending/reassuring by phone." I haven't heard of the council offering a dog walking service, but I know they have been making phone calls to people – especially older ones – who they fear may be isolated because of the pandemic, just to offer them someone to talk to; I assume that this is the befriending service mentioned on the sheet. I infer from this that it's probably an older person I'm delivering to, so I'm surprised to be met by a woman in her twenties. She's wearing leggings and a dirty white vest, piercings all over her face. She's so thin she's barely there, messy hair and wild eyes, scarred arms, bare feet stark and white against the black of the floorboards. She mumbles thanks but won't look me in the eye.

I'm hoping that will be it for the day, but Terry gives me one last drop to finish off. It's in Beeston, on a street I've already visited today. The yard is tidier than a lot of the others I've seen around here, with a big shed and a scarecrow made to look like one of the princesses from *Frozen*. The door's answered by a bear-like Polish woman, who's swaying on her feet like she's been drinking all day and is clouded in lager fumes. She's wearing joggers and a vest and doesn't say thanks, simply snatches the bags from me and turns away inside.

When I get home my wife is watching the news; the Cummings story is still running. According to the latest reports, he actually went to Durham *twice*. The journalists who broke the story only printed half of it, waited for the Government to respond, then published the rest of it.[27] The Prime Minister has still come out and defended Cummings, saying the rules clearly state he was allowed to do what he did. Judging by the response, the public don't appear to agree, and even some Tory MPs are complaining. The Government's defence of Cummings appears to completely contradict their official health policy with regards to Covid-19, and public unrest is growing as a result.

---

27 *The Daily Mirror* and *The Guardian* first broke the story of their joint investigation into Cummings's alleged breach of lockdown rules on 22nd May. On 24th May, *The Observer* and *The Sunday Mirror* published the second part of the story, claiming that Cummings had made a further trip to Durham on 19th April.

Week 8:
Descending into Chaos

Recorded death toll: 38,489

*"I don't think that I am so different and that there's
one rule for me and one rule for other people [...] I
don't regret what I did." – press conference of Dominic
Cummings, chief adviser to the Prime Minister, Monday
25ᵗʰ May 2020*

*Boris Johnson's chief adviser Dominic Cummings gives a press conference
in which he defends his apparent breaking of lockdown rules by visiting
family in Durham. Despite this, at least thirty-five Tory MPs call for
him to resign from his post, and Douglas Ross, a junior minister, resigns
in protest at the Government's defence of Cummings. Shadow Scottish
Secretary Ian Murray responds to the resignation by saying, "Integrity
has been sadly lacking from the Government, especially over the last
72 hours, so I commend him on making this difficult decision. He
understands that it is not acceptable to have one rule for the Prime
Minister's closest adviser, another for everyone else." Labour MP Nick
Thomas-Symonds comments on the Government's response to the
Cummings story, saying, "The attempts from the Prime Minister to
defend the indefensible actions of his most senior adviser are quickly
descending into chaos and undermining trust."*

*On 27ᵗʰ May, figures from the Treasury indicate that the furlough
scheme now covers 8.4 million people, a rise of 400,000 in a week. It
is announced that the track and trace scheme, which had been due to
begin on 1ˢᵗ June, will not be "fully operational at a local level" until the
end of the month. Shadow Communities Secretary Steve Reed responds
to the news, saying, "Test and Trace is the key to easing lockdown
restrictions safely, but instead of the "world beating" system the Prime*

Minister promised by 1ˢᵗ June, the system is in total chaos because the Government got the planning wrong." It's also announced this week that the furlough scheme will finish at the end of October; from August, employers must pay National Insurance contributions; from September, they must contribute 10% of employees' wages, and 20% from October.

At the end of the week, members of SAGE say that it's too early to lift the lockdown restrictions; Professor John Edmunds says that lifting lockdown measures is "a political decision"; Sir Jeremy Farrar says the virus is spreading "too fast to lift lockdown in England" and that the NHS track and trace system[28] "has to be fully working and infection rates be lower" before measures can be lifted; Professor Peter Horby says, "What I would say is that returning to a situation where we lost control again is far worse than another week or two of social measures," and Professor Calum Semple sums it up: "Essentially we're lifting the lid on a boiling pan and it's just going to bubble over. We need to get it down to simmer before we take the lid off, and it's too early."

Monday 25ᵗʰ May

My first drop of the day takes me to Halton Moor. I pass a dustbin wagon on the way, but no other traffic apart from that. The woman at the house speaks to me from an upstairs window. The street is narrow and packed with cars so I leave the van at the top and have to go back to collect the bags. When I come back she has opened the front door; I can see a stairlift, and she's propped up on a pair of metal crutches.

Are you a volunteer, love? she asks.

Of a fashion. I work as a librarian in the real world.

A librarian? Oh, how *lovely*. You can never have too many books, can you?

Definitely not.

How did you come to be doing this, love, if you don't mind me asking? It's a bit different to what you normally do, isn't it?

It sure is.

28 The 'world-beating' track and trace system promised by the Prime Minister cost an estimated 37 billion pounds but never delivered on its mission to stem the tide of the pandemic. A government report in March 2021 said, "There is still no clear evidence to judge NHS T&T's overall effectiveness. It is unclear whether its specific contribution to reducing infection levels, as opposed to the other measures introduced to tackle the pandemic has justified its costs." House Of Commons Public Accounts Committee: Covid-19 Test, Track and Trace part 1, published 10/03/21, accessed via (https://committees.parliament.uk/publications/4976/documents/50058/default/

I spend a couple of minutes telling her about how the council put out a call for volunteers for people to work at the FDC and drive the vans, and how I put my name forward as soon as the email went out.

Thank you so much for everything you and your colleagues are doing, she gushes. It really is *wonderful*. It's an absolute lifesaver for people like me.

On the way to the next one I drive past the children's centre in Osmondthorpe. It's another place I've worked with over the years, providing books and literacy support to a parent and toddler group as well as a parent and baby group. Hopefully it won't be too much longer before I'll be able to start doing more of that kind of outreach work again – I really miss it, and most importantly it's incredibly beneficial to the community. The drop's at a small townhouse to a woman with an Irish name, raven hair down to her shoulders. She's pleased to see me and takes the parcels gratefully.

The last one on this run is in the middle of Harehills; the place looks a wreck. The entire building is swathed in scaffolding, so much of the stuff you can barely see the house beneath it. There are black bin liners piled up four feet high against the side of the house and all manner of rubbish and waste littering the front garden. The note on the job sheet says to call when I get there, so I give the man a ring. A low voice answers, a threatening, drug-fucked growl.

Who's that?

Stu from the council, bud. I've got your food parcel.

Ah, thing is, mate, right, I'm not in, but I'm fucking starving like, know what I mean, could you leave it for us, yeah?

I can't be bothered to argue so I agree to leave the food, even though I shouldn't. Where do you want it?

Stick it in t'red thing, be 'right in there.

Alright, chief.

The red thing he's talking about is a cross-section of a plastic rubble chute of the kind builders run down the side of buildings so they can throw bits of heavy stone into the skip below without the risk of braining anyone; there's a length of it lying on the grass in front of the house. I hide the bags in there, making sure they're not visible from the road, then get on my way.

The first one on the next sheet is Highways, a couple of tower blocks off York Road that I've driven past hundreds of times recently but not visited yet. It feels a little bit edgy. Three men and a pre-teen

163

boy are sitting on the steps near where the intercom system is. They stop talking as soon as they see me walking towards them, and one of the guys – who's riding a chopper – eyeballs me knowingly, then gets on his bike and fucks off immediately. When I buzz the intercom they stop paying attention to me and get back to their conversation. I have a listen and gather that Steve might be looking at five to seven years, the silly cunt. He was unlucky to get caught, like, but still, looks like he's fucked good and proper now.

There's a lull in the conversation while I'm waiting for the man to come down. One of the other men looks at me from behind his fag.

We can let you in if you want.

You're alright, chief. He's coming down now. Ta though.

He shrugs and gets back to his brew.

When the man comes down he's in his 50s, tall and thin, white hair, carrying one of those massive blue Ikea bags that people at uni used to use to put clothes in when moving house. He asks me to leave the stuff on the steps. I offer to put it in the bag for him but he won't come near me, so I do as he says and head off, noting the scores of empty beer cases spilling out of the tops of the bins.

The next one takes me into the heart of Seacroft. On the way I pass two girls in their mid-teens, arse cheeks hanging out of their shorts, boob tubes not doing much in the way of covering them, pushing a pram each; they could just as easily be pushing their siblings as they could their own children. I once met a thirty-two-year-old grandmother at an outreach event on the estate, so anything is possible.

The house has a large front garden. The grass needs a cut but it's tidier than a lot of others in the neighbourhood. There are a few stone statues dotted around, including some pretty birds and one of a little witch. The door's opened by a woman with dreads and a quiet, raspy voice. She's pale and looks like she may be ill, and I wonder whether she might have Covid. The virus hasn't been in my thoughts for a long time while I've been driving, an indication of how far away from its original remit the delivery service has got.

The afternoon turns out to be a real pain. There are some large Romanian families in Harehills that we've been delivering regularly to, and I get given a sheet with a few of their names on it. They need at least three bags per household so it's a massive job loading up the van and the suspension creaks beneath the weight once the back is full; the addresses are all streets that are awkward to drive around, so I'm not looking forward to the trip at all.

The first one is on a street which is so tightly packed with cars that I have no choice but to stick the hazards on and block the road. Harehills is busy and feels faintly threatening today. There's a group of around twenty youths hanging round the shop at the bottom of the road, no social distancing in place at all. A couple of older men come and stand right next the van, smoking and glowering at me as I cross the road to knock at the address. I wait for a few minutes and get back in the van, then the door is opened and a couple of girls in their late teens start waving to me. They're all white teeth and dark eyes, trying to explain in broken English that they were upstairs and didn't hear the door. I don't believe them – I think they were probably spying to see who was there before they opened it, but it doesn't matter to me. We get the food unloaded between us and have a friendly chat despite the language barrier.

I have a strange experience at the next drop. These people sure don't want to answer the door. I knock and I can hear footsteps coming downstairs and some voices whispering. I knock again and wait for ages but no one answers. There's no contact number on the sheet so eventually I get on my way. Like the family in Hunslet a couple of weeks ago, it's chilling to think that people are too frightened to open their front doors, especially when they're starving and they know that food is on the way.

To get to the next job, I have to drive up Harehills Road, crunching through the glass and nitrous cans that litter the roads. This is possibly the most culturally diverse area in the whole city. Polish shops, Romanian shops, Halal butchers, Indian supermarkets, loads of little food places with a delicious mix of smells coming from them, shopfront churches and faith healers of every description. Across the road from the drop there's a group of shirtless Slavic lads, built like brick shithouses, smoking, drinking Zwiec out of cans and glaring at me intensely.

The job turns out to be hugely stressful – a horrendous experience all round. The door is opened by a corpulent man who looks to be in his fifties. I point to the name on the sheet, but he shakes his head. He doesn't speak English, so I show him the address instead.

Is this here?

He narrows his eyes, shakes his head again.

Food? I say. Are you waiting for food? I mime an eating motion with my hands, but he looks at me like I'm crazy. I point to the name one more time, but he looks away. I'm all out of ideas, so I head back out to the van and get ready to leave. It all goes a bit sideways after that.

A little way up the street there are a few people talking on the pavement. I saw them watching the van earlier. As I'm about to drive away, an older woman in a headscarf walks over and taps on the window, so I wind it down.

Is problem? she asks. Is problem?

I shake my head and start trying to explain who I am and why I'm there, but the fat man comes running out of his front yard and half-slaps, half-pushes her in the middle of the chest, nearly knocking her over. Three more lads come diving in and pull her away as he berates her angrily, waving his fists in her face; then one of the lads feigns as if he's about to punch him, and he soon calms down. I'm keen to get the fuck out of here, but I'm stuck; there's a whole gang surrounding the van now. The bottom end of the street is blocked by bollards so I can't just floor it and drive down there, and the street is too narrow to back up at any kind of speed, especially with them all crowding the van.

One of the lads, who looks like he's about thirty and could be the older woman's son, is banging his fist on the side of the van.

What's the problem, what's the problem? he keeps asking.

There's no problem. I've brought some food. Do you know who this is? I point to the name on the sheet, then reach for the van key and press the button on the fob that locks all the doors.

Immediately he starts talking to the fat man and he smiles for the first time. The crowd parts and they back away from the van, trying to explain that they're sorry, but they don't speak English well, they didn't understand. The lads crowd round the back of the van and help unload the food parcels and it's all pretty friendly in the end; I get a few slaps on the back and hands are proffered to shake, but my heart's still palpitating when I leave.

The next family live a couple of streets over, and this one is similarly hard to drive down. There's a man in his forties sitting in the front yard with his wife and two pre-teen girls. The parents are drinking something hot from delicate glasses, the steam from the top mixing with the fag smoke they're both exhaling. In total contrast to the last drop, they're happy to see me, the man sitting there grinning while I lift the bags over the wall. As I'm doing it, a third girl, maybe about fourteen, comes down the street into the yard, giving me a radiant, white-toothed smile when she sees what's in the bags.

Thank you, she beams, with a strong accent

I smile back and give her the thumbs up. You're welcome, I tell her.

The final drop of the day is in Seacroft. Apparently the man at this address has received a food parcel but complained that it wasn't enough so he's phoned up and asked for some more. There's a powerful reek of weed when I get out of the van – you can smell it all over the estates on hot days like this, a constant olfactory hum in the background. The man's round the back getting wasted to some banging techno. I shout and he comes out front, shirtless, not a bit of fat on him, a ribcage so prominent you could play it like a xylophone, tattoos all over including a spider's web on his face. He's got a beer in one hand and the arse end of a spliff in the other.

Cheers pal, he says. I've got five fucking kids here, one bag's not gonna last us right long, know what I mean?

You should have mentioned it on the phone, chief.

I will next time.

Nice one. Enjoy the sun.

The two main events in the news today are Dominic Cummings's press conference about his ill-fated trips to Durham, in which he *still* insists he did nothing wrong. The other is that today's the day the Prime Minister announces that the most intensive part of lockdown is over. Primary schools are free to open from 1st June, and most non-essential businesses will be able to open from 15th June, providing they follow government guidelines around social distancing and other measures meant to ensure that they are "Covid secure".

The wisdom of this decision is questioned by many – according to reports, infection rates now are no better than they were when lockdown started; advisers from the Government's SAGE committee have also said that they think the measures may be being lifted too early, but the Government are determined to press on regardless. The drive to get the economy up and running has trumped all concerns about public health, or so it would appear. The consequences of this in the long-term remain to be seen, but if social media reports are anything to go by, it's fair to say that huge swathes of the public do not share the Prime Minister's optimism at all.

Friday 29th May

Yesterday was a good day. My wife and the kids have been suffering from cabin fever so I suggested we all go out for some fresh air. I took them for a ride out to Ilkley so we could have a walk around the Cow and Calf, a beautiful rock formation at the top of the moor. It was a gorgeous day and there were a lot of people about. We had a lovely time, eating a picnic and cooling our feet in a freezing hilltop stream. We were up there for most of the afternoon and it did us all good.

I'm feeling strained and emotional this morning. The lack of sleep and the constant stress of the last few weeks are starting to catch up with me. I find myself blinking back the tears that keep pricking the backs of my eyes for no reason at all, and I spend most of the morning trying to swallow the lump that's blocking my throat like a stuck gobstopper. I could curl up on the floor and cry if I let myself.

It's gloriously sunny and sure to be hot. The traffic flow has increased again but it's still not back to normal and I find myself wondering if it ever will be. The messages, from my employers at least, seem to suggest that home working is going to become standard practice in the post-virus world, and maybe the same will follow for a lot of other places too. There's long been talk of the virtual office, and now it seems that may become a reality for many. There's also no way the traffic at this time of day will return to pre-pandemic levels until schools have gone back, and although the Government are keen for it to happen, many parents feel differently.

I have three drops in the north of the city this morning, so it should be an easy start. It's all quiet around the university when I pass, save for the gang of workmen in high-vis who are sitting on the steps of the Parkinson building having a tea break. They're a mass of neon yellow, white hard hats, Styrofoam cups and white sandwich bags from one of the shops across the road, faces flushed from working in the sun. It puts me in mind of the pictures from a century or more ago where all the working men were identically dressed in baggy trousers and cloth caps, and all the middle-class men had suits, briefcases and bowlers. *Plus ça change, plus c'est la même chose.*

The first drops are up near the big Asda and Holt Park Active Leisure Centre. These are two more little estates with difficult numbering systems, but somewhere in my brain I'm starting to be able to predict their unpredictability and it doesn't take me as long to find the addresses.

The woman at the first one is a pensioner, smoking in her dressing gown, greasy hair straggling rattily down her neck. She asks me to carry the bags inside; it stinks in the house, a mixture of stale and fresh fag smoke. Everything inside is sticky with nicotine; the carpet is worn away to practically nothing, there's an underlying smell of piss and an excitable dog trying to batter its way through the living room door.

It's a big lad at the next place, early thirties, wearing tight shorts and a vest. His voice is so husky he can barely speak, and I wonder if he might have the virus, the second time this has happened recently after a prolonged period of barely giving it a second thought.

The next run is a crazy one, Lofthouse and then Yeadon. Lofthouse is one of the few bits of the city I don't know at all – in fact, I don't think I've ever been there before today. The drop is in a close of red-brick semis lined with shiny cars and well looked after gardens. There's some bunting up and a couple of St George's flags too, probably leftovers from VE Day celebrations. The house next door even has a red telephone box draped in a Union Jack in the garden, plonked near to a double garage and locked away behind a tall metal gate.

The drop has an overgrown lawn with a few stone ornaments and some massive floral pyjama bottoms drying on a spinner. No one answers the door, but when I get back in the van a woman comes chasing out after me. I get out and take the food to the house for her, planting it inside the front door, which smells like old smoke and laundry liquid.

Lofthouse and Yeadon are at opposite ends of the city, so much so that it takes me forty-five minutes to drive from one to the other. I've done a couple of deliveries in this part of Yeadon before; this turns out to be a strange drop though. When she opens the door, the woman peers at the bags and blows her fag smoke at me disinterestedly.

You can take this back. Both her front teeth are chipped.

Didn't you order some?

I did. But my kids won't eat out of a tin. Is this all you've got?

I'm a bit taken aback. Surely she can't be in such desperate need if she's refusing food? Most people would be grateful to be getting so much shopping for free.

I've a bag of fruit and veg for you in the van.

Give us that then. But you can have this lot back.

I shake my head and take the bags back to the van. When I go back with the fruit and veg she's smoking another fag with her neighbours, not socially distanced at all. I'm pretty annoyed considering how long it's taken me to drive here, but there's not a lot I can do about it.

The next two jobs are in Headingley and are unusual in that they're next door to each other. When I get there, two older ladies are sitting outside, a big Scottish woman in a wheelchair and her Yorkshire friend next door.

Youse are doing a brilliant job, the Scottish woman tells me. You need to get a few pints down your neck tonight, like.

There are two more drops to do when I get back, this time on the Swarcliffe estate. I go to what I think is the first address and speak to a lovely woman and her teenage daughter, but she doesn't know the name on the sheet and it's obvious I'm in the wrong place. I head around the corner up the street to find the next address. It's a house turned into flats and I'm trying to figure out where I need to be when I hear a noise and look up to see two lads in their early twenties, shirtless and shitfaced, wobbling up the street.

Ey, whaddyawantpal? The voice is slurred and aggressive.

Instant fear. They're covered in tattoos and pretty stacked, young lads with broken noses and broken hands, swigging from cans of Guinness and looking like they could inflict some serious damage if they took a dislike to me. I show them the job sheet with unsteady hands and instantly the vibe changes.

That's us! That's us! Ben and Liam, Ben and Liam! They're hugging each other. There are two flats here, bud, we've got one each.

Safe, brother, fuckin' nice one, this is amazin', Ben or Liam says. They're so pissed and happy that they both lean over and shake my hand. I'm a bit taken aback but it's rude to leave them hanging so I shake them back and bang a load of sanitiser on my hands when I get back in the van.

As I'm going back for another load from the van I hear one of them shouting upstairs, 'Ey, Vicky! Fella from t'council's here wi' t'food. You wanna see this fuckin' lot in 'ere!

Saturday 30ᵗʰ May

I had the screaming horrors in the night, something about going to America and being locked up in a Victorian mental institution. The details are sketchy, but the feeling remains, meaning that I'm fragile again this morning and unbelievably tired; I could do with a busy day without too much hanging around. If I fall asleep in the van while waiting for a job, it's going to be difficult to wake me up again.

In the news, another member of the Government's SAGE committee has said that talk of lifting lockdown restrictions has come far too early. I also read an interesting take on the Cummings story this morning: that the Government are happy for the Cummings story to run for now as a distraction so they can get away with lifting the restrictions early, and then they can always sack him in a symbolic gesture later. It's an interesting idea, and I wonder if there could well be some truth to it.

The first job of the day is a quick meds pick-up from Oakwood Lane Pharmacy. It's a place I know well, but I'm so spaced-out that I drive past it three times. Thankfully it's too early for there to be a queue so I get straight in and mercifully the medication is there. It needs delivering to a tower block in Gipton that's not too far away. It's the usual scene when I get there, no one around but a collage of glass and cigarette ends scattered over everything, sticky patches of coagulated gunk where people have been gobbing on the floor, oblivious to, or uncaring about the fact this may spread the virus.

I have to take the lift, redolent with the familiar smell of smoke and disinfectant. I don't like riding in these lifts as they're prone to breaking down, but it gets me to the first floor in one piece. The woman is in her sixties, I think, but I don't get much of a look at her. She opens the door a crack, sticks a claw out, grabs the bags and that's it.

There's a steady flow of traffic on the ring road and on York Road today. All the little sarnie shops are open; the Eldon in town was open for takeaway beer yesterday, and today the car park for the Asda/B&Q/B&M complex at Killingbeck is rammed. Even though it's still a couple of weeks until lockdown is officially lifted, it's obvious people are keen to start getting back to whatever kind of normality they can.

Back at the depot, Sharon asks if I fancy going to LS8.

Whatever, I tell her. It's not a proper Saturday until I've been to Harehills.

The first address is up past Hovingham Primary, a school I've worked with a lot over the years. It has a capacity of 794 pupils, and last time I asked they said they had children speaking something like fifty different languages within the walls. Every year I visit schools near my branches to promote the Reading Agency's annual Summer Reading Challenge; I came to Hovingham when I worked in Harehills, presenting two assemblies to nearly four hundred kids each, many of whom didn't have English as a first language. When I first started working as a librarian I didn't have much experience of public speaking and those kind of assemblies used to fill me with dread, but once I'd done a few I came to love them. Many of the schools I've engaged with over the years have had high numbers of ESOL pupils, but despite the potential language barriers, they're some of my favourite children to work with.

The house looks almost picturesque; there are roses growing around the doorway and the garden is beautifully presented, the lawn close-cropped and green, a few toys and some wellies lying around but no sign of the usual dereliction you find in the area. A youngish woman answers the door, smiling politely beneath her headscarf. She's flanked by a little boy of about three who keeps shouting what sounds like Go away! Go away! Go away! but I take it in good spirit and give him a smile as I'm handing the food to his mum.

The next one is in the Conways, right in the centre of the area. Harehills is packed; probably 80% of the shops are open – not only the ones classed as "essential" – and there are masses of people hanging around the streets. The road is chock-a-block with cars parked on both sides but the people I'm delivering to – an attractive Spanish couple in their twenties – are out in the front yard so I bang the hazards on, block the road and hoof the parcels over the wall for them.

I get another sheet and end up back at the bungalow in Kirkstall where I delivered some food to the woman with the house like an antique shop. Today she's rocking camo pants and a floral dress. The front door is ajar and I can see inside: this time I spot a load of Disney trinkets on a what-not next to the grandfather clock, which still doesn't say the right time. A big dog comes running out with her, tall enough to be able to put its paws on my shoulders if it jumped up at me, but it's a dozy old thing so it's not likely to.

Hope your dog's friendly, love? I laugh as it tries to lick my hand.

Don't worry about her, darling. She's as daft as a brush.

This is the second time in two days I've delivered to an address I've visited before. I wonder how many people are beginning to rely on the service for their meals. People have started asking if it's a weekly service and I know from speaking to other drivers that they've also visited certain addresses numerous times. Given how much money the service costs to run, there's no way it can be sustainable in the long term – but finding an exit strategy is going to be very tricky.

The next drop is at the other end of the city in Tingley and it takes a while to get there, back round the ring road in the usual way. It's a narrow street, fairly tight, containing lots of bungalows with handrails outside. I manage to get the van down it okay and park outside the house. Two little black and brown dogs sit in the window and start yapping madly through the open window when they see me. A loud female voice shouts at them to be quiet. I don't bother knocking because the woman obviously knows I'm there. She talks to me through the window.

Are you from t'council?

That's right. My name's Stu. I've got your food parcels for you.

Just leave it on t'step will yer?

Yeah, alright.

I go back to the van to get the food. When I put it on the doorstep, she opens the door and one of the dogs runs out, starts chasing me up the street. The woman calls after it in her dragon's voice, Come back 'ere yer bloody stupid thing!

It's running after me, barking like mad and snapping at my ankles. I'm trying to stay serious and professional but I'm dying to laugh.

Here y'are love, can yer bring him back in for us? she asks.

It's still yipping at me as I try to round it up and chase it back towards the yard, bouncing backwards and occasionally having a nibble at the end of my boot. At this point, one of the neighbours comes past and I finally let myself laugh – Hope your neighbours don't think I'm robbing your house and the dog's come to see me off!

It takes a while to get the mutt inside, me laughing my tits off by now and the old woman cursing a blue streak the whole time, calling it every name under the sun and threatening to kick it right up the arse. Once that's sorted, the neighbour wants to have a chat.

How do *I* get one of these food parcels, then, love? I haven't had one yet.

I try to explain to her that the service is meant to be for people who are self-isolating, but it's clear that she doesn't understand so in the end I give her the helpline number and tell her to call if she needs anything.

Cheers love, keep up the good work, she says.

It's been a tiring day, sweltering in the van and covering a lot of miles. Thankfully all's well at home when I get back, so I chill in the garden with a couple of beers while the kids climb all over me and tell me about their day. It's a rollercoaster for the little people at the moment – I never know from one day to the next how things are going to be when I get home, but it's lovely to find them happy, and thankfully my wife has had a better day of it too.

Sunday 31st May

I've started going to bed a bit later to see if it helps with my sleep, but it doesn't seem to have made any difference. I stayed up until half eleven last night and was so tired I felt like I could have fallen asleep on the sofa, but the instant I got into bed my brain woke up and started thinking about work again. I lay there tossing and turning until about four, then got up and sat downstairs reading for three hours until the kids woke up. By the time half past eight rolls around and it's time to go to work, I feel like I'm ready for bed.

There's no one about at the first drop in East End Park, save for the grizzled old man on the front step at the house next door, hanging his head and gurning sadly into a can of Stella, looking completely defeated. It takes a while for the woman at the drop to answer. She's maybe about forty, plump with pale skin, wearing a pretty purple and pink head scarf. I have three bags for her so it must be a big family; she doesn't have much English and it's a quick drop.

Next up is a trip to Harehills, which is full of people as usual. The first thing I see on the street is an ornamental lamp, shattered into thousands of multi-coloured pieces right in the middle of the road, like a stained-glass window that's been hit with a hammer. This street is so wrecked it looks like it's been bombed, missing doors and windows everywhere. The house has been painted purple or pink at some point, but all the colour is flaking off to expose the battered brickwork beneath. There's rubbish in the gutters and in the yard: at a glance, I can see a shredded duvet with the insides hanging out, a broken table and a smashed TV; all the usual stuff. The front door has several panes of glass that are cracked, and some of them are missing altogether; the kitchen window has also been broken and never replaced. Amazingly, the place has a FOR RENT sign outside it with a phone number.

The woman who comes out is tall and skinny in a white full-length dress that's so tight it looks like it's been painted on. She's smoking, speaks in sentences full of *sweetie*, *darling* and *love* like a character from *Absolutely Fabulous*; she carries the air of a famous actress who's hit the skids and can't believe where she's ended up.

Some jobs come in marked *URGENT* so I get sent out with those as soon as I get back to the FDC. The first one is in Churwell. It's a pretty street, a cul-de-sac with some really big houses on one side, some luxury cars and quite a few vans. The house I'm delivering to is a smallish semi, the lawn filled with a rotary dryer with some vests and underwear hanging off it. A massive tree blocks the path to the front door; on the drive there's a Ford Fiesta with chunks of bodywork dangling from it. The garage door has a load of old children's toys jammed in between it and the back end of the Fiesta. Next to the front door is a plastic packing crate full of empty wine and sherry bottles.

The man is tall and thin, wearing jeans and a Rhinos top, a couple of tattoos on each arm. Through the door I can see bare walls and a carpet that's worn almost completely through. The place has the vibe of having been a happy family home once but it looks as if they've fallen on hard times. It seems like a lot of people may be following soon: unemployment has rocketed as a result of the pandemic, and economic forecasts predict that things are only going to get worse. Already there's talk that unemployment levels in this country may surpass even those seen under the Thatcher Government, a catastrophic vision that's almost unimaginably bleak. It seems crazy to think that the country may be heading in this direction, but that's the brutal truth; the slide was kick-started by the financial crash of 2008, exacerbated by austerity and has now been compounded by the pandemic.

The next drop is at the opposite end of the city in Farsley. I cruise round the ring road, then down the main street, past the library which looks like a building site at the moment. I used to work at that one once upon a time, too. I start to look for the house but I've no idea where it is, so I give the number a call. I explain where I am and he says he can see me, gives me some directions and eventually I clock him a couple of hundred yards away. He's a young lad, with such a baby face that I bet he isn't even out of his teens. He's built like a garden cane: the clothes he's wearing look like they're meant to be skinny fit, but they're enormous on him. On the job sheet it says they requested baby formula, but we haven't got any. He says it doesn't matter when I tell him, but he looks crushed and it's all I can do to not give him a tenner out of my wallet and send him off to buy some.

A trip to Bramley follows, this address on another haphazard estate but I find the house quickly; it's the only one that has had its door kicked in. It's hard to put an age to the woman who calls down from the upstairs window; she's flabby and wrinkled, another who's clearly not had an easy life. When she comes down I can see she's got some smudged, fading tattoos on her arms, and bruises all over her legs. She's got a pair of crutches and I'm not sure how she's going to get the bags up the stairs, but when I offer to help she looks suspicious and says she can manage.

The next run takes me to Headingley. There are a few more people around when I drive up past the uni, but not many. Hyde Park's got a fair few people in it though – the usual mix of locals and students who've decided to stick around, everyone drinking out of plastic bags and rolling spliffs on the grass. Hyde Park Book Club – a popular local café, bar and arts space – is open for take-away pints and a fair few people are sitting around outside chatting and drinking their socially distanced beers. People seem to be enjoying themselves, and who can blame them after the stress of recent weeks?

I'm dreading trying to get the van down this street because it's so narrow and there are always cars parked on both sides – god knows how you'd get a fire engine or an ambulance down here in an emergency. The house has a big front garden hemmed in by a tall, messy hedge, and there's a lot of room around the side too. There are not one but two leather three-piece suites in various stages of decomposition; there's a stack of furniture too – a bedside table, a dining chair, something that looks like it could be from a nest of tables – all piled up in a heap. There's a children's trampoline on the straggly lawn, hundreds of fag ends.

I knock and wait, knock and wait. There's no answer, but when I'm getting into the van a woman comes out and collars me. She's in her sixties, wearing a flower-patterned dress and smoking a fag. I take the bags back up for her as she's apologising, laughing and telling me she was asleep. The inside of her house reeks of smoke and looks like a charity shop – stuff everywhere, no rhyme or reason to any of it.

From here it's a short drive to Burley. I have to drive past the back of Burley Park, resplendent in the sun, and that's full of people too. The drop is on another maddening estate on two levels, but thankfully I can see the place straight away and manage to park outside. The only word to describe this guy is *grey*; he has grey stubble, grey hair, grey skin, grey eyes. He's tall and tragically underweight, fixes me with the thousand-yard stare when he opens the door, then his gaze turns to his feet and he never looks up from them again. He has orange fingers and a brownish lump on his bottom lip where his cigarette must fit. I can't see much past the front door, but I can smell the house from here, that lingering perfume of fag smoke and old sweat that's so repulsively familiar to me now. He reminds me of the lad in Garforth on my first day of deliveries – he looks like he's in urgent need of support, but it's doubtful whether he's getting any. He takes the food without a word and shuts the door in my face.

There's one more to do at the town end of Belle Vue Road, but there's no answer at the drop and the man doesn't answer his phone. It's a little before three when I get back to the FDC and I'm expecting the usual Sunday afternoon slowdown, but Sharon gives me a sheet with a few drops in LS9. The first of these is at Roxby Close tower block in Burmantofts; I park the van and head on down. The woman answers when I buzz, but the intercom is busted and she can't understand me properly through the crackling. Luckily she can see me. She waves down from the balcony on the third floor and says she'll come to meet me. She's wearing colourful African dress and a striking headscarf, and there's a faint London twang when she speaks.

I've got three bags of dry food for her plus the fresh bag and the fruit and veg so I offer to carry them inside. It smells of weed as soon as the door opens; you could probably get high by osmosis if you hung around here for too long. The lift is minging too, a few fag ends in it, and the woman's complaining because some kids have chucked Ribena all over it and her feet keep sticking to the floor.

Spalding Towers is so close by that I don't even bother moving the van. The area around the intercom hums with the aroma of stale piss. I'm met by a woman with two pre-school age children at her side and a baby that can't be more than a couple of months old strapped to her chest in a sling. Her face lights up when she sees me.

God bless you my child, she says, hands pressed together in benediction, bowing to me. It's a humbling to be confronted by such gratitude, and as usual I don't know how to deal with it other than to mumble my goodbyes and try to choke down the lump in my throat.

After a failed drop nearby, the woman who meets me at the last job of the day is in her early fifties, straight blonde hair down to her shoulders and wearing a short grey cotton summer dress.

I feel really, really embarrassed, she tells me when she opens the door, eyes downcast and despondent.

There's nothing to feel embarrassed about, I tell her. We're here to help.

I know love, but I shouldn't need it at my age. Thirty-five years I've been working and I still can't pay all me bills.

She looks so sad. I mumble something about times being hard, then tell her it's her lucky day. The last person on my sheet wasn't in, so I've got a load of extra stuff in the van; she can have double everything as long as she doesn't tell anyone.

Oh, love, are you sure?

Of course. I'll go get it for you.

You're an absolute star, love, you've no idea what this means to me. This'll help me *so* much. Her lip wobbles and her voice catches in her throat. She's so grateful that for an awful minute I think she's about to burst into tears and I just *know* that if she does I will too, but she pulls herself together and thanks me as I leave. If she's been working on a low income for all that time, probably three quarters of it has been spent under Conservative governments; that may well explain why she's still struggling to make ends meet.

It's been a bruising day. If the gratitude of the woman at Spalding Towers left me feeling humbled, the quiet desperation of the woman at the last drop floored me completely. I keep telling myself that this is just a job and that I need to leave what I'm seeing at work, but the poverty and hardship being endured by the people I'm meeting every day continue to haunt me, and the fact that I'm going home and writing about it every night feels important but isn't helping me to compartmentalise. Doing the delivery job has been a great experience and is one that I wouldn't swap for the world, but I'm starting to feel incredibly burned out.

Week 9:
Lifting Restrictions

Recorded death toll: 40,552

"We took the right decisions at the right time." – Health Secretary Matt Hancock, responding to comments from Professor John Edmunds of the Government's SAGE committee that not implementing lockdown measures earlier "cost a lot of lives", Sunday 7th June 2020

The week begins with some lockdown restrictions being lifted. Car and caravan showrooms, non-food selling outdoor markets and outdoor sports amenities may reopen. Schools can reopen, but some local authorities ignore government advice and keep them closed. Gatherings of up to six people are now permitted.

The chair of the UK Statistics Authority says the Government's handling of data with regards to testing is "still far from complete and comprehensible". Shadow Health Secretary Jonathan Ashworth says, "This intervention from the UK statistics authority is damning. For test and trace to be effective, we all need confidence in the data. The Health Secretary [...] must stop including mailed tests as completed."

The Government is to stop its weekend briefings, citing low viewing figures as the reason. On 5th June, the official number of recorded deaths passes the 40,000 mark. On 7th June, no deaths from Covid-19 are recorded in Scotland or Northern Ireland. The figure for England and Wales on the same day is 77.

Monday 1st June

For a change, I actually had some sleep last night, although I'm at a loss as to why. I probably got about five hours over the course of the night, which may not sound like a lot, but is unheard of for me this year. Strangely though, I feel *more* tired than before. I think once the brain gets some sleep after a prolonged period without it, it starts to realise what it's been missing and craves even more. I'm taking it as a positive sign though, and I hope that tonight brings more of the same.

A lot of primary schools are back today, and it's also the first day of lockdown measures officially starting to lift so I'm curious to see how the traffic is going to be on the roads. I pass a dad at the top of my street with two little boys in uniform, but that's the only sign of schools being open. He was riding a mountain bike in shorts and shades and didn't exactly look like he was going to drop them off and go to work. The head teacher of my children's school has taken the decision that it's still not safe to open and that the risks to staff and pupils outweigh the benefits of opening up. She's deferred it for a week, with a decision on reopening next week to be made nearer the time.

It's a quiet morning, with a couple of drops in Morley and Tingley to start the day. Driving up the road to get on the motorway I spy two planes in the sky and I'm struck by the thought that they now seem like a really odd sight. I spot a couple more later on and have the same reaction – *oh look, a plane.* How strange that something once so commonplace has become such a novelty. I wonder how many people are on them, and where they're going.

The M1 is busy this morning. There are a lot of HGVs and haulage vehicles, but there are a lot more cars around today too, and I find myself getting boxed in more than once, which would have been unheard of even a week ago. In Tingley I drive around the back of one of the primary schools and see half a class of tiny kids – reception age by the look of them – being marched out to the playground. They're all socially distanced, teachers making sure they keep apart, so there's none of the usual bustle and jostle you'd see in kids of that age as they spill outside. They look like a line of forlorn soldiers waiting for a battle they don't want to fight, subdued in dejected silence. It's incredibly sad and it reinforces my conviction that keeping my own daughter at home is definitely the right thing to do.

The address I am delivering to isn't far from the school, a big terrace down a wide street. It takes so long for the woman to answer the door that I'm returning to the van, thinking she isn't in, when she calls me back. I go to the door and she's sitting on the step smoking a fag and putting the ash into a skull-shaped ashtray, the ultimate memento mori. She's in her fifties, witchy grey hair down to her waist, wearing a big dress with pink and purple flowers all over it. Her arms, legs and chest are covered with tattoos, and she has an unusual number of facial piercings.

She asks if I'm from the Salvation Army. I start to explain but then her daughter shows up. I have a go at introducing myself but she just stands at the top of the path with her hands on her hips, refusing to speak and gawping at me until I leave.

It's busy in Morley. I've worked around here quite a bit over the last couple of years and the level of traffic I'm seeing today is probably consistent with what you'd expect to see at this time on a Monday. Morrisons car park is packed. There are bags and bags of litter in the park – they must be awaiting collection by the council. There's been a disgusting amount of litter left around the country's beauty spots these last few weeks, so much so that it's even been on the news. With so many restrictions in place, it seems as if more people have been heading out as there's nowhere else they can go, but not all of the new visitors seem to know how to respect the countryside. My hometown is at the foot of the Yorkshire Dales and I've always loved being outside, so to see places like Ilkley Moor and Otley Chevin being mistreated by so many careless people makes me very sad indeed.

On the way back up the motorway I notice that already the signs about the NHS have gone. Now they say DON'T DRIVE TIRED. SERVICES OPEN and things like that.

The drop in Armley is off Town Street, up past the library and the temperance hall. When I find the address it's surreal – someone in the flat above the front door is listening to an audiobook of Winnie the Pooh at ear-splitting volume, and the sound is filling the street. I stand there listening disinterestedly until the young woman comes down to meet me, wearing bright pyjamas and sucking on an orange Callippo. She doesn't thank me.

Town Street is mad busy, big queues outside all the usual shops and lines of traffic too. On the gable end of one of the shops is a big mural saying LOVE ARMLEY, with peace signs and hearts spray-painted all around it. It's a laudable sentiment, but one that is in stark contrast to the local charity shop over the road which has had its front window shattered.

The next one is for a young lad, baseball cap on and hood up even though it's a hot day and he's inside. He looks and sounds stoned, shakes my hand when I leave. A lot of people I've talked to have baulked at stories of people shaking my hand, but it's not a problem for me – I just sanitise my hands when I get back in the van.

I know the next drop is going to be a pain when on the job sheet it says Flat 8 First Floor Rear. I get there, and so it proves. Access to the back of the parade is down a narrow ginnel that I can't get near in the van, and I wouldn't fancy walking down it if I could, even in daylight. I park on the front of the street, outside a house that's had all the downstairs doors and windows kicked in. When I give the guy a ring, he leans out of an upstairs window and waves down, says he'll come meet me round the front. He's a tall, thin man with a slight Scottish accent and a yellowish hue to his skin. He looks like he's stoned out of his mind, red eyes peering out from over the top of his surgical mask.

The drop that follows is off the main strip in Armley, down a narrow, potholed lane. It's a development of houses with an Anchor care home at the top, but the whole thing is hemmed in by four tower blocks including Burnsall Court, another one named after a Yorkshire village. I pull into a cul-de-sac down at the bottom and park outside a little block with six flats in it. I ring the buzzer and the woman comes straight out. She might be anywhere between forty and sixty, it's hard to say. Her skin is rubbery, sallow, and she has swollen ankles with bruises and bandages all over her legs.

Back at the depot Sharon has a few lists. I take a single one in Yeadon because it should kill off the day. I fall foul of York Road, which is shut and end up in Burmantofts, which is like a car park and it takes me half an hour to get through all the traffic. When I finally get there I ring the buzzer at the flat and at first there's no answer. I'm about to phone but a woman shouts through the downstairs window. She's wearing a grey tracksuit, dirty blonde hair and shocking pink lipstick. She's in her twenties probably, with a smoker's voice and skin.

Ta love, is all she says as I hand her the parcels through the window.

It's been a fairly uneventful day at work, and at home it's much the same. My wife and the kids have had a lazy time in the garden, interspersed with a bit of TV and video games. For a change the kids behave at bedtime and I get them settled fairly early. Once they're in bed there's not a whole lot to do and not a whole lot to talk about either, so my wife and I watch a film in companionable silence and grab an early night.

My hopes for a second night of good sleep turn out to be in vain, however. It's a torturous bout of tossing and turning, punctuated with screaming nightmares of which I can't remember a thing. I feel ruined in the morning, and I'm thankful it's a Tuesday so I can work from home and try to pull myself together with some menial admin tasks.

Saturday 6th June

The final day of collecting detailed journal entries for this book ends with what is unquestionably the most difficult drop I have.

The morning is notable for a couple of things, not least a delivery in Harehills to a Romanian family in a run-down terrace, at which I counted seven children all under the age of about twelve in the living room. I had four dry bags of food for them, plus the usual chilled items and some fruit and veg, but with so many mouths to feed it's uncertain how long the food will last.

On another job I try to deliver to a flat in Swarcliffe near the children's centre, to a place opposite the wreckage of some pre-fabricated flats that are in the process of being demolished, a big yellow bulldozer parked at a precarious angle atop a pile of rubble, PVC and broken glass. There's no one in at the drop, and when I phone up, the girl I speak to – who sounds so young she can't be out of her teens – tells me tearfully that she's had to come to her mum's house because the electricity meter has run out and she hasn't got any money to put in it. She says she'll be back later when she's borrowed some money off her mum, and asks if I can leave the food outside for her. She sounds like she needs all the help she can get so I agree to leave it in the wheelie bin outside, which has been emptied that morning. Her story is a reminder that some people don't even have the money to pay for the gas or electricity they need to cook the food we deliver to them, and that so much more help is needed.

The afternoon starts with what should, on the face of it, be a straightforward job. There's one address on the sheet, in Morley. I need to collect a prescription for them and deliver a food parcel to the same address while I'm there. It should be an hour of a job, but it ends up taking the whole shift.

I head off down the motorway and park on a side street in the middle of Morley so I can go to the Boots in the shopping centre. I arrive in the middle of an apocalyptic hailstorm and get soaked on the way to the chemist, shivering in the cold as the day started off with bright, warm sunshine and I'm only wearing a t-shirt. When I go into the pharmacy, the staff recognise me because I've been here a few times before.

You picking something up for the council again, love? the woman behind the counter asks.

Yeah, you know me too well, I answer. It's for this woman here. I show her the name on the job sheet.

She squints at it, shakes her head. Don't think it's one of ours, love, I don't recognise the name and the address is a new one on me too. Just wait there a sec, I'll have a look for you.

She moves off a little to the left, takes a box from behind the counter and starts rifling through a stack of prescriptions. She checks through the whole box a couple of times and shakes her head again. It's not here, love, she tells me. Are you sure you're in the right chemist?

I show her the job sheet and point to the column where it shows the address of the pharmacy I'm supposed to be collecting from.

That's definitely us, she says. But it isn't here. I'll see if anyone else knows anything about it. Julie! She calls to one of her colleagues. This gentleman's here to pick up a prescription for the council but I can't find it. Could you have a look for us?

Julie comes over, looks at the name on the sheet and shakes her head. Definitely not one of ours, she says. Have you picked something up for this woman before?

No, I don't think so.

Best thing to do, she says, is give her a ring and ask the woman herself, she'll definitely know.

No worries, I tell her. I need to drop some food off at her house anyway, I'll ask her when I go.

I thank them both, wave my goodbyes and go outside, dashing back through the hail, thousands of tiny golf balls bouncing and clattering onto the pavement all around me. I put the heater on in the van in a vain attempt to warm myself up and dry off my t-shirt, which is clinging to my body like a second icy skin. The address isn't one I'm familiar with, but it turns out it's only a five-minute drive away, so the heater doesn't have much time to take effect and I'm still shivering when I arrive.

The drop is on one of a strip of bungalows on a wide street, opposite a big red-brick estate full of houses and flats. It has a disabled access ramp around the front, and signs all over the fence saying *No Parking, Access Required At All Times*. There are some other signs too, mostly saying *Beware of the dog*. I hop out of the van, push the gate open, walk up the ramp and bang on the door. This prompts an immediate flurry of barking from inside, but it's nothing to worry about. Judging by the shrill yapping emanating from behind the door, it can't be a big dog.

I'm coming, says a muffled voice from behind the door.

There's a note on the job sheet saying that it may take a while for this person to answer, and I'm there for about five minutes waiting for her to come. The woman who opens the door is probably about fifty, big boned and heavy set, wearing a flimsy cotton nightie and not much else. Her face is white, wracked into a grimace of pain, and she's breathing heavily, bent almost double against the doorframe with tears in her eyes.

Thank god it's you, she says, looking at my badge. Have you got my morphine?

I've brought you some food parcels, I tell her. I'm meant to get your meds too but they've sent me to the wrong chemist. I show her the job sheet.

No, it's not that one, she shakes her head. You need to go to the one near Morrisons. Do you know it? She's taking in big gulps of air between every word she says, her whole body shaking. I've never seen anyone in so much pain in all my life and my muscles tense up in sympathy.

Let me bring your food in, I tell her, then I'll go get your prescription.

Thanks so much, love, she tells me. I need to go sit down. She turns to shuffle back inside, but in the time it takes me to go back to the van for the food and bring it back to the house, she's barely moved three feet. She's in so much pain it's a wonder she can stand up.

Shall I put it in the kitchen? I ask.

Yeah, just through there, she wheezes, waving an arm.

The kitchen is a bombsite, stuff all over the counters, a couple of bags of rubbish hanging off the door handle, clutter all over the floor. The dog is going mental in what I presume is the living room; I can hear it jumping up and trying to claw its way through the wood. I put the bags down and go back into the hallway, where the woman is still standing in the same place.

Are you alright? It's a silly question but I'm not sure what else to say.

I just need my morphine, love, she says. It's my back. I'm in agony with it. I'll be better when I've had that.

It's the one near Morrisons, you say? Give me ten minutes, I'll be back as soon as I can.

I get into the van and hurtle to the chemist and back, getting drenched in another hailstorm in the process. When I knock on the door, the dog starts going crazy again. I wait for a while but she doesn't come, so in the end I open the door a crack and stick my head inside. Straightaway I can hear crying, mixed with screams of pure, animal pain.

It's Stu from the council, I say, I've got your medicine.

She doesn't answer, carries on wailing and my body starts to shake as the adrenaline begins to flow. I follow the sound and find her laying on a bed in a dark, dingy room piled high with so many boxes I can barely get inside. She has tears streaming down her face and she can barely catch her breath.

I've got your medicine, I say again. Can you sit up?

You'll have to help me, she gasps, please. Oh Christ it hurts it hurts it hurts.

Ok, can you put your arms around my neck? I bend over and she creaks into motion. I'm only a couple of feet away from her and the small exertion of reaching for me makes her start screaming again, deafening and shrill with her face so close to my ear. I'm sorry, love, I'm sorry, she keeps gasping over and over again. Finally she manages to get her arms around my neck, clinging on for dear life like a scared and lonely child.

Okay, I'm going to pull you up now, I tell her. Is that alright?

She nods and I start to ease her up. The screaming stops but her whole body is shaking and she bites her lip so hard she draws blood. It takes a couple of minutes to get her upright and she's exhausted by the effort.

Can you get me the morphine? she gasps, in between big, shuddering intakes of breath.

I open the bag, pass her the box and the plastic pipette that comes with it, watch as she takes out a brown bottle, sucks a bit of the transparent liquid into the tube and drops it on her tongue. Her hands are shaking so hard it's a wonder she can hold the stuff, like a lifelong alcoholic in the throes of the worst delirium tremens imaginable. I'm not quite sure what to do so I stand in silence for a couple of minutes, watching her do it, and I can actually *see* when the morphine hits her. The shaking subsides, her body relaxes a little and her breathing slows down a touch.

Oh god, she says, thank you so much.

Is that any better? I ask.

She gulps, nods, yes, thank you. Thank you.

I think you need to go to the hospital, I tell her.

She shakes her head and frowns like a little girl. No. I can't. The doctor keeps telling me that, but I can't leave Alfie. There's no one else to look after him.

Alfie? Is that your dog? I can still hear it yelping in the other room, the occasional bump as it hurls itself against the door.

Yeah. He can be a right nuisance but I love him to bits.

I bet. I'm sure that you could get someone to look after him.

No. There's no one. Maybe Jean from over the road, but I don't have her phone number.

It's an awkward situation. According to procedure I shouldn't even be in the house, but there's no way I can leave her here like this.

Well, I start, not entirely sure what I'm going to say. I can't leave you like this. I really think I should call an ambulance.

You can't, she says, you just can't. What about Alfie?

Alfie will be fine. Listen, do you mind if I make a quick phone call? I'm going to step outside for a couple of minutes so I can talk to work and let them know what's going on. Is that alright with you?

You do what you need to do, love, she says. I need to lay down again. And with that she grits her teeth, bites her lip and struggles back into a horizontal position.

I go outside and dial Sharon's mobile number. I'm shaking now. I'm comfortable with my ability to deal with the situation, but my body is experiencing something akin to a shock reaction as my brain tries to come to terms with the awful state of the woman inside. Thankfully, Sharon answers immediately. I explain the situation and tell her the woman needs help, but it's the first time anything like this has happened to me on the job and I'm not sure what to do.

Don't worry, love, she tells me. You keep doing what you're doing – I'll speak to some people at this end, then I'll give you a ring back in five minutes and we'll sort it out from there.

Okay. I'll go back in and sit with her till you call.

When I go back in, the morphine has worked its way fully into her system and she looks a little more relaxed. The shaking that had been wracking her frame has stopped and her breathing is more or less back to normal, but her eyes are glazed over and when she speaks it's in a whisper.

Don't worry, I tell her, they're going to ring me back in a minute and we're going to see what we can do to help. What's your name? In all likelihood her name was written down on the job sheet, but in the rush of the moment I've forgotten it.

Leslie, she whispers, my name is Leslie.

I think I told you before, but my name is Stu. It's nice to meet you. I try to laugh.

She tries to laugh with me. Nice to meet you too. Bloody hell, what a state. A couple of tears spring in the corner of her eye and trickle slowly down her cheek as she chokes back a sob and bites her lip again.

We have a chat while I'm waiting for work to call. She tells me that she has a growth in her back that's pressing down on her sciatic nerve, and it means she can't feel anything below her waist. All she can feel is excruciating pain where the nerve is trapped, so of course she can't walk. The doctors want her to go to hospital, but she's adamant that she won't leave the dog. I'm worried about what will happen to poor little Alfie, she says, tears in her eyes again.

I understand that, I tell her, but I'm worried about *you*. I think if the doctor says you need to go to hospital that's probably where you should be. I think you need an ambulance, but I can't *make* you get one.

I can't carry on like this, she says. I know I need some help, but I can't leave him.

Just then my phone rings, so I tell her I'll have to go outside to take the call. When I answer it, it's Tina, who's been helping Sharon co-ordinate the deliveries today.

How're you doing, Stu? she asks. Tina and I used to work together a couple of years ago and it's a relief to hear a familiar voice.

I've been better, I tell her, but this poor woman's in a right fucking state. What are we gonna do?

She says they've looked into it and the only thing I can do for now is give her doctor a call. Given that it's Saturday I don't think the doctors will be open and I say as much, but Tina says to give it a try and then call her back.

When I go back in I relay the conversation to Leslie and ask her the name of her doctor's surgery. She tells me, and I do a quick Google search on my phone to get the number. As predicted, it's closed.

The way I see it, I tell her, there are two things we can do. I can either phone an ambulance and get them to have a look at you, or I can just leave you here like this and I'm definitely not going to do that. What will you do when I'm gone?

She sighs with her whole body. You're right, love, she says.

Like I said, I can't *make* you go to the hospital, but we need to get someone to have a look at you, and the only way we can do that is to phone an ambulance. They might take you to hospital, they might not, but that's up to them. I don't really think I can leave you here without getting you some help though. I'm sure the ambulance people will have dealt with things like this before – they'll be able to tell us who we can call to make sure Alfie's okay.

She doesn't look convinced, but she nods her assent. Okay, love. You're right.

Are you giving me permission to call an ambulance for you?

She nods again.

Okay. I need to call work, then I'll come back in here and call 999, is that alright?

Another nod. Thank you, Stu.

I go back out and speak to Tina, tell her that I've got the woman to agree to ambulance and that I'm going to go back in to ring one.

Well done, love, she says, it sounds like you're having a hell of a time. I'm going to send a female driver down to you as soon as I can, just for safeguarding reasons. You know you're not meant to be in the house on your own with her?

I know, but what the hell else am I supposed to do?

You're doing the right thing, she says. Someone will be down soon. You call the ambulance and keep me up to speed with what's happening, okay?

Sure.

I go straight back in to make the 999 call. I'm on the phone for about ten minutes, explaining the situation to the woman on the end of the phone, acting as intermediary when she's asking questions about whether the patient has ever had heart problems, any difficulties breathing, and lots of other things besides. There are multiple questions relating to Covid-19 too, as they have to ascertain whether or not Leslie is displaying any symptoms. Once the call is done, she says the ambulance is coming with the blue light on so they'll be there as quickly as they can.

I explain this to Leslie, send a quick text to Tina to tell them the ambulance is on its way. While we're waiting, I ask Leslie how long she's been like this, and am shocked when she tells me it's been months. The doctors have given her a wheelchair, but the bungalow is too small for her to be able to use it. The council are meant to be moving her somewhere bigger and she's all packed up ready to move – hence all the boxes – but something's been held up somewhere along the line and she's not sure when she's going to be able to go to the new place. She's desperate to get away; there are people selling drugs on the estate and the dealers used to stash their gear behind her garden hedge when the police were after them. On more than one occasion people have tried to break in, so she's had CCTV fitted in the garden and all around the house and is constantly frightened.

At that moment comes a female voice from outside. Hello?

At first I think it must be the driver Tina has sent down, but then the voice says, Leslie, are you alright? Leslie?

Jean? Jean, I'm in here, Leslie says.

I go into the hallway and greet a slight woman in late-middle age, greying brown hair and a concerned expression on her face. I introduce myself and tell her what's happened.

Thanks for looking after her, love, she says. I saw the front door open and I was worried. There's a lot of druggies on the estate and I thought maybe someone had broken in or something, it wouldn't be the first time. Is she in the bedroom?

Sure. I'll leave you to it and go wait for the ambulance.

We dance around each other in the cramped hallway, and I hear Jean say, Bloody hell, love, what have you done to yourself now? as I go outside. At that point another council van pulls up with Kayleigh, one of the other drivers inside. We have a quick chat, and within a couple of minutes the ambulance arrives. I point the paramedics into the bungalow and we stay outside.

Thanks bud, one of them says. We'll take it from here.

I can hear quiet voices but I can't make out what they're saying. Five minutes later they come outside with Leslie strapped to a stretcher and wrapped in a blanket, screaming in pain again as they heft her into the back of the ambulance. From underneath the blanket I can see her hands balled up into fists so tight it looks like her fingers are going to break with the pressure, her white knuckles looking like they're about to burst right through the wrinkled skin. Jean follows them, patting Leslie on the arm as they carry her in, then comes back to where Kayleigh and I are standing by the door. Inside the house, Alfie is still going crackers.

It's taken me an age to get her to agree to the ambulance, I tell Jean. I've been here all afternoon. She was worried about who was going to look after the dog.

I don't mind doing it, she says, I've got a key for the house.

She mentioned your name but she said she didn't have your number.

Bloody hell, she sighs. Course she's got it. It's the pain. And the morphine, like. She forgets, you see. She taps the side of her head.

Are you going to mind the dog then?

Yeah, I don't mind letting him out. I'm only across the road. She points across to the estate as a police car pulls up nearby.

Ah shit, I think that's my house, she says, pulling the front door closed and locking it. I'd better go see what they want. If they're looking for my lad again I'll throttle him. Don't worry about Alfie, I'll take him for a walk once I've spoken to that lot. And with that, she skips off down the ramp and runs across the road, shoving a fag in her mouth and lighting it without breaking step.

Well done, Stu, Kayleigh says, you did a bloody good job there. Hope you've got no plans for tomorrow – you're gonna have a mountain of paperwork to fill in.

What's the craic now? I'm a bit dazed by what's happened and I don't really know what to do. The adrenaline's still surging and I'm shaking pretty hard, head spinning as I try to process it.

She looks at her watch. Four o'clock. Might as well get yourself off, that's what I'm doing. I'll see you tomorrow if you're in.

We walk down the path together, climb into our respective vans and I give her a wave as she drives off. I give Tina a quick call to tell her everything is sorted. Good work, love, she tells me. It's happened to me a couple of times, that, when you're with someone and you know you *have* to help. I'll give you a buzz tomorrow so we can talk about the paperwork, and if you wanna come in a bit late it's fine. In the meantime, bugger off home and get some cider. You deserve it.

The drive back to LBS is a blur, but I manage to get the van back there and pick up the car. I'm in a bit of a fog, my mind replaying the afternoon over and over again, like a YouTube clip that's set to repeat. Not long afterwards I find myself standing in the kitchen at home with an ice cold can of Stowford Press in my hand and nine more in the fridge. The first can lasts about fifteen seconds.

Christ, what's happened to you today? my wife asks. You look like you've seen a ghost.

I crack another can and drain it immediately, hoping the alcohol will settle my nerves and stop the shaking, but it only makes things worse.

I'll tell you in a bit, I say. I need to sit down.

I take myself off into the living room and distract myself with the kids for a while, listening to them tell me how they went for a walk to the park but got soaked in the hail and there was so much of it on the ground it looked like it had been snowing. It dawns on me then that I'm still drenched from being caught out in it myself and I realise I'm absolutely frozen. No wonder I'm still shaking. I drink another can and head upstairs, spend about half an hour in the shower with the water so hot it feels like it could strip the skin from my flesh. It's lovely while I'm in there, but I start shaking again as soon as I get dressed. The shock is wearing off a bit now, but the cold has got in my bones and I don't manage to get warm again for the rest of the evening.

In the end I drink all the cider and stumble up to bed at half past eleven, the shock of the afternoon's events blurred and softened by the alcohol haze. I'm bone tired and half-cut, wiped out from the stresses of the day, and for a blissful change I fall asleep instantly.

Afterword – one year on

Death toll: at least 129,000[29]

"I am deeply sorry for every life that has been lost. And of course, as Prime Minister, I take full responsibility for everything that the Government has done." – Prime Minister Boris Johnson's press conference, Tuesday 26th January 2021

The easing of the lockdown restrictions proved to be a false dawn. Despite the Prime Minister's promise of "a significant return to normality" by Christmas, cases continued to rise as society opened up again. A surge in infections in Leicester led to localised restrictions being put in place at the end of June; subsequently, new legislation was passed to allow local lockdowns to be imposed, with Greater Manchester and parts of East Lancashire and Yorkshire being among the first areas affected as early as the end of July. By mid-September, former Chief Scientific Adviser Sir Mark Walport was warning that the country was "on the edge of losing control" of the virus; a little over a week later, the Prime Minister told the House of Commons that the nation had reached "a perilous turning point" and more restrictions were introduced. By the beginning of October, it was estimated that around 25% of the population of the UK was living under some kind of localised restrictions.

Later that month, the Prime Minister announced a new three tier system of restrictions for England, with areas being categorised by levels of risk – medium, high, or very high. On the same day, minutes published from a SAGE meeting in September showed that the committee had recommended a short "circuit breaker" lockdown to slow the spread of the virus, warning that "not acting now to

---

29 Figure correct at the time of writing, August 2021.

reduce cases will result in a very large epidemic with catastrophic consequences in terms of direct Covid related deaths" and that "the burden of a large second wave would fall disproportionately on the frailest in our society, but also those on lower incomes and BAME communities."[30] Responding to this, Labour Leader Sir Keir Starmer called for the immediate imposition of a short national lockdown, telling the Prime Minister, "You know that the restrictions you're introducing won't be enough [...] You can't keep delaying this and come back to the House of Commons every few weeks with another plan that won't work. So act now."

The Government continued to delay; by the end of October, the UK had recorded over 1 million Covid cases. Despite having previously compared it to "a nuclear deterrent", the Prime Minister announced a second national lockdown – excluding the closure of schools – to run throughout November, after which the UK would revert to the tier system. During this time, having seemingly weathered the fallout from his well-publicised trips to Durham, Dominic Cummings stepped down from his role as chief adviser to the Prime Minister.

The death toll continued to rise, passing 60,000 as lockdown ended at the beginning of December and climbing to 70,000 by Christmas Day; an exponential rise in cases led to the declaration of a state of emergency. There was a brief relaxation of restrictions for Christmas in some areas of the country, but a full national lockdown – this time including the closure of schools – was announced on 4th January 2021.

Despite the lockdown, the death count climbed stratospherically; on 26th January, the Prime Minister announced to the nation that over 100,000 people in the UK had died from Covid-19, saying, "it is hard to compute the sorrow contained in that grim statistic" and stressing that the Government "did everything we could." Speaking to the BBC Radio 4's *Today* programme, Shadow Health Secretary Jonathan Ashworth responded by saying, "Monumental mistakes have been made." In reply, Communities Secretary Robert Jenrick acknowledged that, "There will be some things that we could have done differently with the benefit of hindsight."

30 SAGE, (2020). Summary of the effectiveness and harms of different non-pharma-ceutical interventions [online]. Available from: https://assets.publishing.service.gov.uk/government/uploads/system/uploads/attachment_data/file/925854/S0769_Summary_of_effectiveness_and_harms_of_NPIs.pdf

A step-by-step plan to lift the lockdown and fully open up society was announced at the end of February, with 21st June 2021 being given as the earliest date at which all forms of restriction on social contact could be lifted. The Prime Minister stressed that the process would be driven by "data not dates" and that the lifting of measures would be "cautious but irreversible."

Throughout the year, the government response to the pandemic continued to come under fire, with revelations about a lack of transparency in the procurement of PPE contracts in the early part of the outbreak continuing to become public well into 2021. In February, the High Court ruled that "There is now no dispute that in a significant number of cases [Health Secretary Matt Hancock] breached his legal obligation" by not publishing details of these contracts within thirty days of them being signed, prompting the Good Law Project's legal director Gemma Abbott to say, "We have a government contemptuous of transparency and apparently allergic to accountability."

Further controversy erupted in early March when it was announced that NHS staff – of whom the Prime Minister had previously said "I can't thank them enough. I owe them my life." – were to be offered a mere 1% pay rise; Shadow Health Secretary Jonathan Ashworth branded the offer "a disgrace". The Prime Minister responded by saying, "What we have done is try to give them as much as we can at the present time." Health Secretary Matt Hancock also defended the offer, calling it "what we think is affordable." Patricia Marquis of the Royal College of Nurses warned that many would be forced to leave the profession, citing the fact that "this slap in the face from the Government really just has reinforced the belief that they are not valued either by the Government or perhaps some of the public in the way they would want to be." Shortly afterwards, Jenny McGee, a nurse who cared for the Prime Minister while he was hospitalised with the virus left her position in the NHS, saying, "We're not getting the respect and now pay we deserve. I'm just sick of it.," before going on to say that, "Lots of nurses felt the Government hadn't led very effectively – the indecisiveness, so many mixed messages. It was just very upsetting." Sir Keir Starmer responded by saying Ms McGee's resignation was "a devastating indictment of Boris Johnson's approach to the people who put their lives on the line for him and the whole country."

Despite concerns over supplies, the full vaccine roll-out, begun at the beginning of the year, proceeded at a rapid pace; by the end of March, 30 million people in the UK had received their first of two doses of the vaccine, and the early stages of the Government's plan to lift restrictions came into force. On 8th March all schools were reopened and people were allowed to meet up with one other person from outside their household in an outdoor environment. Care home residents were also allowed to have one visitor. The second phase kicked in on the 29th of the month, where the rules were relaxed to allow up to six people or two households to meet up in an outdoor setting, including private gardens. Outdoor sports facilities such as basketball and tennis courts were also re-opened.

The Government's criteria for unlocking society continued to be met in the spring. Amid falling infection rates and low levels of hospital admissions, non-essential retailers were allowed to open from 12th April, with re-opened hospitality venues allowed to serve food and alcohol in an outdoor setting. By the end of the month, ONS reports indicated that for the first time since the previous autumn, Covid-19 was no longer the leading cause of death in England and Wales, with dementia, Alzheimer's and heart disease now back in their usual places at the top of the list.[31]

Concerns were raised in April and May about a new mutation of the virus – first identified in India in October 2020 and which came to be known as the Delta variant – that had found its way into the UK and was feared to be more transmissible than the strain which had caused the devastating wave of infections in the UK over the winter. Early data showed, however, that vaccines seemed to be effective against it; by the middle of May, 36 million adults in the UK had had their first dose of the vaccine, and 20 million had had their second, so the Government made the decision that it was safe to push ahead with the next step of their roadmap. On 17th May more restrictions were lifted, meaning that indoor hospitality could reopen, as well as indoor entertainment such as cinemas, museums and children's play areas, although all of these would still be subject to social distancing regulations; in addition, groups of two households or six people were allowed to meet indoors

---

31 Office for National Statistics, (2021). Monthly mortality analysis, England and Wales: March 2021 [online]. Available from: https://www.ons.gov.uk/peoplepopulationandcommunity/birthsdeathsandmarriages/deaths/bulletins/monthlymortalityanalysisenglandandwales/march2021

and groups of up to thirty people were allowed to meet outdoors. This was greeted with a huge wave of enthusiasm by the general public, who seemed to feel that the end may be in sight at last.

The following week, the former chief adviser to the Prime Minister Dominic Cummings appeared before a hearing of the Commons Health and Social Care and Science and Technology Committees, who were holding a joint enquiry into how the Government handled the early stages of the pandemic. Since stepping down from his role in November, Cummings had been a vocal critic of the Prime Minister and the statements he made to the inquiry reflected this. He began by acknowledging his own role, saying "senior ministers, senior officials, senior advisers like me fell disastrously short of the standards the public has a right to expect from the Government during a crisis like this." Over the course of a seven-hour session, he made numerous claims about the Government's handling of the crisis, saying, amongst other things, that Health Secretary Matt Hancock was guilty of "criminal behaviour that caused serious harm" and saying that he "should have been fired for at least fifteen to twenty things, including lying to everyone on multiple occasions."

The Prime Minister also came in for scathing criticism, with Cummings alleging that before he contracted the virus himself, Boris Johnson said, "I'm going to get Chris Whitty to inject me live on TV with Covid-19 so everyone realises it's nothing to be frightened of"; he also claimed the Prime Minister dismissed the virus as "a scare story". In reference to the Prime Minister's alleged reluctance to implement a "circuit-breaker" lockdown in September, he said, "All credible serious people in my opinion were saying essentially the same thing so I was very, very clear with him about it. He wasn't taking any advice, he was just making his own decisions, he was going to ignore the advice. Cabinet wasn't involved or asked." This, Cummings claimed, led to a drastic deterioration in his relationship with the Prime Minister, and by the time he stepped down from his role in November, "Fundamentally, I regarded him as unfit for the job."

At Prime Minister's Questions, which took place at the same time as the hearing, Sir Keir Starmer responded to the evidence given so far, referring to "a lack of planning, poor decision making and [...] transparency." The following day he spoke about the hearing again, saying the Cummings claims demonstrated "the chaos and incompetence of the decision making in the Government." The day after the hearings, the Prime Minister announced that he was optimistic the UK was on track to lift all restrictions as planned, saying "I don't see anything currently in the data to suggest we have to deviate from the roadmap."

On 1st June, the UK reported no deaths from anyone within 28 days of a positive test for the first time since the Pandemic began. This should have been cause for great optimism, however only two days earlier, Professor Ravi Gupta of Cambridge University and a member of the Government's New and Emerging Respiratory Virus Threats Advisory Group told BBC Radio 4 that the UK was showing "the signs of an early wave", raising concerns that a sudden spike in infections may overwhelm the NHS at a time when it was trying to cope with the huge backlog of patients from the previous twelve months.

In the run-up to 14th June, the date on which the Prime Minister was due to announce whether or not measures would be lifted on the 21st, the mood was cautious. With infection rates – 90% of which were thought to be caused by the new Delta variant – rising fast, Vice President of the Association of Directors of Public Health Jim McManus said the Government had "a fiendishly difficult decision" to make, going on to say that if we "invest that little bit of time to keep us going forwards, it will stop us going backwards." Foreign Secretary Dominic Raab also hinted at a potential delay, telling the BBC's *Andrew Marr Show*, "The key point is we want to move out of lockdown irreversibly. [...] We don't want to yo-yo back in and out of measures." The Prime Minister himself echoed this, saying, "The roadmap was always cautious but irreversible, and in order to have an irreversible roadmap, we have to be cautious."

A delay in unlocking appeared to be inevitable, and this was confirmed by the Prime Minister's press conference on 14th June. Alluding to the fact that "we're seeing cases grow by about 64% every week [...] and the average number of people being admitted to hospital in England has risen fifty percent week on week", he said that "even if the link between infection and hospitalisation has been weakened, it has not been severed," and warned that if unlocking went ahead as planned, "there is a real possibility that the virus will outrun the vaccines and that thousands more deaths would ensue that could otherwise have been avoided."

He gave a new date for the full unlocking of society, saying, "I am confident we will not need any more than four weeks and we won't need to go beyond 19th July." It is to be hoped that his confidence is well-founded and that the much-anticipated Freedom Day will finally go ahead on the date he specified, although one thing the virus has taught us more than anything, as Chancellor of the Duchy of Lancaster Michael Gove told BBC Breakfast the day after the announcement was made, is that we "can never predict the future with perfect confidence." Despite the success of the vaccine rollout, it is clear that while the end may appear to be in sight at last, the restrictions necessitated by Covid-19 are going to have to remain in place for at least a little while longer.

On 25th June, Health Secretary Matt Hancock issued a public apology after pictures of him kissing a female aide with whom he had allegedly been having an extramarital affair, in flagrant breach of his own social distancing guidelines, were published by *The Sun* newspaper. The following day, he resigned.

July 19th – so-called 'Freedom Day' – finally saw almost all legal restrictions on social interaction in the UK come to an end. While the public celebrated, Prime Minister Boris Johnson, who warned in a press conference marking the occasion that "this pandemic is far from over", spent the day is self-isolation, after being identified as a close contact of someone who had tested positive for Covid-19. While the general mood was one of cautious optimism, largely attributable to the apparent success of the vaccine roll-out, scientists warned that the effects of lifting all restrictions would be impossible to predict; as we move into the autumn, the future path of the pandemic in the UK is still very much uncertain.

*

The Food Distribution Centre finally closed its doors in September 2020, having been operational for 23 weeks, during which time it is estimated that almost 63,000 food bags had been made up into 33,900 food parcels and distributed to the public.[32] As is clear from the figures, it was a huge operation, but it formed only one part of Leeds City

---

32 Leeds City Council, (2020). Update on Coronavirus (Covid-19 Pandemic:
    Response & Recovery Plan [online]. Available from: https://democracy.leeds.gov.
    uk/documents/b23642/Late%20Item%20of%20Business%20Agenda%20Item%20
    10%20Update%20on%20Coronavirus%20Covid-19%20Pandemic%20Response%20
    Recover.pdf?T=9

Council's response to the pandemic. The cost was enormous. As early as June, the council's Chief Financial Officer Victoria Bradshaw was quoted as saying that the authority faced a potential overspend of £197.6m for the financial year 2020-21. Despite the Government's claim that it was giving local authorities "unprecedented support", Leeds City Council Chief Executive Tom Riordan hinted at huge cuts to public services, saying, "The potential implications are as serious as it gets. If we anticipate that we can't balance our budget, we have to take steps to pare our spending right back to just the things we have a legal duty to provide. That would rule out many of the services we provide in the city today. For example, all the cultural institutions we fund [...] are non-statutory. We would basically have to take very draconian measures."

This grim outlook was replicated across the country. In August, the Institute For Fiscal Studies published a report into the financial implications of the pandemic for local authorities which gave the stark warning, "The public health and economic effects of the Covid-19 crisis are creating a perfect storm for councils' finances, simultaneously increasing spending and reducing incomes"[33] and forecasting that based on the figures available at the time, councils nationwide could face an overall shortfall of 2 billion pounds even when government aid was taken into account.[34] Not long afterwards, the BBC reported that 9 in 10 councils across the country would fail to balance their books at the end of the financial year.

In February, new Leeds City Council Leader James Lewis addressed a meeting to discuss budget plans for the upcoming year, warning that Leeds was "under the shadow of the biggest crisis facing our city and the world in over 75 years," and declaring that "Our city continues to be held back by the incompetence of Westminster, with a public service and transport infrastructure starved of funding." As part of the budget, council tax was increased by 1.9%, with the adult social care precept climbing by 3% in an attempt to offset some of the losses incurred due to the pandemic. These rises, plus the prospect of cutting nearly 800 full-time equivalent posts were aimed at making savings in the region of 87.5 million pounds by March 2022, with substantial additional savings needing to be made for the following two years.

33 Ogden, K., and Phillips, D., (2020). *Covid-19 and English council funding: how are budgets being hit in 2020-21?*, Institute For Fiscal Studies, p.5
34 Ibid, p.9

For Leeds and many other cities like it, the outlook for public services looks bleak for the foreseeable future as authorities continue to battle with the legacy of the austerity years, compounded by the unparalleled financial upheaval caused by the pandemic.

*

I continued my work delivering food parcels for the whole period during which the FDC was open. In the months between the middle of June, which provided the endpoint for the journal entries featured in this book, and the closure of the FDC, I witnessed the same problems of poverty, social inequality, addiction, starvation, poor mental health and people living in slum-like conditions on a daily basis. The issues I paid witness to and the frequency with which I saw them highlight the sheer *scale* of the problem, the vast numbers of vulnerable people affected. I was only one of a large team of drivers, and every single one of them could have written a book of their own detailing the hardships they witnessed every day. These issues are not problems specific to Leeds or even the North of England; they're endemic in towns and cities throughout the UK.

According to a recent government briefing paper, for the year 2019/20, 14% of the population (9.2 million people) were living in absolute poverty *before* housing costs were taken into account, with this figure rising to 18% (11.7 million people) *after* housing costs.[35] The same paper goes on to discuss the potential effects of the pandemic on poverty in the UK, stating, "Early analysis suggests that poverty will increase over the next few years, and that low income households are particularly vulnerable to the economic effects of the pandemic."[36] The Institute for Fiscal Studies report quoted in the introduction to this book echoes this statement, stating, "The economic implications of the Covid-19 pandemic will mean a reduction in household incomes as workers lose their jobs, earnings fall, and plummeting share prices and interest rates lead to lower incomes from savings and investments"[37],

---

35 Francis-Devine, B., (2021). House Of Commons Library Briefing Paper Number 7036, Poverty in the UK: Statistics, p.4

36 Ibid, p.20

37 Bourquin, P., Joyce, R., Keiller, A N., (2020) Living standards, poverty and inequality in the UK: 2020. *Institute for Fiscal Studies*, p.8

before going on to say, "the Covid-19 pandemic is likely to lead to [...] increases in absolute poverty in the coming years" and that "the measures that have been taken to limit the spread of the virus also mean that falls in income are likely to be sharper among certain types of workers and households than others."[38]

These kinds of statistics and analyses are striking in themselves, but one of the aims of this book was, as Engels had it, to show "more than an abstract knowledge of [my] subject"; in other words, to try to put a human face on this tragedy by lifting some individuals out from the amorphous mass of percentage points and infographics that proliferate through myriad television reports and reams of newsprint, and try to show how their lives are affected by these issues in a concrete way.

From a narrative point of view, the main problem this presented was who and what to leave out. During the time period covered by the journal entries in this book, I met scores of people who ended up not being included in these pages; when you factor in all the people I met over the rest of the summer, this figure rises into the hundreds, each one of them an individual with their own lives, worries and support needs. To include every single one of them would have led to the book being repetitive in the extreme, not to mention unimaginably long.

During every edit, the text was stripped back so that less noteworthy incidents were left out and a coherent narrative could be developed. Some things were easy to remove; many encounters were fleeting and banal to document; for example, all the people who refused to come to the door and asked for the food to be left outside. There were also countless occasions when people weren't in when I attempted to make a delivery, which would have added no value at all to the content.

Other things were harder to omit; I saw many, many people who appeared to be on the verge of starvation, but there was no way they could all be included when the encounters were so brief. A lot of the food drops involved little conversation, nothing more than a handing over of the bags and a quick thank you, sometimes not even that. To have left *all* these in would have detracted from the narrative flow of the book, but it was still a tough choice to make as each individual life is as valid as the next; these men, women and children are already invisible in the eyes of some sections of society, and I didn't want to feel as if I was erasing them twofold by leaving them out. I hope that I have

38 Ibid, p.24

been able to use the cases of the few who did make it in to represent the lives of the many that were omitted and all the others like them.

*

When the FDC finally closed its doors, I went back to my usual role as a Communities Librarian and continued to work from home as I had been doing at the beginning of the initial lockdown.

Home life was tough over the summer of 2020; our daughter was able to spend two weeks at school before the summer holidays and was all the happier for it, while our son had to endure the whole six months stuck at home at great cost to his mental health, and he was delighted to finally get back to the classroom in September.

The third, post-Christmas lockdown was a terrible time for us, as it was for most people. Having worked through the first lockdown, I bore the brunt of the childcare during Lockdown Three as the charity shop my wife manages continued to trade online while I worked from home. The children were experiencing something of a post-Christmas crash and were looking forward to getting back to school, so it was a crushing disappointment to them both when, after a single day in the classroom, we had to tell them school was closed again and we had no idea when it might re-open. It was a torrid couple of months trying to entertain, reassure and occasionally home-school two traumatised, distressed little ones and it was sweet relief for all concerned when schools finally re-opened in March 2021.

It's still difficult for me to process the events of the last twelve months, as I'm sure is the case for most people. My overriding feeling is one of sadness, not only for all the lives lost but for all the lives put on hold, the families unable to see each other, the bereaved relatives unable to bury their loved ones, the children unable to see their friends, the small businesses lost and lives wrecked as the pandemic wreaked havoc on the economy, the catastrophic effects on the physical and mental health of adults and children alike, the unutterable psycho-logical violence perpetrated on the national psyche by the endless chopping and changing of restrictions, the interminable lockdowns.

The main thing I think that has really been demonstrated is the inherent wrongness of the capitalist system that allows companies like Amazon to report a huge increase in profits during the pandemic, while smaller businesses fold in their thousands and people who work in precarious, low-paid sectors such as retail and hospitality bore the brunt of job cuts[39]; it's yet another stark demonstration of the way the system is set up to increase the wealth of a tiny minority at the expense of everyone else, a repetition of the same old story of financial inequality that only seems to get worse with the passage of time.

Another obvious thing the pandemic has highlighted is the value of the NHS; so many of the measures introduced to control the virus were brought in because of fears that the NHS would be overwhelmed and unable to cope with patient numbers. Since the financial crash of 2008 and the years of austerity that followed, cuts to funding have meant that the NHS budget rose by an average of 1.4% per year between the years 2009-19, compared with an average rise of 3.7% per year since the NHS was established. This has led to serious staff shortages, with hospitals, mental health services and community providers reporting shortages of 84,000 full-time equivalent posts, 38,000 of which are for nurses; there is also a shortage of 2,500 GPs, with fears that this could rise to 7,000 in the next five years.[40]

According to a House of Commons Health and Social Care Committee report entitled *Workforce burnout and resilience in the NHS and social care*, published 8th June 2021, "Against a context of workforce shortages, funding pressures and reconfiguration of services, concerns about the morale of the NHS and social care workforce are not new. Even before the pandemic, one third of the doctors who responded to a survey published by the BMJ in January 2020 were described as burned out, with those in emergency medicine and general practice most impacted."[41] It then goes on to say that "the covid-19 pandemic had increased workforce pressures exponentially. 92% of trusts told NHS Providers they had concerns about staff wellbeing, stress and

39 According to Forbes, "Amazon delivered a record performance in 2020 with annual revenue up 38% to $386 billion, a yearly increase of over $100 billion. Net profit for Amazon was up 84% for the year as compared to last year." [https://www.forbes.com/sites/shelleykohan/2021/02/02/amazons-net-profit-soars-84-with-sales-hitting-386-billion/?sh=6aa4f0fd1334]

40 Fund Our NHS, (2020). Staff shortages [online]. Available from: https://nhsfunding.info/symptoms/10-effects-of-underfunding/staff-shortages/

41 House of Commons Health and Social Care Committee (2021). Workforce burnout and resilience in the NHS and social care [online]. Available from: https://committees.parliament.uk/publications/6158/documents/68766/default/, p.3.

burnout following the pandemic"[42] and "Workforce burnout was described by many as the highest in the history of the NHS and care systems and as such, it is an extraordinarily dangerous risk to the future functioning of both services."[43] The report states that this issue "needs to be tackled now if we are to attract and retain skilled staff, keep them physically and mentally well, and provide high quality care to patients and service users"[44] but "This will not happen until the service has the right number of people, with the right mix of skills across both the NHS and the care system."[45]

It's clear from that significant investment is needed to safeguard the future of the NHS and its staff, not just to cover the possibility of a future pandemic, but to keep the organisation functioning effectively. What is *not* clear, however, is where the money may come from, or whether the political will to find the incalculable sums involved exists within the current administration.

A joint letter calling for an international vaccine treaty, signed by more than twenty world leaders, including Boris Johnson, and published in newspapers across the world, recently claimed that "There will be other pandemics and other major health emergencies. No single government or multilateral agency can address this threat alone. The question is not if, but when." If this is the case, it strikes me that something must be done to redress the huge inequalities in wealth distribution in order to ameliorate the economic impact when a global crisis like this happens again.

The collapse of the Soviet Bloc in 1989 led to the development of what theorist Mark Fisher called Capitalist Realism, i.e. "the widespread sense that not only is capitalism the only viable political and economic system, but also that it is now impossible to even *imagine* a coherent alternative to it."[46] It would appear to me that the pandemic has shown that we *have* to find a viable alternative as soon as possible in order to protect the lower-paid and most vulnerable members of society in the event of a future health crisis. Ideas such as Universal Basic Income have long been derided by critics as expensive and unworkable, but would that kind of scheme, properly administered and funded, be any more expensive than the furlough scheme that is estimated to have

42 Ibid
43 Ibid, p.5
44 Ibid
45 Ibid, p.14
46 Fisher, M., (2009). *Capitalist Realism – is there no alternative?*, Zero Books, p.2.

cost upwards of *50 billion pounds* from the end of March 2020 to April 2021?

In a speech given to the House of Commons at the end of June 2020, the Prime Minister promised that his government would "[use] this crisis finally to tackle this country's great unresolved challenges of the last three decades, to build the homes, to fix the NHS, to solve social care, to tackle the skills crisis, to mend the indefensible gap in opportunity and productivity and connectivity between the regions of the UK, to unite and level up..."

It is to be hoped that he will be as good as his word but, given that at the time of writing the government is still under fire amidst accusations of rampant cronyism, and the National Audit Office has set up multiple enquiries into government lobbying, it could be argued that there is little reason to be confident. As Labour Leader Sir Keir Starmer has pointed out, "Every day there are new allegations about this Conservative government: dodgy PPE deals; tax breaks for their mates; the Health Secretary owns shares in a company delivering NHS services. Sleaze, sleaze, sleaze [...] with this scandal now firmly centred on [the Prime Minister], how on earth does he expect people to believe that he is the person to clean this mess up?"

Some may say this is an assessment with which it is difficult to argue, although with the next UK General Election not set to take place until May 2024 and the Conservative Party consistently ahead in the opinion polls, it would appear that for better or worse, the current Prime Minister is the only man for the job; for the time being, at least.

Post Script

Just after this book was completed, in January 2022, the government was rocked by a series of newspaper reports alleging that the Prime Minister and other government officials attended numerous social gatherings during lockdown – including a party for the Prime Minister's birthday – in flagrant disregard of the public health guidelines they themselves had set. In the wake of these reports, and Sue Gray's subsequent investigation, the Prime Minister faced a huge amount of criticism from the press and public alike. Despite calls to resign from politicians of all colours, including some in his own party, the Prime Minister stubbornly refuses to give up his office, and as we go to print – 3rd May 2022 – he remains in power.

On 22nd February 2022, the Prime Minister announced that all Covid restrictions would be lifted by 1st April, a move which Labour leader Sir Keir Starmer described as "a half-baked announcement from a government paralysed by chaos and incompetence." On the day the announcement was made, there were 41,130 recorded Covid infections and 205 deaths, bringing the total number of recorded deaths in the UK to 160,815.

Acknowledgements

First and foremost, I'd like to express my unending gratitude to my wonderful wife Ania and our beautiful children Luka and Kita, who had to endure the full horrors of the first lockdown and subsequent school holidays together during the five months I was out working in the van. This book is lovingly dedicated to them. Thanks also to my mam, dad and sister who've been unbelievably supportive of me over the years and never doubted that one day a book would appear with my name on the cover.

Huge thanks to everyone at Bluemoose, especially Kevin Duffy, who was completely on board with this project before he'd read a single word of it, and also to my editor Annie Warren, who has been an absolute delight to work with throughout. Thanks also to Fiachra McCarthy for the brilliant cover design.

I'm indebted to my good friend Heidi James for relentless motivation, occasional arse-kickings, endless conversation and some invaluable editorial advice when I was getting the first couple of drafts of this into shape; also to Chris White, motivator-in-chief for the last two decades and so often my first reader, who remains a far better judge of my work than I am. Thom Cuell has been on hand with some savvy industry advice and much-needed pep talks at various points over the last two or three years, so thanks very much to them too.

Cheers to Chris Nickson for pointing me in the direction of some really useful background reading about the history of different areas of Leeds. Fraternal fist-bumps Gav Musto, Steve Clough and Ian McArdle; thanks also to Greg Stringer and my old friend Ali Millar at Leeds Libraries.

Massive respect to the warehouse staff, drivers, support staff and everyone else who worked on the Food Distribution Project from March to September 2020.

Special thanks to Jenn Ashworth.